Investigating Terrestrial Ecosystems

CONTOURS: STUDIES OF THE ENVIRONMENT
Second Edition

EDITOR AND PRINCIPAL AUTHOR
William A. Andrews
Professor and Chairman of Science Education
Faculty of Education, University of Toronto

Investigating Terrestrial Ecosystems
Investigating Aquatic Ecosystems
Investigating Environmental Issues
Investigating Natural Resources

THE MEANING OF THE CONTOURS SYMBOL

The symbol for *Contours* embodies two basic elements: the Greek letter theta and receding and rising contours. The letter theta is the first letter of the Greek word *thanatos*, meaning death, which has come to symbolize the urgency with which we must examine our "use" of our home, Earth. The receding and rising contours within the letter theta represent the conflicting sides in every issue and the need for careful study and analysis of those issues.

William A. Andrews

EDITOR AND PRINCIPAL AUTHOR
Faculty of Education, University of Toronto

Donna K. Moore

David and Mary Thomson Collegiate Institute

Investigating Terrestrial Ecosystems

Prentice-Hall Canada Inc., Scarborough, Ontario

NORTHWEST COMMUNITY
COLLEGE

Canadian Cataloguing in Publication Data

Andrews, William A., date
    Investigating terrestrial ecosystems

Includes index
For use in high schools
ISBN 0-13-503186-9

1. Ecology.   2. Biotic communities.   3. Adaptation
(Biology).   I. Moore, Donna K., date   II. Title.

QH541.A57   1986   574.5′264   C86-093116-1

Prentice-Hall, Inc., Englewood Cliffs, New Jersey
Prentice-Hall International, Inc., London
Prentice-Hall of Australia, Pty., Ltd., Sydney
Prentice-Hall of India, Pvt., Ltd., New Delhi
Prentice-Hall of Japan, Inc., Tokyo
Prentice-Hall of Southeast Asia (Pte.) Ltd., Singapore
Editora Prentice-Hall do Brasil Ltda., Rio de Janeiro
Prentice-Hall Hispanoamericana, S.A., Mexico

ISBN 0-13-503186-9

Communications Branch, Consumer and Corporate Affairs Canada,
has granted use of the National Symbol for Metric Conversion.

Project Editor: Lesley Wood
Production Editor: Miriam London
Production: Joanne Matthews
Illustrator: James Loates
Composition: CompuScreen Typesetting Ltd.
Cover Illustration: Julian Mulock

Printed and bound in Canada by Bryant Press

6 7 8 9 10 BP 98 97 96 95 94

Policy Statement

Prentice-Hall Canada Inc., Educational Book Division, and the authors of *Investigating Terrestrial Ecosystems* are committed to the publication of instructional materials that are as bias-free as possible. The student text was evaluated for bias prior to publication.

The authors and publishers also recognize the importance of appropriate reading levels and have therefore made every effort to ensure the highest degree of readability in the student text. The content has been selected, organized, and written at a level suitable to the intended audience. Standard readability tests have been applied at several stages in the text's preparation to ensure an appropriate reading level.

Research indicates, however, that readability is affected by much more than word or sentence length; factors such as presentation, format and design, none of which are considered in the usual readability tests, also greatly influence the ease with which students read a book. These and many additional features have been carefully prepared to ensure maximum student comprehension.

Contents

UNIT TWO: TERRESTRIAL ECOSYSTEMS

UNIT THREE: BIOMES OF NORTH AMERICA

Acknowledgments

The authors wish to acknowledge the competent professional help received from the staff of Prentice-Hall Canada Inc. in the production of this text. In particular, we extend our thanks to Lesley Wood and Mia London for their editorial work and to Joanne Matthews for her coordination of the production aspect of this book. We also thank Steve Lane for his assistance in the planning and development of this text. This book owes its final shape and form largely to the efforts of Joe Chin.

We wish, further, to thank the many teachers who reviewed the manuscript and offered constructive criticism. Our thanks also go to the students who volunteered to serve as models in the photographs. In particular, we wish to acknowledge the assistance of Sandra McEwan and her Science Club at Anderson Collegiate and Vocational Institute, and students from the classes of Donna Moore at David and Mary Thomson Collegiate Institute. We are grateful for the photographs that these people and those mentioned in the photo credits below provided in order to make our book more appealing and useful.

We would be remiss if we did not express our appreciation of the imaginative, attractive, and accurate artwork of James Loates and the cover illustration drawn by Julian Mulock. Finally, we extend a special word of appreciation to Lois Andrews for her skillful and dedicated preparation of the final manuscript and index.

W.A. Andrews
Editor and Principal Author

Photo Credits

Every reasonable effort has been made to find copyright holders of the following material. The publishers would be pleased to have any errors or omissions brought to their attention. For permission to use the following material in this textbook we thank:
Figs. 1-0; 1-3, A; 1-3, B; p. 24, middle; 2-1, C; 2-6, A; 2-6, B; 4-9; 4-23; 6-3; 8-2, A; 8-2, B; 8-7, A; 9-18; 9-27; 9-33; 9-37; 10-2; 10-10, A; 10-18; 10-25: Ontario Ministry of Natural Resources. Fig. 1-3, E: courtesy of NASA. Fig. 1-6: Bill Stanley and Associates/Miller Services. Fig. 5-9; U.S.D.A. Photo by Bluford W. Muir. Figs. 2-12; 10-28; 13-11: U.S.D.A. Photos. Fig. 8-1: courtesy of J.C. Ritchie. Figs. 8-10; 8-11; 11-6; 11-8; 12-6: U.S. Fish and Wildlife Service. Fig. 12-2: Duncan M. Cameron, Jr. Fig. 8-7, B: U.S. Forest Service. Fig. 9-1: U.S.D.A. Photo by Freeman Hein. Figs. 9-3; 13-8; 13-19: Donna K. Moore. Fig. 9-21: National Museums of Canada, National Museum of Natural Sciences, Neg. #J9086. Fig. 9-23: Serge Jauvin/Miller Services. Figs. 9-26; 10-22; 10-24: Harold M. Lambert/Miller Services. Fig. 10-20: Norman R. Lightfoot, Federation of Ontario Naturalists. Fig. 10-23: Jeanne White/Miller Services. Fig. 11-5: U.S.D.A. Photo by Leland J. Prater. Figs. 11-17; 12-10: Ontario Ministry of Agriculture and Food. Fig. 13-13: Nancy J. Purcell. All other photos by W.A. Andrews.

To the Student

Ecology is the study of the relationships between living things and their environments. Such relationships occur everywhere on earth. They occur in freshwater ecosystems such as ponds, lakes, and streams. They occur in terrestrial (land) ecosystems such as forests, grasslands, and deserts. They occur in marine (saltwater) ecosystems such as oceans and tidal marshes. They even occur in the soil under terrestrial, freshwater, and marine ecosystems.

You begin your study of ecology by learning the basic principles of ecology in Unit 1 of this book. Then in Unit 2 you discover how those principles operate in local terrestrial ecosystems. Finally, in Unit 3, you use your knowledge to investigate the biomes of North America.

Why study ecology? There are two good reasons. First, it's fun; you will enjoy doing the activities in this book and figuring out how everything is related. But there is a more important reason. Just about everyone knows that relationships exist between all things on earth. And most people know that the well-being of humans depends upon the well-being of all other parts of the natural world. In other words, most people know how important ecology is. But most people do not know enough about ecology to help look after this earth and the life on it. As a result, environmental problems are quite common. Noise, water, and air pollution plague cities. Agricultural land is being lost through soil erosion and urbanization. And natural resources such as forests and wildlife are being exploited.

The purpose of this book is to help you understand the ecology of our main terrestrial ecosystems. Then you should be ready to help solve and prevent environmental problems. Two other books in this series will give you further ideas on how to do this: *Investigating Environmental Issues* and *Investigating Natural Resources*.

UNIT ONE

What Is Ecology?

Fig. 1-0 The deer interact with both their living and non-living environments. How do the deer depend on plants? How do the plants depend on the deer? How do the deer depend on the water? Do the deer affect the water in any way? What animals interact with the deer?

Every living thing on earth interacts with other living things. It also interacts with its non-living environment—air, water, and soil, for example. Even humans interact with their living and non-living environments. Can you think of ways you depend on other living things? How do they depend on you? How do you depend on your non-living environment? And how do you affect it?

Ecology deals with the relationships between organisms and their environments. This unit is an introduction to ecology. It teaches you the basic principles of ecology that you will use in Units 2 and 3 as you study natural ecosystems.

1 Interdependence of Living Things
2 Structure of an Ecosystem
3 Flow of Matter and Energy in Ecosystems
4 Ecological Succession

1 Interdependence of Living Things

Environment ... ecology ... habitat ... ecosystem ... food chain.... We often hear these words today. That's because people are becoming concerned about their environment. They care about clear air and clean water. They care about our forests, farms, and wildlife. But caring isn't enough. We have to work together to protect our environment. However, before we can act to protect our environment, we need to understand how it works. And that's what this chapter is all about.

1.1   What Is Ecology?

Fig. 1-1   What organisms make up the living environment? What factors make up the non-living environment?

Some Questions to Think About

Imagine that you are the person who photographed Figure 1-1. Everything around you is your environment. Part of your environment is living. The dog, cattle, grass, and trees are examples. And part of your environment is non-living. Soil, air, water, wind, light, and temperature are examples.

Can you think of ways that you interact with the other animals? That is, how do you depend on the cattle, and how do they depend on you? How do the dog and cattle depend on one another? How do you interact with the trees? For example, what do they do for you, and what do you do for them? How do the cattle interact with the grass? Does the dog interact with the grass? Do you? And how do the living things interact with the non-living factors? For example, how do the trees and cattle depend on the soil? And how do they affect the soil? How do the grass, dog, and you depend on temperature? How do the plants and animals depend on the air? How do they affect the air?

Before you go on, you should do two things:

1. Discuss the questions in the previous paragraph with other people in your class.

2. Make a list of other relationships not mentioned in the questions.

A Definition of Ecology

No organism lives completely on its own. It depends on other organisms and they depend on it. It also depends on the non-living environment in which it lives, and it affects that environment. Ecology is the study of the relationships between organisms and their environments. That is, ecology describes and explains how organisms interact with other organisms and with their non-living environments.

Section Review

1. What makes up an organism's environment?
2. **a)** Describe how the trees and cattle in Figure 1-1 affect the soil.
   b) Describe how the soil affects the trees and cattle.
3. What is ecology?

1.2   Ecology and Levels of Biological Organization

From Cell to Individual

All living things are made of cells. In the more complex organisms, cells are organized (put together) to form tissues. For example, muscle cells are organized into muscle tissue. Tissues, in turn, are organized into organs. Your heart is an organ. It is made up of muscle tissue, nerve tissue, connective tissue, and other tissues. Then organs are put together to form organ systems. For example, your digestive system is an organ system. It consists of several organs including your stomach, intestines, and liver. Finally organ systems are organized into an organism, or individual. Among your organ systems are the breathing system, digestive system, circulatory system, and skeletal system.

Cell, tissue, organ, organ system, and organism (individual) are called levels of biological organization. They describe how various levels of life are put together.

From Individual to Biosphere

As Figure 1-2 shows, the "putting together" of levels of life does not stop at the organism (individual) level. That's because no organism lives completely

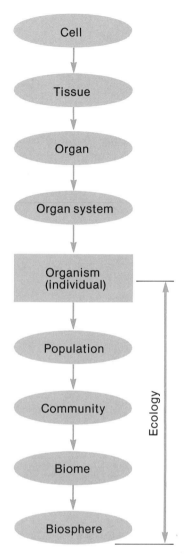

Fig. 1-2 Levels of biological organization.

on its own. It interacts with other organisms. Such interactions form levels of biological organization above the individual level: population, community, biome, and biosphere (Fig. 1-3). Ecology deals mainly with these levels. Let's look more closely at their meanings.

Population   A population is a group of individuals of the same species, living together in the same area. The geese in level 2 of Figure 1-3 are an example. The pond with the geese in it might also have a bullfrog population. It might also have a water lily population and a perch population.

Community   A community is *all* the living things in an area. A community consists of several populations. The pond community in level 3 of Figure 1-3 is an example. Look closely and you will see a goose population and a duck population. The pond community also has many populations which you cannot see in this photograph—a water lily population, a perch population, a snail population, and many others.

Biome   A biome is a large geographic area with a characteristic climate. Canada has only seven main biomes. The United States has the same seven and three additional ones. The whole earth has only 10 or 15 main biomes. Look ahead to Figure 7-14, page 140, to see where these biomes occur.

A biome consists of several communities. The coniferous forest that stretches across Canada and into Alaska is a biome. Like all biomes, it has a characteristic set of plants and animals. These plants and animals occur in the communities which make up the biome. Among the communities which make up the coniferous forest biome are lake communities, pond communities, and bog communities.

Biosphere   The biosphere is the region on earth in which life exists. Organisms live in the lower part of the atmosphere. They also live in almost all bodies of water on earth. They live on the soil and in the first metre or two of the soil. This thin layer from the lower atmosphere to the bottom of oceans makes up the biosphere.

The biosphere is made up of biomes. Among them are the desert biome, tundra biome, grassland biome, and coniferous forest biome.

Section Review

1. Name, in order, the four levels of biological organization that follow the cell level.
2. Name, in order from smallest to largest, the four levels of biological organization that are a part of ecological studies.
3. State in one sentence the meaning of each of these terms: population, community, biome, and biosphere.

Individual (Level 1)

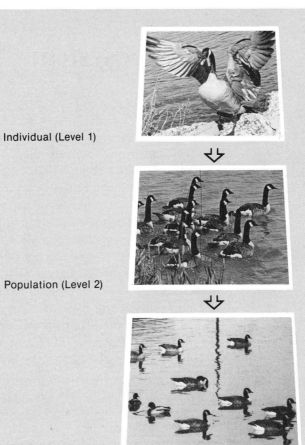

Population (Level 2)

Community (Level 3)

Biome (Level 4)

Fig. 1-3 Individuals of the same species make up a population; populations make up a community; communities make up a biome, and biomes make up the biosphere.

Biosphere (Level 5)

1.3   The Ecosystem Concept

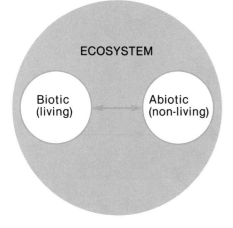

Fig. 1-4   An ecosystem has two interacting parts, biotic and abiotic.

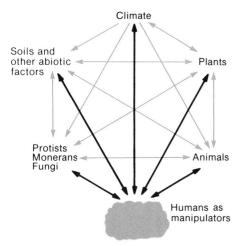

Fig. 1-5   The main parts of most ecosystems. Each part, biotic or abiotic, is affected by the other parts. Can you name some other abiotic factors which could be placed in this diagram?

What Is an Ecosystem?

An ecosystem is an interacting system that consists of groups of organisms and their non-living environment. Thus an ecosystem has two main parts, a biotic (living) part and an abiotic (non-living) part (Fig. 1-4). The biotic part includes all the living things in the ecosystem—animals, plants, fungi, protists, and monerans. The abiotic part includes all the non-living factors in the ecosystem—water, soil, temperature, light, wind, and others.

As Figure 1-5 suggests, climate is the overriding factor which determines the general nature of an ecosystem. If the climate is always dry and hot, the soil will likely be sandy. And the plants, animals, and other life will be special organisms that can exist in desert conditions. If, however, the climate is wet and hot, the soil will likely be soggy and rich in decaying organic matter. Here, organisms that like tropical rain forest conditions will flourish.

Remember, *all* parts of an ecosystem are interrelated. Each part is affected by *all* the other parts, just as the arrows suggest. Thus, if the plants in an ecosystem change, the soil, animals, and all other factors will change. The chain of events that occurs when one factor in an ecosystem is changed is long and complex but these events are certain to happen.

An ecosystem can be any size. Any community of living things interacting with its environment is an ecosystem. A woodlot is an ecosystem. So is a city park, a lake, a pond, and the whole Arctic tundra or the Florida everglades. Even a classroom aquarium or a handful of soil is an ecosystem.

Humans and Ecosystems

Humans are animals. Therefore, like other animals, we fit into the interactions shown by the green arrows in Figure 1-5. However, unlike other animals, we change ecosystems in dramatic ways. We manipulate ecosystems as shown by the grey arrows. For example, we remove the natural grasses of the prairies and replace them with grasses that we want, such as wheat. We replace deer, ground squirrels, and other grassland animals with cattle, sheep, and other domestic animals. We use herbicides to kill plants that we do not want. We till the soil so that it will grow what we want it to grow. We fertilize and irrigate the soil. We clear mountain slopes to make room for new homes, shopping plazas, schools, and roads. We even change the climate by polluting the air and by cloud seeding.

All these things are not necessarily "bad". Humans do have to eat and have a place to live. Sometimes, though, the *way* we do these things is "bad". We often do not consider the ecological results of our actions. We should always remember that we are part of the ecosystem. We depend on *all* the other parts. Therefore, our survival as a species depends on all the other parts of the ecosystem. We must develop an ecological awareness of our actions.

An Example: Effects of Clear Cutting

Suppose that a lumber company completely cleared a forested area of trees. We call this clear cutting (Fig. 1-6). What effects would this have on the forest ecosystem? The trees would no longer add humus to the soil since they could no longer drop leaves onto the ground. Snails, slugs, earthworms, bacteria, and fungi thrive on leaf litter. Therefore, their numbers would decrease. Some species might vanish completely. Animals that feed on these organisms would be affected. Soil might erode because the leaf canopy would no longer be present to absorb the energy of a heavy rainfall. If the soil were washed away, many plant species would disappear. The animals that eat these plants would move away or die of starvation. Plants that require shade and moisture, such as ferns, would die. Broad-leafed plants like Jack-in-the-pulpit and trillium cannot live in direct sunlight. Therefore they, too, would die.

On the other hand, many species of plants that require bright sunlight might then be able to grow in the area. Grasses, goldenrod, and other sun-loving species might gradually become established. Shrubs and tree species that could not grow in the shade of the forest might appear. New insect populations might be established. New bird populations might appear. Mammal species, such as white-tailed deer, might increase in numbers.

The changes which would occur because of clear cutting are not all "bad". But the original ecosystem would be gone, perhaps forever. And nearby ecosystems would also be affected. How would a nearby stream be affected? How would a lake in the clear-cut area change? How could humans lessen the "bad" changes?

Fig. 1-6 This clear cut area was once a dense stand of coniferous trees.

Section Review

1. **a)** What is an ecosystem?
    b) Name the two main parts of an ecosystem.
2. Explain why climate is the overriding factor determining the general nature of an ecosystem.
3. Name five ecosystems of differing sizes.
4. What is meant by "Humans as manipulators" in Figure 1-5?
5. Why should we always consider the ecological consequences of our actions?
6. Explain why clear cutting of a forest often increases the number of deer in the area.

1.4   ACTIVITY   Making a Model Ecosystem

In this activity you will build a model ecosystem. Then you will study how it works. The basic principles you learn here also apply to natural ecosystems such as lakes and forests. How many of these principles can you discover?

Problem

What are the basic parts of an ecosystem? How does an ecosystem work?

Materials

large bottle or jar with top (at least 3-4 L)
table lamp with 60 W bulb
khuli loach or another plant-eating fish
strands of an aquatic plant (3 or 4)
pond snails (8-10)
clean gravel and/or sand

Procedure

a. Place sand or gravel to a depth of 2-3 cm in the jar.
b. Fill the jar with water. If you use tap water, let the jar stand with the top removed for 48 h. This lets the chlorine leave the water.
c. Add a few strands of an aquatic plant. Any submerged aquatic plant will do. *Cabomba* (fanwort) and *Ceratophyllum* (hortwort or coontail) do particularly well in closed ecosystems.
d. Add 8-10 pond snails to the water.
e. Place a khuli loach in the water. You may use one or two small guppies instead of the khuli loach. Or you could use both types of fish.
f. Put the top on the jar and seal it tightly.
g. Place a table lamp with a 60 W bulb in it close to the jar, as shown in Figure 1-7.

Fig. 1-7 A model ecosystem. Where do the plants, fish, and snails get their nutrients? Why is light needed? Why don't the organisms die with the top on?

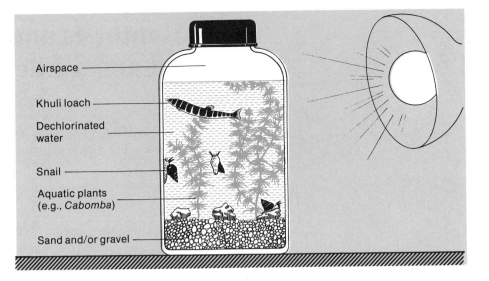

Airspace
Khuli loach
Dechlorinated water
Snail
Aquatic plants (e.g., *Cabomba*)
Sand and/or gravel

h. Place the setup in a location away from windows and other places where light and temperature conditions change greatly during the day.

i. Leave the lamp on 24 h per day or place it on a timer that provides at least 16 h of light per day. Do not depend on your memory to turn the light off and on!

j. A healthy ecosystem of this kind will have a pale green colour in the water. This colour is caused by algae. They develop from spores present on the plants and animals. Algae are important in the ecosystem. They provide both food and oxygen for the animals. Move the light closer if the water does not develop a green colour after 4-5 d. Move it further away if the green becomes intense.

k. Observe your ecosystem closely from time to time for several months. Make careful notes of any changes in it.

Discussion

Many days may pass before you can answer all these questions. Also, you must read on in order to get the knowledge you need to answer some of these questions.

1. Your ecosystem is called a **closed** ecosystem. How does it differ from a natural ecosystem?
2. Why do you think we used a closed ecosystem for this activity?
3. From what source do the plants and algae get carbon dioxide for photosynthesis?
4. From what source do the organisms (plants, animals, and algae) get oxygen for respiration?
5. How do the plants get the nutrients they need?
6. How do the animals get the nutrients they need?
7. Why is the light required?
8. What do you think will happen if a fish or snail dies?

Photosynthesis and Respiration—Maintaining a Life Balance

You need to know what photosynthesis and respiration do before you can understand how ecosystems such as the bottle in Section 1.4 and forests function. You probably have studied these processes before. Therefore the discussion here is brief.

Respiration

The cells of all living things need a constant supply of energy. They use the energy to carry out essential cell processes such as growth, repair, and reproduction. Where do they get this energy? They get it by oxidizing or "burning" a fuel, just as you get energy to heat your home by burning a fuel. The fuels used by cells and those used in your home are more similar than you might expect. Both are organic in nature. That is, they consist of compounds containing carbon atoms. When you burn wood, coal, or fuel oil, the carbon atoms in the organic compounds separate from one another. This separation is caused mainly by the oxygen that must be present for things to burn. As the atoms separate, the chemical energy of the bonds that held them together is released. Generally, it is released in the form of heat and light. Carbon dioxide and water are formed as by-products.

The "burning" of fuels within cells is called respiration. The main fuel for this oxidation reaction is glucose. Glucose is a simple sugar found in many foods. You can prove to yourself that glucose is an organic compound by heating a small amount of it in a test tube. Try it! Glucose, in the presence of oxygen, burns readily when heated. To permit "burning" at temperatures that will not damage the organism, cells have catalysts. They lower the temperature at which glucose oxidizes. Organic catalysts that operate in living cells are called enzymes. When glucose is oxidized in living cells, energy is released and carbon dioxide and water are formed as by-products. The following word equation summarizes the process of respiration:

$$\text{Glucose} + \text{Oxygen} \xrightarrow{\text{enzymes}} \text{Energy} + \text{Carbon Dioxide} + \text{Water}$$

The chemical equation is:

$$C_6H_{12}O_6 + 6\ O_2 \xrightarrow{\text{enzymes}} \text{Energy} + 6\ CO_2 + 6\ H_2O$$

The energy released is used by cells for their life processes.

Photosynthesis

Where do cells get the glucose in the first place? That depends on the type of cell. If the cell is in a green organism, it makes its own glucose. A cell of this type contains chloroplasts. They, in turn, contain the chlorophylls that help

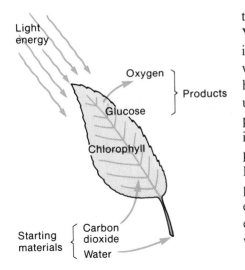

Light energy

Oxygen ⎫
          ⎬ Products
Glucose ⎭

Chlorophyll

Starting ⎧ Carbon
materials ⎨ dioxide
          ⎩ Water

Fig. 1-8 A summary of the process of photosynthesis.

the cell change light energy into stored chemical energy. How is this done? You read earlier that energy is released when large molecules are broken up into smaller ones. It seems reasonable to expect, then, that energy is used up when smaller molecules are combined to form larger molecules. That is what happens during photosynthesis. As the name implies, light energy (photo) is used to build (synthesize) complex substances out of simpler substances. This process occurs only in green organisms like plants. The cells of these organisms take in carbon dioxide and water. Then, with the assistance of chlorophyll and light energy, they make organic compounds like glucose (Fig. 1-8). In addition, a very important by-product is formed, oxygen gas. During photosynthesis, then, light energy is changed to and stored as chemical energy in the bonds between the carbon atoms in glucose molecules. This energy can be released at some later time by oxidation of the glucose. The word equation and the chemical equation for photosynthesis are:

$$\text{Carbon Dioxide} + \text{Water} + \text{Light Energy} \xrightarrow{\text{chlorophyll}} \text{Glucose} + \text{Oxygen}$$

$$6\ CO_2 + 6\ H_2O + \text{Light Energy} \xrightarrow{\text{chlorophyll}} C_6H_{12}O_6 + 6\ O_2$$

Both photosynthesis and respiration are much more complex than these equations suggest. These are merely summation equations. That is, they show the starting materials and the final products. Other complex reactions take place between these stages.

Obviously not all cells can photosynthesize. If a cell is in an animal, for example, it cannot make its own glucose. As a result, it must get it from the environment. This is why herbivores eat plants and why carnivores eat herbivores. A predator may not eat glucose directly when it eats its prey. But its digestive enzymes soon form glucose out of many of the food materials in the prey.

Section Review

1. Why do cells need energy?
2. How do cells get the energy they need?
3. Write a word equation for the process of respiration.
4. How do green organisms get the glucose they need for respiration?
5. How do animals get the glucose they need for respiration?
6. Write a word equation for the process of photosynthesis.

1.6 ACTIVITY Earthworm Ecology

Earthworms, like all organisms, interact with their abiotic environment. They have adapted to certain conditions of light, moisture, soil acidity, temperature, and other abiotic factors. In this activity you will discover the abiotic conditions that earthworms prefer.

Problem

What abiotic conditions do earthworms prefer?

Materials

shallow tray
rich organic soil
water
earthworms (5)

one or more of:
sand
light source
soda water
baking soda solution
cold packs (2)

Procedure

a. Copy Table 1-1 into your notebook.

Table 1-1 Earthworm Ecology

Abiotic factor	Predicted behaviour of earthworms	Experimental result
Soil organic content		
Soil acidity		
Light intensity		
Soil moisture		
Soil temperature		

b. Complete the column in Table 1-1 titled "Predicted behaviour of earthworms". Think about where you have seen earthworms and about the following questions as you do so.
If earthworms are given a choice, will they select
1. sandy or rich organic soil?
2. acidic, neutral, or basic soil?
3. a light or dark area?
4. water-logged, dry, or moist soil?
5. warm, hot, or cold soil?

c. Your class has been divided into 5 groups for this activity. Join the group to which you were assigned.

Soil Organic Content Group

d. Put moist sand to a depth of 5 cm in one half of the tray (Condition A in Fig. 1-9).

Fig. 1-9 Which condition will the earthworms select?

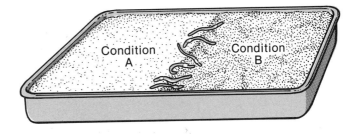

e. Put rich organic soil to a depth of 5 cm in the other half of the tray (Condition B in Fig. 1-9). The soil should have the same "wetness" as the sand.

f. Place the 5 earthworms in the centre of the tray.

g. Note the locations of the earthworms every 3 min for 15 min. Record the average of your results in your table.

Soil Acidity Group

d. Put rich organic soil to a depth of 5 cm in the tray.

e. Moisten one half of the soil with soda water, an acid (Condition A in Fig. 1-9).

f. Moisten the other half of the soil with baking soda solution, a base (Condition B in Fig. 1-9). Make sure this half is moistened the same amount as the other half.

g. Place the 5 earthworms in the centre of the tray.

h. Note the locations of the earthworms every 3 min for 15 min. Record the average of your results in your table.

Light Intensity Group

d. Put rich organic soil to a depth of 5 cm in the tray.

e. Cover half of the tray with dark paper (Condition A in Fig. 1-9).

f. Put a bright light over the other half of the tray (Condition B in Fig. 1-9).

g. Place the 5 earthworms in the centre of the tray.

h. Note the locations of the earthworms every 3 min for 15 min. Record the average of your results in your table.

Soil Moisture Group

d. Put *dry*, rich organic soil to a depth of 5 cm in one half of the tray (Condition A in Fig. 1-9).

e. Put *moist* (but not soggy), rich organic soil to a depth of 5 cm in the other half of the tray (Condition B in Fig. 1-9).

f. Place the 5 earthworms in the centre of the tray.

g. Note the locations of the earthworms every 3 min for 15 min. Record the average of your results in your table.

h. If time permits, repeat this experiment using soggy soil instead of dry soil for Condition A.

Soil Temperature Group

d. Put rich organic soil to a depth of 5 cm in the tray.

e. Place a cold pack at 0°C or below in the soil at one end of the tray (Condition A in Fig. 1-9). Make sure this pack was in a freezer overnight.

f. Place a cold pack at about 40°C in the soil at the other end of the tray (Condition B in Fig. 1-9). Make sure this pack was in 40°C water for several minutes.

g. Place the 5 earthworms in the centre of the tray.

h. Note the locations of the earthworms every 3 min for 15 min. Record the average of your results in your table.

Discussion

Answer these questions after the groups have shared their results.
1. What soil conditions do earthworms seem to prefer?
2. Why don't all the earthworms select exactly the same conditions?
3. Suppose you wanted to catch some earthworms. What two things could you do to get them to leave their burrows?

Main Ideas

1. Ecology is the study of the relationships between organisms and their environments.
2. There are four levels of biological organization smaller than the individual (organism): cell, tissue, organ, and organ system.
3. Ecologists study four levels of biological organization larger than the individual (organism): population, community, biome, and biosphere.
4. An ecosystem is an interacting system that consists of groups of organisms and their non-living environment.
5. All ecosystems operate on the same basic principles.

Key Terms

abiotic
biome
biosphere
biotic

community
ecology
ecosystem
population

Chapter Review

A. True or False

Decide whether each of the following statements is true or false. If the sentence is false, rewrite it to make it true. (Do not write in this book.)

1. Ecology deals just with relationships between organisms.
2. A community is made up of several populations.
3. The abiotic part of an ecosystem consists of non-living factors.
4. Canada has more biomes than the United States.

B. Completion

Complete each of the following sentences with a word or phrase that will make the sentence correct. (Do not write in this book.)

1. The fish, snails, plants, and algae make up the ▩▩▩ part of your model ecosystem.
2. A ▩▩▩ is a large area with a characteristic climate.
3. A tissue is made of similar ▩▩▩ .
4. The ▩▩▩ is the region on earth in which life exists.

C. Multiple Choice

Each of the following statements or questions is followed by four responses. Choose the correct response in each case. (Do not write in this book.)

1. All the bullfrogs in a pond are best called a
   a) population **b)** community **c)** ecosystem **d)** organism
2. Look at Figure 1-10. All the plants in this pond are best called the
   a) pond ecosystem   **c)** pond plant population
   b) pond plant ecosystem   **d)** pond plant community
3. The Arctic tundra of northern Canada and Alaska is best called a
   a) biosphere **b)** biome **c)** community **d)** population

Using Your Knowledge

1. Study Figure 1-11 carefully. Now explain what this drawing represents.
2. Identify each of the following as a population, community, or biome:
   a) the deer in a field
   b) all the corn plants in a cornfield
   c) all the living things in a forest
   d) the brook trout in a stream
   e) the prairies of the United States and Canada
   f) the giant sequoia redwood trees of Yosemite National Park in California
   g) the polar bears which live around the Beaufort Sea
   h) all the organisms in the Florida everglades

Fig. 1-10   Are all the plants in this pond an ecosystem, community or population?

Fig. 1-11 What does this diagram represent?

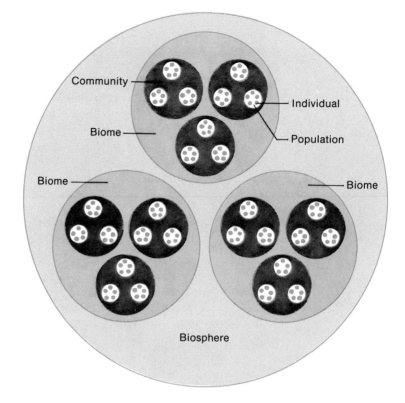

3. a) What is the difference between a community and an ecosystem?
   b) Ecologists often speak of a plant community and an animal community. What do you suppose they mean by these terms?
4. Identify each of the following as a community, an ecosystem, or neither of the two:
   a) a handful of soil   c) the water, soil, and other abiotic factors in a lake
   b) a coastal marsh   d) all the life on a mountain

Fig. 1-12 What communities make up this alpine area?

5. Name at least five different communities which make up an alpine biome (Fig. 1-12).

6. **a)** If hunters shot all the deer in a forest, what changes might occur in the forest?

   b) If hunting were totally banned in the forest, what changes might occur?

Investigations

1. Visit an ecosystem such as a pond, meadow, park, lake, woodlot, or beach. Compare that ecosystem to your model ecosystem. Record your comparisons in a table like Table 1-2.

Table 1-2 Comparing Ecosystems

Model ecosystem	Corresponding part(s) of the natural ecosystem
table lamp	
sand and/or gravel	
tap water	
snails	
algae	
plants	
khuli loach	
guppies	

2. You read in Section 1.3 that human activities such as clear cutting can cause ecological problems. Identify an ecological problem in your area. Write a paper of about 500 words on its causes, effects, and possible solutions.

3. Photograph an ecosystem and include photographs of the various levels of organization within it. Prepare a poster with these pictures or show your slides to the class.

4. Choose an open area near your home or school. Research its history through interviews with people who live nearby or through library references. Describe the changes in biotic and abiotic factors that have occurred in this area over a long period of time (e.g. 100 years).

2 Structure of an Ecosystem

An ecosystem has two main parts, a biotic part and an abiotic part. The biotic part includes all the living things in the ecosystem: plants, animals, fungi, protists, and monerans. The abiotic part includes all the non-living factors in the ecosystem: water, soil, temperature, light, wind, and others. This chapter looks at the nature of these biotic and abiotic parts and how they are related.

2.1   Habitat and Niche

Habitat

The habitat of an organism is the place in which it lives. An ecosystem such as a woodlot has many habitats. For example, the habitat of an earthworm is the rich woodlot soil. The habitat of a land snail is the moist leaf litter. The habitat of a blue jay is the branches of the trees. And the habitat of a porcupine is the larger branches of the trees in a forest.

Habitats may overlap. For example, the porcupine may seek out a meal of bark in the branches that are also the habitat of the bluejay. It may also step on the habitats of the earthworm and snail as it walks to a river for a drink. However, since these animals do not eat the same food, no problems result when their habitats overlap.

Niche

The niche of an organism is its total role in the community. For example, the niche of a deer is to feed on grass and other plants, to become food for

Red fox

Red squirrel

White-tailed deer

Fig. 2-1 Can you describe the habitat and niche of each of these animals?

wolves, to provide blood for blackflies and mosquitoes, to fertilize the soil with its wastes and so on. The niche of a frog in a pond is to feed on insects, to become food for snakes and other animals, and many other things.

Comparing Habitat and Niche

Fig. 2-2 What are the habitat and niche of this hawk, the Northern harrier?

Many people confuse habitat and niche. This may help you remember the difference. Think of the habitat as the "address" of the organism. And think of the niche as the organism's "occupation", or "job" (Fig. 2-1).

The niche of an organism decides its habitat. For example, the niche of the hawk in Figure 2-2 is, in part, to feed on mice which live in grassy areas. Thus these hawks are found much of the time in grassy areas. They cannot find the food they need in a forest. In other words, their niche is mainly in the grassy area, not the forest. Thus their habitat is usually the grassy area.

Competition

Fig. 2-3 Cattle cannot compete with bighorn sheep in the sheep's summer habitat, the mountains. But the two species do compete when the sheep move to their winter habitat in the valleys.

If two species have the same habitat and similar niches, they will **compete** with one another. For example, cattle and bighorn sheep often winter in the same mountain valley in the Rocky Mountains (Fig. 2-3). That is, they have the same habitat. Both species eat grass and other plants. That is, they have similar niches. In time, then, they will compete for available food and space in the valley. When this happens, one species will often crowd the other out. Cattle are able to use the resources of the valley better than bighorn sheep. With the help of humans, they are simply better adapted to the habitat than bighorn sheep. As a result, cattle are fenced out of the winter grazing grounds of bighorn sheep in some areas. If this were not done, bighorn sheep could eventually disappear from those areas.

In general two species cannot occupy *exactly* the same niche in the same habitat. If they try, they end up competing for food and space. Only one species can win such a competition. The other will either die off or move away and fill the same niche in another habitat.

Section Review

1. What is the difference between habitat and niche?
2. What happens if two species with similar niches move into the same habitat?
3. Describe the habitat of the snails in the model ecosystem you set up in Section 1.4.
4. What is the niche of the snails in the model ecosystem?

2.2   Trophic (Feeding) Levels

As you know, all organisms in an ecosystem depend on one another and on their physical environment. In this section we will look at how organisms depend on one another for food.

Every organism belongs to at least one of three main feeding levels: producers, consumers, and decomposers. Ecologists call feeding levels trophic levels. Let's see what these are.

Producers

All living things need energy to support life processes. Plants, many protists, and many monerans contain chlorophyll. Therefore they can carry out photosynthesis. That is, they store some of the sun's energy in starch, sugar, and other molecules. They make, or produce, their own food. Therefore they are called producers.

Organisms that produce their own food are also called autotrophs ("self-feeders"). They occupy the trophic level of producer. The trees of a forest, the cacti of a desert, the grasses of a lawn, and the diatoms in the ocean are all producers.

Consumers

Consumers are organisms that feed on other organisms. Most consumers are animals, and they feed on plants or other animals. Consumers are also called heterotrophs ("other feeders").

Animals that feed directly on producers are called first-order consumers, or herbivores ("plant-eaters"). Deer, rabbits, cattle, and mice are herbivores. Animals that eat other animals are called carnivores ("flesh-eaters"). Wolves, polar bears, eagles, mountain lions, and sharks are carnivores.

Those carnivores which feed on herbivores are called first-order carnivores. (They can also be called second-order consumers. Why is this so?) The wolf is a first-order carnivore when it eats a deer. The fox is a first-order carnivore when it eats a mouse. And you are a first-order carnivore when you eat chicken, beef, or pork. (Technically, you would have to do your own killing.)

Fig. 2-4 This ground squirrel eats grass, seeds, and a variety of plants. It also eats grasshoppers. What kind of consumer is it: herbivore, carnivore, or omnivore?

Fig. 2-5 A predator-prey relationship exists between owls and mice. Which one is the predator? Which one is the prey?

Those carnivores which feed on first-order carnivores are called second-order carnivores (and also third-order consumers). If a mountain lion kills and eats a fox, it is a second-order carnivore. You are a second-order carnivore when you eat trout. (These fish feed mainly on other fish and insects that are herbivores.)

Some ecosystems have still higher orders of carnivores. And all ecosystems have top carnivores. What do you suppose that means?

Some animals are both herbivores and carnivores (Fig. 2-4). For example, the red fox does not eat just mice, birds, and rabbits. It also eats seeds and fruits it finds in the meadows and woods. In fact, during the summer and fall some foxes eat little else except plant material. Animals which are both herbivores and carnivores are called omnivores ("all-eaters"). Are you a herbivore, carnivore, or omnivore?

Carnivores which feed on live animals are called predators. The animals which are eaten are called prey. The owl in Figure 2-5 is a predator. And the mice it eats are the prey.

Animals which feed on dead organisms (both plant and animal) are called scavengers. Snails and crayfish are scavengers in ponds because they eat dead plants and animals. Crows, magpies, and vultures are also scavengers. You may have seen one of these birds feeding on an animal carcass on the roadside. Some animals may be predators one day and scavengers the next. The wolf is an example. It may kill a deer and eat part of it one day. Then it may return to the kill and feed on the remains for several days afterwards. Fungi and bacteria which feed on dead organisms (both plant and animal) are called saprophytes.

Decomposers

All ecosystems also contain a feeding level called decomposers. These organisms are mainly bacteria and fungi such as yeasts and moulds. They break down (decompose) and feed on non-living organic matter such as dead plants, dead animals, and animal wastes.

All organisms eventually die. And all animals produce wastes. If decomposers were not present, dead organisms and wastes would soon smother the earth. But decomposers perform an even more important function than breaking down organic matter. As they break down or feed on the organic matter, they return valuable nutrients to the soil. These nutrients can now be used again to help producers grow. For example, decomposers break down the leaf litter in a forest. Nutrients are then released from the leaves into the soil from which the nutrients can be obtained by trees.

The moulds that often grow on bread and fruits are also decomposers. They break down the bread and fruits as they feed on them. Some of the nutrients in the bread and fruit become part of the moulds. Other nutrients are released into the environment.

1. Name the three trophic levels.
2. a) What are producers?
   b) Name five producers.
   c) Why are producers also called autotrophs?
3. a) What are consumers?
   b) What is the difference between a first-order and a second-order consumer?
   c) How do herbivores, carnivores, and omnivores differ?
   d) What is a top carnivore?
4. What is the difference between predator and prey?
5. a) What is a scavenger?
   b) Name five scavengers.
6. a) What are decomposers?
   b) Give two reasons why decomposers are important.
7. a) What are the producers in your model ecosystem?
   b) Name the consumers in your model ecosystem. What do they eat?
   c) How do you know your model ecosystem contains decomposers?

2.3 Food Chains and Food Webs

Food Chains

Fig. 2-6 You can easily see that this food chain begins with a producer. Most food chains are like this. Some, however, seem to begin with dead plants and animals. Yet even these begin with producers. Can you explain why?

Organisms in an ecosystem may be linked together in feeding relationships called food chains. For example, clover is food for the groundhog. The groundhog, in turn, is food for the coyote. This simple food chain is shown in Figure 2-6.

Many food chains follow the pattern shown in Figure 2-6. That is, they begin with producers and move through herbivores to carnivores. Some food

PRODUCER　　　　　HERBIVORE
Clover　　　　　　　Groundhog

CARNIVORE
Coyote

chains however begin with dead plants or animals. An example is a crayfish feeding on a dead fish in a pond. In a sense, however, even this food chain began with a producer. The fish, when it was alive, was in a food chain that began with a producer. It may have eaten smaller animals which, in turn, had eaten algae or plants.

Though many food chains have just the three steps shown in Figure 2-6 (producer, herbivore, carnivore), others can be quite long. That's because they have several "orders" of carnivores. In other words, they have more predator-prey relationships. Figure 2-7 shows a food chain in which there are three orders of carnivores. Even a long food chain like this usually has the

Fig. 2-7 This food chain has the three main trophic levels—producer, consumer, and decomposer. (Decomposers are "busy" at all steps in this food chain when organisms die.) The consumer level in turn is divided into four sub-levels.

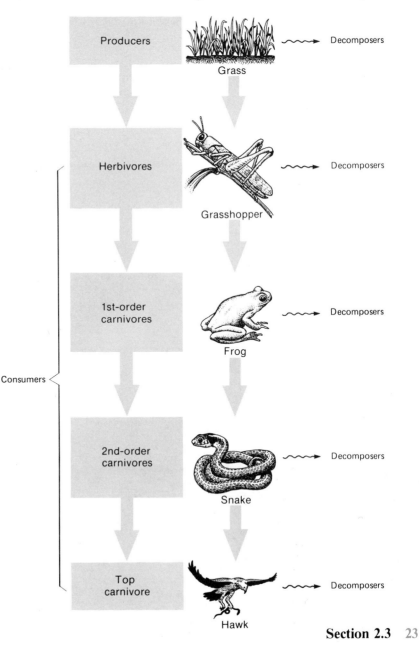

three main trophic levels—producer, consumer, and decomposer. The decomposers feed at all levels along the food chain. The consumer level, in this case, is divided into four sub-levels—herbivore, first-order carnivore, second-order carnivore, and top carnivore. Thus it is proper to say that the grasshopper occupies the trophic level of herbivore. And, the snake occupies the trophic level of second-order carnivore.

Food Webs

Most organisms are in more than one food chain. A certain species of plant, for example, could be eaten by several species of animal. And a certain species of animal could have more than one source of food. For example, a rabbit could be part of the following food chains:

grass ⟶ rabbit ⟶ wolf
clover ⟶ rabbit ⟶ wolf
clover ⟶ rabbit ⟶ fox
grass ⟶ rabbit ⟶ owl
grain ⟶ rabbit ⟶ hawk

Because organisms are often in more than one food chain, the food chains in an ecosystem are connected. The connected food chains are called a **food web**. Figure 2-8 shows a food web with food chains in both aquatic and terrestrial environments. Follow the arrow in this food web to find out what eats what.

Fig. 2-8 This food web involves both aquatic and terrestrial environments. Which organisms bridge the gap between water and land?

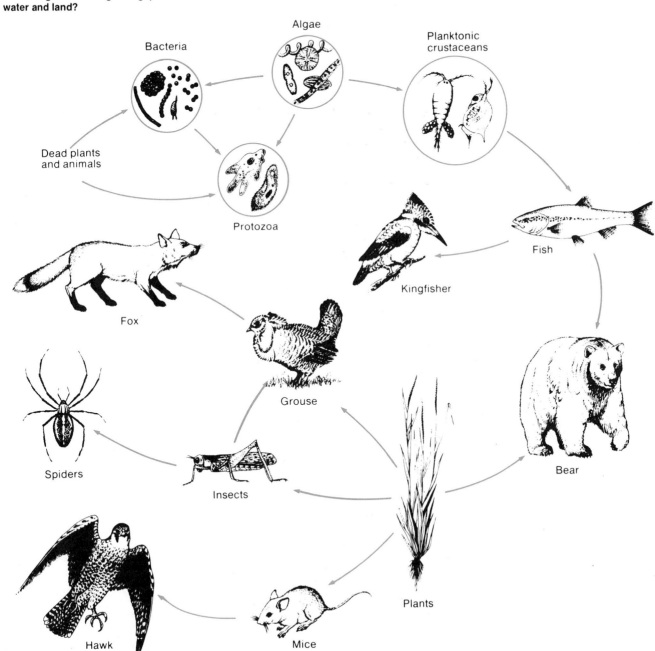

Bacteria

Algae

Planktonic crustaceans

Dead plants and animals

Protozoa

Fish

Kingfisher

Fox

Grouse

Bear

Spiders

Insects

Plants

Hawk

Mice

1. What is a food chain?
2. What is the general pattern for food chains that begin with producers?
3. Why do food chains get longer when there are more predator-prey relationships?
4. What is a food web?
5. List four food chains that are in the food web in Figure 2-8. Indicate the niche of each organism in each food chain.
6. List three food chains in your model ecosystem. Indicate the niche of each organism in each food chain.

Trophic Levels in a Lawn or Meadow

2.4   *FIELD TRIP*

There are three main trophic levels: producers, consumers, and decomposers. Consumers, in turn, can be divided into many smaller levels. Herbivores, first-order carnivores, second-order carnivores, and scavengers are examples.

In this activity you will visit a meadow or lawn. A meadow (unmown area) is best since it will have more life in it. At the site you will search for organisms. How many can you find? What trophic levels are they in?

Problem

What organisms are present in a lawn or meadow? What trophic levels do they occupy?

Materials

plastic jars with tops (5)   trowel
hand lens   sweep net
white tray   Field Guides for identification
                                       of plants and insects

Procedure

a. Copy Table 2-1 into your notebook. Make it a full page long.

Table 2-1 Study of a Meadow or Lawn

Species (name or sketch)	Trophic level and sub-level

Fig. 2-9 Sorting through soil and plant litter for animals.

b. Look at the vegetation closely. How many kinds of plants are present? If you know them, put their names in your table. If you don't, make a sketch of each of them. What trophic level do the plants belong to? Write your answers in the table.

c. Use the trowel to collect some topsoil and plant litter. Put this in the tray and spread it out. Then search for animals (Fig. 2-9). Watch them with the hand lens. You may wish to put them in jars to examine them more easily. Put their names (or sketches) in the table. What trophic level and sub-levels are the animals in? Put your answers in the table.
Note: You won't get all the sub-levels. But if you watch the animals closely, you will get some of them.

d. Sweep the vegetation with the sweep net as shown in Figure 2-10. Transfer the animals to jars. Watch them with the hand lens. Put their names (or sketches) in the table. What trophic level and sub-levels are the animals in? Write your answers in the table.

e. Are there any decomposers present? What is your evidence?

f. Release all animals when your study is complete.

Walking direction

Fig. 2-10 Move the net from side to side as you move along. Note how the animals are trapped when you are done sweeping.

Discussion

1. List as many food chains as you can for this ecosystem.
2. Create a food web for this ecosystem.
3. What would happen if all the producers died?
4. What might happen if all the herbivores died?
5. What larger animals may be involved in the food chains of this ecosystem? Was there any indirect evidence of their presence?
6. What evidence did you see that decomposers are present?

2.5 Ecological Pyramids

Pyramid of Numbers

Consider this simple food chain:

wheat ⟶ mouse ⟶ owl

A mouse that eats only wheat must eat a few hundred kernels a day to stay alive. (This number is found on 10 or 20 wheat plants.) However, the owl needs only five or so mice a day to survive. Many food chains show a similar numerical relationship. That is, many producers feed fewer herbivores which, in turn, feed still fewer carnivores. Such relationships are often represented by a pyramid of numbers (Fig. 2-11).

Fig. 2-11   A pyramid of numbers involving wheat, mice and an owl.

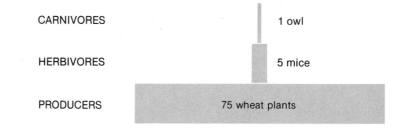

CARNIVORES	1 owl
HERBIVORES	5 mice
PRODUCERS	75 wheat plants

Not all pyramids of numbers have such a regular shape. In fact, some don't look like pyramids at all! For example, you may have seen tent caterpillars feeding on an apple tree (Fig. 2-12). One apple tree feeds thousands of caterpillars. The caterpillars, in turn, feed just a few thrashers (a type of bird). And several hundred lice may feed on the thrashers. This pyramid of numbers is shown in Figure 2-13.

Although it is simple, the pyramid of numbers is not used much by ecologists. The pyramid treats individuals of all species as though they were identical. For example, a cactus, a rabbit, and a fly each count as one unit. And a fifty tonne whale is equal numerically to a bacterium. The pyramid ignores differences in size. Yet, to a hungry fox size is important. One rabbit makes a better meal than one mouse!

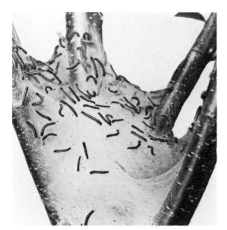

Fig. 2-12   This "tent" is home for hundreds of tent caterpillars. These animals eat the leaves of the tree.

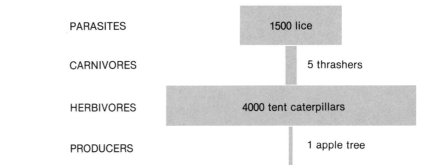

PARASITES	1500 lice
CARNIVORES	5 thrashers
HERBIVORES	4000 tent caterpillars
PRODUCERS	1 apple tree

Fig. 2-13   Another pyramid of numbers. Parasites are organisms that feed on other organisms without killing them.

Pyramid of Biomass

To get around this fault in the pyramid of numbers, ecologists often use a pyramid of biomass. Each trophic level in the pyramid shows the biomass (total mass of the organisms) at that level. Here is an example that uses a food chain of which you may be a part:

$$\text{grain} \longrightarrow \text{chicken} \longrightarrow \text{human}$$

Chickens eat grain, and humans eat chickens. About 30 g of grain are needed to form 10 g of chicken. Yet that 10 g of chicken will form less than 1 g of human (Fig. 2-14).

Fig. 2-14 A pyramid of biomass. Note how the mass decreases as we move along the food chain.

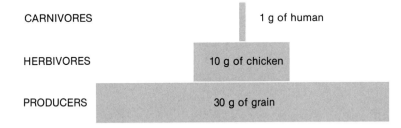

CARNIVORES — 1 g of human

HERBIVORES — 10 g of chicken

PRODUCERS — 30 g of grain

A pyramid of biomass is more useful than a pyramid of numbers. It makes more sense to equate 1 g of rabbit with 1 g of mouse than to equate one rabbit with one mouse. However, 1 g of rabbit and 1 g of mouse are not the same. They won't supply a fox with the same amount of energy. Different types of tissue have different energy contents. The most noticeable difference occurs between plant and animal tissue. You can usually obtain about 20% more energy by eating 1 g of animal than you can by eating 1 g of plant.

Pyramid of Energy

Some animals eat plants to obtain energy for life processes. Other animals eat animals to obtain their energy. Regardless of the source, all animals need energy to live. And the more easily they can get this energy, the better. Therefore, the efficiency with which energy is passed along the food chain is more important than either the numbers of organisms or their biomasses. Therefore, ecologists today direct most of their attention toward pyramids of energy. You will learn about these in Chapter 3.

Section Review

1. What is a pyramid of numbers?
2. Why do some pyramids of numbers not have a pyramid shape?
3. What is the main fault with a pyramid of numbers?
4. What is a pyramid of biomass?
5. Why is a pyramid of biomass more useful than a pyramid of numbers?
6. What is the main fault with a pyramid of biomass?
7. Why do ecologists today deal mainly with pyramids of energy?

2.6 Special Feeding Relationships

Many unusual ecological relationships exist between organisms. One of these is called symbiosis. The word symbiosis means "living together". Symbiosis is a close association between two organisms of different species in which at least one of the two benefits. There are three kinds of symbiosis: parasitism, mutualism, and commensalism. In each of these relationships, organisms provide food and/or other benefits for other organisms without being killed and eaten themselves.

Parasitism

Parasitism is a symbiotic relationship between two organisms in which one organism benefits and the other suffers harm. The organism that benefits is called the parasite. The organism that is harmed is called the host. The mosquito is a parasite. When you provide it with a blood meal, you are the host.

Fleas, lice, ticks, and blackflies are common parasites. Humans, other mammals, and birds are their common hosts. Tapeworms are parasites that live in the intestines of humans, cattle, and other animals. Many plant diseases are also caused by parasites. Rusts, smuts, and mildews are examples.

Most parasites do not kill their hosts. If they did, they would lose their food supply. Besides, it isn't nice to kill a host who just gave you a free meal!

Mutualism

Mutualism is a symbiotic relationship between two organisms in which both organisms benefit. For example, the relationship in a lichen is mutualism. A lichen consists of an alga and a fungus, growing together in a close relationship (Fig. 2-15). The alga contains chlorophyll. Therefore it can make food. It shares this food with the fungus. The fungus, in turn, provides the alga with water, minerals, and support.

Another example of mutualism occurs on the roots of legumes (peas, beans, alfalfa, clover, soybeans). A bacterium called *Rhizobium* lives in nodules on the roots of legumes (Fig. 2-16). These bacteria change atmospheric nitrogen into nitrates. The legume plants absorb these nitrates and use them to make proteins. In return, the legumes provide the *Rhizobium* with food, water, and a home.

Commensalism

Commensalism is a symbiotic relationship in which one organism benefits and the other neither benefits nor suffers harm. An example occurs in the

Fig. 2-15 This lichen looks like one organism. However it is really two, a fungus and an alga living in a close relationship called mutualism.

Fig. 2-16 The roots of a soybean plant. Note the lumps (nodules) on the roots. These nodules contain the *Rhizobium* bacteria.

Fig. 2-17 Commensalism. The lichen, Old man's beard, is growing on a spruce tree. The spruce tree is not harmed. Nor does it get any benefits from the lichen. The lichen, however, receives several benefits by growing on the spruce tree. What are some of these?

coniferous forests of the northern parts of Canada and the United States (Fig. 2-17). A lichen called "Old man's beard" uses the spruce tree as a home. It gets water and some minerals from the bark. But it does not usually harm the tree. Nor does the tree get any benefit from the lichen. Sometimes the lichens get very dense and then can harm the trees. What would you now call the relationship?

Section Review

1. Define symbiosis.
2. What is parasitism? Use an example to illustrate your answer.
3. What is mutualism? Use an example to illustrate your answer.
4. What is commensalism? Use an example to illustrate your answer.

2.7 Abiotic Factors in Ecosystems

Fig. 2-18 This fox is in a clearing in the forest. What abiotic factors affect this fox?

An ecosystem has two main parts, a biotic part and an abiotic part. So far in this chapter we have directed our attention to the biotic part. This section gives you an overview of the abiotic part. You will study this part in detail in later chapters of this book.

The fox in Figure 2-18 was photographed in Gros Morne National Park in Newfoundland. Think about this animal's environment. What abiotic factors affect the fox? In what ways?

Terrestrial Ecosystems

The fox lives in a terrestrial (land) ecosystem. These ecosystems are affected by five main abiotic factors. They are temperature, moisture, light, wind, and soil conditions.

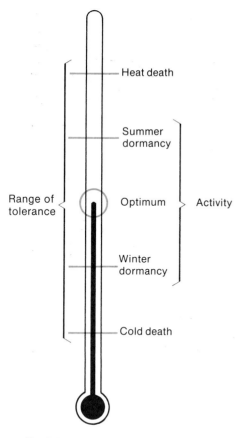

Heat death

Summer
dormancy

Range of
tolerance

Optimum   Activity

Winter
dormancy

Cold death

Fig. 2-19   Range of tolerance to
temperature. Note that the organism goes
dormant (inactive but not dead) if the
environment gets too hot or too cold. Why
is this?

Each organism has a range of tolerance for each of these factors (Fig. 2-19). This range depends on the factor and on the organism. When the range is exceeded in either direction, the organism suffers. Within each range of tolerance there is a point at which the organism lives best. This point is called the optimum. However, conditions are seldom at the optimum. Therefore organisms with the broadest range of tolerance generally survive best.

In Unit 2 you will learn about the interdependence of biotic and abiotic factors in terrestrial ecosystems.

Aquatic Ecosystems

Many abiotic factors also affect aquatic (water) ecosystems. For example, life in a stream may be affected by temperature, speed of the water, nature of the bottom, light, oxygen, and many other factors (Fig. 2-20). A fast cool stream with lots of oxygen will likely support trout. But a sluggish, warm, polluted stream will not.

Life in a pond or lake may be affected by temperature, light, depth, nature of the bottom, oxygen, and many other factors. And life on the seashore may be affected by wave action, the salt content of the water, and the tides, as well as other factors.

You can learn about the interdependence of biotic and abiotic factors in aquatic ecosystems in *Investigating Aquatic Ecosystems*.

Section Review

1. What five abiotic factors affect life in terrestrial ecosystems?
2. What is meant by each of these terms: range of tolerance, optimum?
3. a) Name five abiotic factors which affect life in a stream.
   b) Name five abiotic factors which affect life in a lake.
   c) Name three abiotic factors which affect life on the seashore.

Fig. 2-20   Can you name some organisms
which would thrive in this fast stream?

Effect of Temperature on Germination and Seedling Growth Rate

2.8 *ACTIVITY*

When a seed is planted in the proper environment, it **germinates**. The tiny plant that forms is called a **seedling**. Both the germination of the seed and the growth of the seedling are affected by many abiotic factors. Temperature is one of these.

In this activity you will study the effects of temperature on the germination and growth of several types of plants. Gardeners plant certain seeds in the early spring while the soil is still cool. They plant others in the late spring when the soil is much warmer. See if you can find out why they do this.

Problem

How does temperature affect germination and seedling growth rate?

Materials

trays about 10 cm x 30 cm (4)
potting soil
thermometer
seeds of radish, spinach, tomato,
    pea, bean, squash, corn (any 5
    or 6 will do)

marking pen
markers (20-25)
refrigerator
incubator
water

Procedure

a. Fill the 4 trays with soil.

b. Label the trays "freezer", "refrigerator", "room", and "incubator".

c. Plant 8 radish seeds in 2 rows at one end of each tray (Fig. 2-21). Use the planting depth indicated on the seed package. Mark the rows.

d. Now plant 8 spinach seeds in 2 rows next to the radishes in each tray. Mark the rows.

e. Continue this process with all the types of seeds provided.

f. Water the trays until the soil is damp but not soggy.

g. Put the "freezer" tray in the freezer and the "refrigerator" tray in the refrigerator. Put the "room" tray in a dark cupboard at room temperature. Put the "incubator" tray in an incubator at 35°C-40°C.

h. Copy Table 2-2 into your notebook.

i. Observe the trays every day. Water them when necessary. Record in your table the day when seedlings first appear. Also, record the day when they are 1 cm tall (on average).

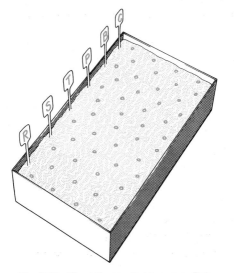

Fig. 2-21 Plant the seeds 4 in a row. Put the rows 2-3 cm apart.

Table 2-2 Temperature and Growth Rate

Species	Day plants first appear				Day plants are 1 cm tall			
	Freezer	Refrigerator	Room	Incubator	Freezer	Refrigerator	Room	Incubator
radish								
spinach								
tomato								
pea								
bean								
squash								

Discussion

1. Why was the "room" tray placed in the dark?
2. Did all seeds and seedlings respond to temperature in the same way? Why or why not? (*Hint*: Use the information on range of tolerance and optimum temperature given in Section 2.7.)
3. Which seeds would you plant in the early spring? Why?
4. Which seeds would you plant in the late spring? Why?
5. How does this activity show that biotic and abiotic factors are interdependent?

Main Ideas

1. The habitat of an organism is the place in which it lives.
2. The niche of an organism is its total role in the community.
3. Two species with the same habitat and similar niches will compete with one another.
4. There are three main trophic levels: producers, consumers, and decomposers.
5. Organisms are linked together in food chains and food webs.
6. Ecological pyramids can be used to represent trophic levels.
7. There are three types of symbiotic relationships: parasitism, mutualism, and commensalism.
8. Abiotic and biotic parts of an ecosystem are interdependent.

Key Terms

autotroph	heterotroph	producer
carnivore	host	pyramid of biomass
commensalism	mutualism	pyramid of energy
consumer	niche	pyramid of numbers
decomposer	omnivore	range of tolerance
food chain	parasite	saprophyte
food web	parasitism	scavenger
habitat	predator	symbiosis
herbivore	prey	

Chapter Review

A. True or False

Decide whether each of the following statements is true or false. If the sentence is false, rewrite it to make it true. (Do not write in this book.)
1. The habitat of an animal is the place where it lives.
2. Carnivores eat both plants and animals.
3. Trees are producers.
4. A parasite usually kills its host.
5. Both organisms benefit in the symbiotic relationship called mutualism.

B. Completion

Complete each of the following sentences with a word or phrase that will make the sentence correct. (Do not write in this book.)
1. Grass is called a ▨▨▨▨ because it makes its own food.
2. If a wolf eats a mouse, the wolf is a ▨▨▨▨ order carnivore.
3. Animals that prey on live animals are called ▨▨▨▨ .
4. Nutrients are returned to the soil by organisms at the trophic level of ▨▨▨▨ .

C. Multiple Choice

Each of the following statements or questions is followed by four responses. Choose the correct response in each case. (Do not write in this book.)
1. A groundhog lives in a burrow but also spends time in nearby fields. This is a description of the groundhog's
   a) niche   b) habitat   c) community   d) ecosystem
2. A skunk eats living grubs and worms. It also eats fruits of some plants. It even eats garbage. The skunk is best described as an
   a) omnivore   b) herbivore   c) carnivore   d) scavenger

3. Consider this food chain:

algae ——→ small animals ——→ minnows ——→ trout ——→ humans

The trout in this food chain are
a) first-order carnivores
b) second-order carnivores
c) third-order carnivores
d) top carnivores

4. A hawk swoops down from the sky and kills and eats a rabbit. This hawk is a
a) scavenger   b) prey   c) predator   d) decomposer

5. The temperature at which an organism lives best is called the
a) range of tolerance
b) summer dormancy
c) winter dormancy
d) optimum temperature

Using Your Knowledge

1. Consider the following food chain as you complete Table 2-3 in your notebook.

algae ——→ water fleas ——→ minnows ——→ trout ——→ bear

Table 2-3 Trophic Levels

Organism	Trophic or sub-trophic level
algae	
water fleas	
minnows	
trout	
bear	

2. Draw pyramids of numbers for these food chains:

dead fish ——→ moulds

grass ——→ rabbits ——→ wolves ——→ fleas

3. Why must all ecosystems have decomposers?

4. Select five foods that you ate during the last three meals. Draw the five food chains that include those foods and you.

5. Barnacles, an animal, usually live attached to rocks. But some barnacles attach themselves to the skin of whales. They do not help or harm the whales in any way. What kind of symbiotic relationship is this? Explain your answer.

Investigations

1. Go on a hike to a nearby park. Make notes on the habitat and niche of at least five animals. Binoculars would be helpful. You might also wish to photograph the habitats.
2. Write a short paper (about 150 words) on a parasite that causes a human disease.
3. Plan and carry out an experiment to show the effects of light on germination and seedling growth.
4. Plan and carry out an experiment to show the effects of moisture on germination and seedling growth.
5. Consult books in the library and find an example of mutualism which is not described in this text.
6. Consult books in the library and find an example of commensalism which is not described in this text. Write a short description of it.
7. Make a poster of a food web with at least 5 organisms and 3 trophic levels in it. Use pictures cut from magazines or take your own pictures or draw them. Be sure all the organisms belong to the same ecosystem. Also, be sure you connect them correctly with arrows.

3

Flow of Matter and Energy in Ecosystems

All living things need matter and energy. Matter is needed to make new cells and to repair worn-out parts; energy is needed to "power" life processes such as movement and growth.

How does energy get into an ecosystem? How does it reach every organism in the ecosystem? How does matter get into an ecosystem? And how does each organism in the ecosystem get the matter it needs? This chapter explains how matter and energy move into and through ecosystems.

3.1   Flow of Energy in Ecosystems

Spend a few quiet moments some day near the woods, beside a stream, in a meadow, or in a park (Fig. 3-1). You'll probably be surprised by the constant activity around you. Birds are constantly searching for food. Squirrels dart everywhere. Insects hop, crawl, and fly in all directions. Activity is the essence of life. And to have activity, energy is needed. Where do organisms get their energy? What happens to energy in ecosystems?

Energy from the Sun to Carnivores

All the energy used by living things comes, in the first place, from the sun. Producers store some of the sun's energy in the foods they make by photosynthesis. They use some of this food for their own life processes. The rest is stored. Herbivores get their energy by eating producers. And carnivores get

Fig. 3-1 All living things need energy. This includes trees, mammals, insects, and fish which may be in this area. How do they get their energy?

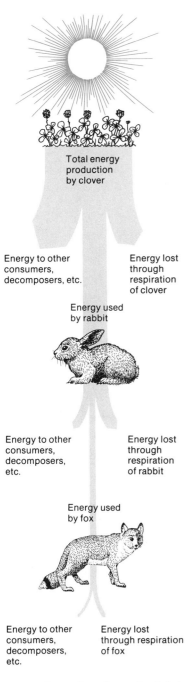

Total energy production by clover

Energy to other consumers, decomposers, etc.

Energy lost through respiration of clover

Energy used by rabbit

Energy to other consumers, decomposers, etc.

Energy lost through respiration of rabbit

Energy used by fox

Energy to other consumers, decomposers, etc.

Energy lost through respiration of fox

Fig. 3-2 Energy flow along a food chain.

their energy by eating herbivores or other carnivores. Thus, the sun's energy is passed along food chains to carnivores.

Energy Flow Is One-Way

The passing of energy along a food chain is not very efficient. A great deal is lost at each trophic level. As an example, consider this food chain:

clover ⟶ rabbit ⟶ fox

Follow Figure 3-2 as you read on. The clover, through photosynthesis, stores some of the sun's energy in foods. Much of this energy is lost as heat through respiration by the clover. However, when the rabbit eats the clover, the rabbit gets some of the stored energy.

Like the clover, the rabbit loses much of the energy it took in through life activities such as respiration. When the fox eats the rabbit, the fox gets some of the energy stored in the rabbit. It does not get all this energy, however. For instance, bones cannot be digested by the fox.

The fox also loses much of the energy it took in through life activities such as respiration. Parasites and decomposers also use some of the fox's energy. In the end, little energy remains to be passed on to higher trophic levels.

As Figure 3-2 shows, energy is gradually lost along a food chain. Much of this energy leaves the food chain as heat. It cannot be recaptured by any organisms in the food chain. It is lost forever to that ecosystem. Thus energy flow is one-way along a food chain. For an ecosystem to keep operating, energy must always enter it from the sun.

In Section 2.5 you saw that there are three kinds of ecological pyramids: pyramids of numbers, biomass, and energy. The most important of these is the pyramid of energy. How well an ecosystem functions depends on how well each trophic level captures energy and passes it on to the next level. This is much more important than the numbers of organisms or their sizes (biomasses).

Since energy is lost along a food chain, all pyramids of energy look like the one in Figure 3-3. They taper off to almost nothing. Each level in this pyramid represents the total energy flow at that level. The total amount includes the energy tied up in the formation of new cells and that given off by respiration.

Fig. 3-3 A pyramid of energy for a terrestrial ecosystem. Each numeral represents the total energy flow at that level in kilojoules per square metre of land surface per year.

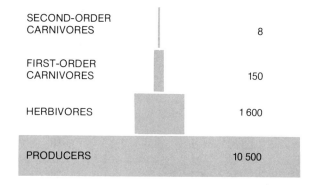

SECOND-ORDER CARNIVORES   8

FIRST-ORDER CARNIVORES   150

HERBIVORES   1 600

PRODUCERS   10 500

Section Review

1. Describe the path of energy from the sun to carnivores.
2. Describe how energy is lost along a food chain.
3. What is meant by the phrase "energy flow is one-way in ecosystems"?
4. Account for the shape of a pyramid of energy.
5. Why is a pyramid of energy more useful to ecologists than a pyramid of numbers or biomass?
6. Describe the flow of energy through your model ecosystem.

3.2   Flow of Matter in Ecosystems

Nutrients: The Elements of Life

An ecosystem needs more than energy to function. It also needs matter. Matter is used by organisms in the ecosystem for life processes such as growth. Most ecosystems need over 20 elements. Among these are nitrogen and oxygen. Just the plants in most ecosystems need 16 elements. Because these elements are so important to living things, they are called nutrients.

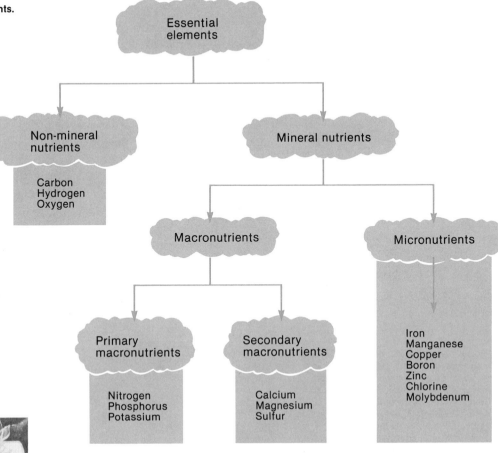

Fig. 3-4   Classification of plant nutrients.

Essential elements

Non-mineral nutrients

Carbon
Hydrogen
Oxygen

Mineral nutrients

Macronutrients

Micronutrients

Iron
Manganese
Copper
Boron
Zinc
Chlorine
Molybdenum

Primary macronutrients

Nitrogen
Phosphorus
Potassium

Secondary macronutrients

Calcium
Magnesium
Sulfur

Fig. 3-5   This 4-9-15 fertilizer is 4% nitrogen, 9% phosphorus, and 15% potassium. All three nutrients are needed in relatively large amounts for plant growth.

Figure 3-4 shows a classification system for the 16 elements which most plants need. As you can see, three elements are classified as non-mineral nutrients and the others as mineral nutrients. Mineral nutrients are those which originally entered the ecosystem from bedrock. Non-mineral nutrients entered the ecosystem in the form of water and carbon dioxide.

The three non-mineral nutrients (carbon, hydrogen, and oxygen) are often called the building blocks of life. Every organism, including you, is almost entirely made of them.

The mineral nutrients are divided into macronutrients and micronutrients. (*Macro* means large and *micro* means small.) The macronutrients are required in greater amounts than the micronutrients. Of the macronutrients, the three primary macronutrients (nitrogen, phosphorus, and potassium) are needed in the greatest amounts. In fact, commercial fertilizers usually contain these three nutrients (Fig. 3-5). Magnesium, a secondary macronutrient, is one of the atoms in a chlorophyll molecule. Thus all plants and algae need this nutrient. Iron, a micronutrient, is needed to make hemoglobin molecules in red-blooded animals.

Most ecosystems need a few more nutrients than the 16 that plants require. For example, most of the animals in ecosystems need sodium and cobalt. And the plants that grow in salt marshes along the oceans generally need sodium.

Nutrient Cycles

In Section 3.1 you learned that energy is lost along a food chain. Little or no energy is left at the end of the food chain to be recycled to the producers. This is not, however, the case for nutrients. Nutrients flow through the food chain back to the start of the cycle. Producers get their nutrients from the soil, water, and air. Herbivores get these nutrients when they eat the producers. Carnivores get the same nutrients when they eat the herbivores. Then decomposers break down animal wastes and dead organisms. Their action releases the nutrients back into the soil, water, and air so producers can use them again. In this way, nutrients are recycled through an ecosystem. The path each nutrient follows is called a nutrient cycle. Figure 3-6 compares energy flow and nutrient recycling in an ecosystem. Study this comparison closely. Then read the next four sections. They show you how four basic nutrient cycles operate.

Fig. 3-6 Energy flow and nutrient cycles in an ecosystem. The green arrows show the direction of energy flow. Note that energy is lost at each level (wavy lines). The black arrows show the path of nutrient flow. Note that nutrients complete the cycle. The broken green arrow represents both energy and nutrient flow to decomposers as they break down dead producers.

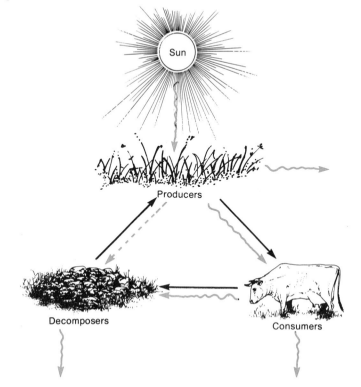

Section Review

1. Why are some elements called nutrients?
2. What is the difference between mineral and non-mineral nutrients?

3. Name the three primary macronutrients.
4. Discuss two examples which show that micronutrients are important to ecosystems.
5. What evidence do you have that nutrient cycles exist in your model ecosystem?

3.3   The Water Cycle

The hydrogen and oxygen atoms in water are nutrients organisms need. These nutrients are recycled through ecosystems as follows.

Water vapour enters the atmosphere through transpiration from vegetation. (Transpiration is the loss of water through pores in the leaves of plants.) It also enters the atmosphere by evaporating from bodies of water and the soil (Fig. 3-7). In the cool upper atmosphere this vapour condenses, forming clouds. In time, enough water collects in the clouds to cause precipitation. When this happens, some of the water that falls on the ground runs along the surface of the ground to a stream, pond, or other body of water. This water is called surface runoff. But some of the water also soaks into the ground by a process called percolation. Some water percolates down to the bedrock. Then it becomes ground water and gradually runs back to lakes and other bodies of water.

Fig. 3-7 The water cycle.

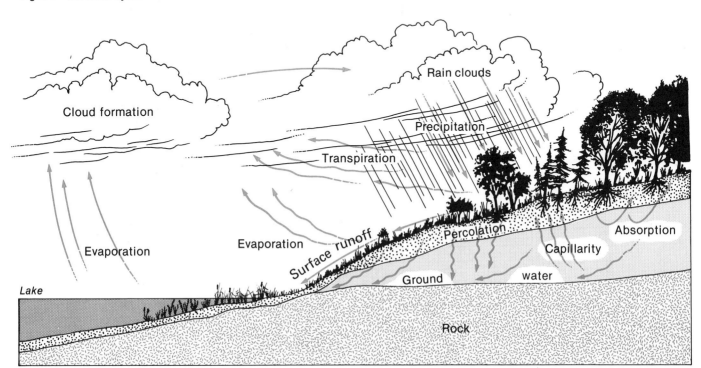

Some of the water in the soil moves up to the roots of plants by **capillarity**. The roots absorb the water. This is how most plants get the hydrogen and oxygen they need. Animals can obtain water by eating plants or by eating other animals. Of course, they can also obtain it by drinking water directly from a body of water.

Finally, when plants and animals die, they decompose. During this process, the water in their tissues is released back into the environment.

Section Review

1. Why is the water cycle important?
2. Make a point form summary of the water cycle.

3.4   The Carbon Cycle

Carbon is another nutrient that all organisms need. In fact, it is the basic building block of all living things. Like water, carbon moves through an ecosystem in a cycle (Fig. 3-8). Here is how the cycle works.

Carbon is present in the atmosphere as carbon dioxide. Producers (plants and algae) use it to make food. Now the carbon is in the producers. Herbivores eat the plants and carnivores eat the herbivores. Now the carbon is in the animals. Both plants and animals respire. Their respiration returns carbon dioxide to the atmosphere. Decomposers break down dead plants and animals as well as animal waste. This, too, returns carbon dioxide to the atmosphere.

Some organic matter does not decompose easily. Instead, it builds up in the earth's crust. Oil and coal were formed from the build-up of plant matter millions of years ago.

At one time, the carbon cycle was almost a perfect cycle. Carbon was returned to the atmosphere as quickly as it was removed. Lately, however,

Fig. 3-8 The carbon cycle.

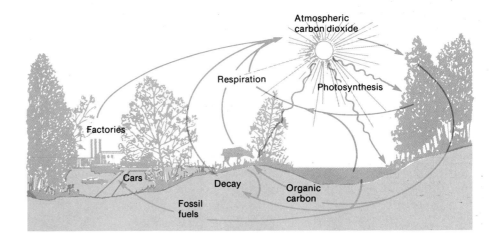

the increased burning of fossil fuels has added carbon to the atmosphere faster than producers can remove it.

The cycle just described happens on, in, and above the land. A similar cycle also occurs in aquatic ecosystems such as lakes and oceans. In fact, water (mainly in the oceans) holds over 50 times as much carbon dioxide as the air.

Section Review

1. Why is the carbon cycle important?
2. Make a point form summary of the carbon cycle.
3. Describe the carbon cycle as it might occur in a lake. Begin with carbon dioxide in the water.

3.5   The Nitrogen Cycle

Nitrogen is another important nutrient. All living things need nitrogen to make proteins. Let's see how this nutrient is recycled in ecosystems (Fig. 3-9).

Almost 78% of the atmosphere is nitrogen (N_2). However, neither plants nor animals can use this form of nitrogen directly. Usually the nitrogen must be in the form of a nitrate (NO_3). Then plant roots can absorb it. Lightning forms some nitrate. It causes oxygen and nitrogen in the atmosphere to join. *Rhizobium* bacteria can do the same thing. You may recall that these bacteria live on the roots of legumes (Section 2.6, page 30). Many bacteria and blue-green algae also form nitrates. The changing of nitrogen to nitrates is called nitrogen fixation.

Plants use the nitrates they absorb to make plant proteins. Animals get the nitrogen they need to make proteins by eating plants or other animals.

When plants and animals die, bacteria change their nitrogen content to ammonia. The nitrogen in the urine and fecal matter of animals is also changed to ammonia by bacteria. The pungent odour of outhouses, chicken pens, hog yards, cat litter boxes and wet baby diapers is ample evidence of this fact. (If you are not sure what ammonia smells like, smell some ammonium carbonate . . . *cautiously!*) Ammonia, in turn, is converted to nitrites and then to nitrates by bacteria. This completes the main part of the cycle. Bacteria convert some nitrites and nitrates to nitrogen (N_2) to finish the cycle. The nitrogen cycle need not and often does not involve this last step.

Many plants are able to use some ammonia directly. Therefore all of it does not have to be converted to nitrate before plants absorb it.

Section Review

1. Why is the nitrogen cycle important?
2. Make a point form summary of the nitrogen cycle.

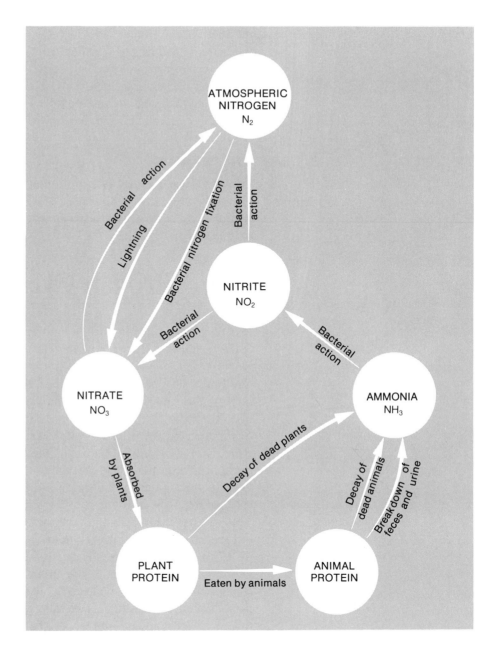

Fig. 3-9   The nitrogen cycle.

3.6   The Phosphorus Cycle

Phosphorus is another nutrient which is important to all living things. Many important molecules within cells contain phosphorus atoms. For example, adenosine triphosphate (ATP) is a phosphorus-bearing compound found in every living cell. There it plays a key role in energy storage and supply.

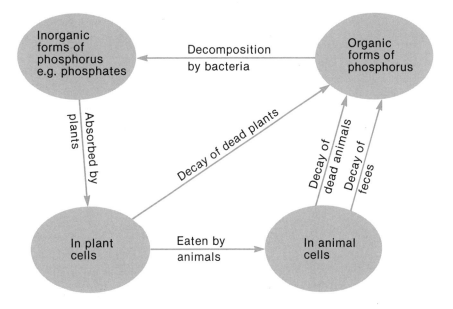

Fig. 3-10   The phosphorus cycle.

Phosphorus, like other nutrients, follows a cycle through ecosystems. Let us begin in the upper left corner of Figure 3-10 and trace this cycle.

Phosphorus normally occurs in water and soil in inorganic compounds. Phosphates (PO_4) are a common form. These compounds are absorbed by plants and used to make organic compounds such as ATP. When animals eat plants, phosphorus is passed on to them. When dead plants, dead animals, and fecal matter decay, organic forms of phosphorus are released into the water or soil. Bacteria decompose these organic forms into inorganic forms. And the cycle begins again.

Section Review

1. Why is the phosphorus cycle important?
2. Make a point form summary of the phosphorus cycle.

Upsetting the Nutrient Balance in an Ecosystem

3.7   *ACTIVITY*

Nutrients pass through cycles in ecosystems. They move from producers through consumers. They are then returned to producers by decomposers. Also, the nutrients in dead producers are recycled to producers by decomposers. As a result, a **balance** usually exists in an ecosystem. That is, some of each nutrient is in the producers. Some of it is in the consumers. And some of it is in the free state, ready to be absorbed by producers.

What do you suppose would happen to an ecosystem if we added extra nutrients in the free state? How might this affect the cycles? the producers? the consumers?

In this activity you will make a simple aquatic ecosystem. Then you will add some lawn fertilizer to it. This fertilizer contains three main nutrients: nitrogen, phosphorus, and potassium.

Problem

How will lawn fertilizer affect the balance in an ecosystem?

Materials

wide-mouthed jars, with a capacity
   of at least 1 L (2)
pond water (2 L)
strands of *Cabomba, Elodea,* or
   other aquatic plant, each about
   10-20 cm long (6)
pond snails (6)

Procedure

a. Fill both jars with pond water.
b. Add half the *Cabomba* to each jar.
c. Add 3 pond snails to each jar.
d. Label one jar "Control". Label the other jar "Experimental" (Fig. 3-11).
e. Add a *very small* pinch of lawn fertilizer to the experimental jar.
f. Place the jars, side by side, in a bright location.
g. Observe the jars each day for 2-3 weeks. Make notes on any changes in the appearance of the *Cabomba* and the snails.

Fig. 3-11 How will fertilizer affect the experimental jar?

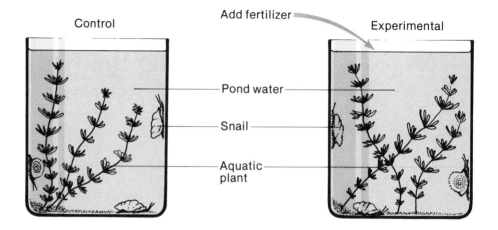

1. What are the producers in your ecosystems?
2. What are the consumers in your ecosystems?
3. **a)** What important invisible organisms are in your ecosystems?
   b) What is their role?
4. What is the purpose of the control?
5. Why are the jars placed side by side?
6. **a)** Describe the changes the fertilizer caused in your ecosystem.
   b) Explain these changes.
7. Explain why sewage can cause plant and algal growth in lakes.

3.8 Summary of the Structure and Functioning of Ecosystems

An ocean, pond, forest, desert, park, alpine (mountain) meadow, and your model ecosystem don't look much alike. But they are all ecosystems. Therefore they have a common structure, and they function in the same basic way. You learned about the structure of ecosystems in Chapter 2 and about how they function in this chapter. Let's list those things ecosystems have in common.

- Most ecosystems have the same three biotic parts: producers, consumers, and decomposers. The actual species will, of course, differ from ecosystem to ecosystem.

- A highly interdependent relationship exists between the biotic and abiotic parts of an ecosystem.

- Energy flow in ecosystems is one-way. Energy is gradually lost along food chains. Little or none is recycled to producers. Therefore energy must always enter the ecosystem from the sun.

- Most ecosystems need the same 20 or so nutrients. These nutrients are recycled within each ecosystem.

Section Review

1. Make a summary of the four things most ecosystems have in common.

Main Ideas

1. Energy flow in ecosystems is one-way; energy is not recycled.
2. Ecosystems need energy input from the sun.
3. Most ecosystems need the same 20 or so basic nutrients.
4. Nutrients are recycled in ecosystems.

Key Terms

capillarity	nutrient
energy flow	nutrient cycle
mineral nutrient	percolation
nitrogen fixation	pyramid of energy
non-mineral nutrient	transpiration

Chapter Review

A. True or False

Decide whether each of the following statements is true or false. If the sentence is false, rewrite it to make it true. (Do not write in this book.)

1. Energy is recycled in ecosystems.
2. Nutrients are recycled in ecosystems.
3. A pyramid of energy can be inverted.
4. Carbon dioxide is returned to the atmosphere by decomposers.
5. Water reaches the bedrock by a process called capillarity.

B. Completion

Complete each of the following sentences with a word or phrase that will make the sentence correct. (Do not write in this book.)

1. The elements that are needed in ecosystems are called ▨▨▨ .
2. Bacteria on the roots of legumes can form ▨▨▨ from nitrogen and oxygen.
3. Mineral nutrients originally entered the ecosystem from ▨▨▨ .
4. Nutrients needed in trace amounts are called ▨▨▨ .
5. The inorganic form of phosphorus in soil and water is normally ▨▨▨ .

C. Multiple Choice

Each of the following statements or questions is followed by four responses. Choose the correct response in each case. (Do not write in this book.)

1. A homeowner left the grass clippings on the lawn when it was mowed. She discovered that the lawn needed less fertilizer than it did when she collected the clippings. This is because
   a) energy flow is one-way
   b) energy must enter the lawn ecosystem from the sun
   c) the clippings help retain water
   d) nutrients are recycled
2. A secondary macronutrient required by all plants and algae is
   a) carbon b) nitrogen c) magnesium d) oxygen
3. Oxygen, hydrogen, and carbon are best classified as
   a) non-mineral nutrients   c) macronutrients
   b) mineral nutrients   d) micronutrients
4. The carbon cycle is no longer a perfect cycle because of
   a) the increased burning of fossil fuels
   b) the lack of enough decomposers
   c) the lack of enough herbivores
   d) a decrease in total respiration on earth

Using Your Knowledge

1. An oxygen cycle exists in nature. Ecologists often consider it along with the carbon cycle. They call the result the carbon-oxygen cycle. Why does it make sense to do this?
2. It has been suggested that to make the best use of food on this crowded planet, we should all become herbivores. In other words, we would no longer eat cattle, pigs, and fowl. Instead, we would eat the plants that these animals would normally have eaten. What do you think of this idea? Why?
3. Many farmers raise cattle by the hundreds in large enclosures called feedlots. The urine and feces from feedlots often pollute nearby streams and lakes.
   a) Name two macronutrients that could enter aquatic ecosystems from feedlots.
   b) Explain why feedlots produce these two nutrients.
   c) Explain what could happen to a lake if these nutrients entered it.
4. Recently, many people have suggested diverting the course of several Arctic rivers. Instead of emptying into the Arctic Ocean, they would flow southward. The water would be used to irrigate arid regions in the American southwest. This would increase the productivity of the area.
   a) In general, what do you think of this proposal?
   b) Use your knowledge of the water cycle to predict some effects of such a diversion.
   c) What effects might such action have on the climate of North America?

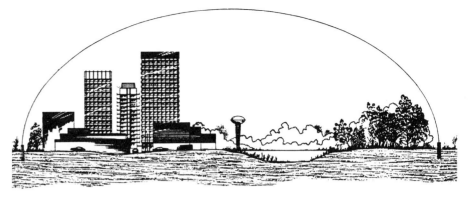

Fig. 3-12 Can this ecosystem function on its own?

5. Imagine that your home community, with some of the surrounding countryside, is enclosed in a large, clear plastic dome as shown in Figure 3-12. Could this closed ecosystem function normally over a period of a year, just as the ecosystem bottle in Section 1.4 does? Support your answer by referring to nutrient cycles and energy flow.

Investigations

1. Repeat Activity 3.7, but this time add just one macronutrient (nitrogen, phosphorus, or potassium) instead of lawn fertilizer. Describe and explain your results. *Note:* Nitrogen may be added by using a nitrate salt like sodium nitrate. Phosphorus may be added by using a phosphate salt like sodium phosphate. And potassium may be added by using a potassium salt like potassium chloride.
2. If lawn clippings are left on a lawn, the nutrients will be recycled. This saves valuable fertilizer. If, however, the clippings are long, they may smother the grass. In this case they should be raked up. But they need not be wasted. Find out what composting is. Then build a simple demonstration compost heap for recycling grass clippings.
3. Design and build a model terrestrial ecosystem.
4. a) Carefully remove a legume plant (soybean, clover, or vetch) from the soil. Examine the *Rhizobium* nodules on its roots, using a hand lens or dissecting microscope. Sketch what you see.
    b) With the assistance of instructions from a microbiology text, extract the nitrogen-fixing bacteria. Stain them and then examine them with a microscope. Sketch what you see.

4

Ecological Succession

You have probably noticed that a vacant lot, left untouched, does not remain in its original state for long. It may have started out with bare soil. But it soon becomes overgrown with grasses and weeds. As time passes taller weeds dominate the shorter ones. In a few years shrubs may appear. Several years later small trees may begin to colonize the area. If you could camp out under one of these trees for a few hundred years, you would witness one of nature's most remarkable phenomena—**ecological succession**. What is succession? Why does it occur?

4.1   Succession on Sand Dunes

A well-defined succession occurs on sand dunes. Let's examine this environment to find out what succession is and why it happens.

The Sand Dune Environment

Sand dunes commonly form on the leeward side of large lakes (the shore toward which the wind blows). They also form on ocean shores. Some of the most famous dunes in the world occur around the Great Lakes (Fig. 4-1). Figure 4-2 shows how they form. Wave action piles sand on the beach where the sun and wind dry it out. Then winds blow the sand inland. This often creates large mounds of sand called **sand dunes**.

Such an area is a harsh environment for any organism. Some of the harsh conditions are:

- lack of moisture
- few available nutrients
- intense light
- strong winds
- shifting sands
- high day temperatures
- low night temperatures

In spite of these conditions, some organisms do establish communities on sand dunes. And, as you know, their presence changes the environment. The changed environment then supports different organisms. These organisms, in turn, change the environment again. And on it goes.

This interaction of biotic and abiotic factors makes a sand dune a region of change. Let us take an imaginary trip through time to see exactly what happens. Imagine that you are sitting on a sand dune. It has no life on it, other than you. This dune is located on the shore of one of the Great Lakes. You are going to sit there for several hundred years and watch succession occur.

Fig. 4-1   Sand dunes commonly form along large lakes and the oceans. The Warren Dunes (A) formed on the Lake Michigan shore. The Prince Edward Island National Park Dunes (B) formed on the Atlantic Ocean shore.

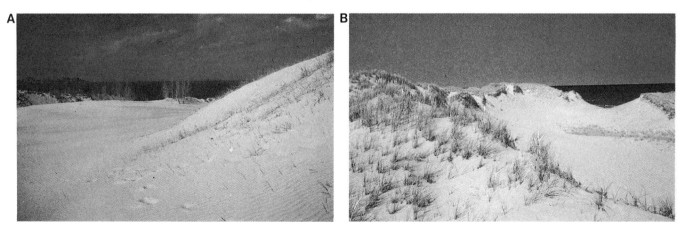

Fig. 4-2   Formation of a sand dune.

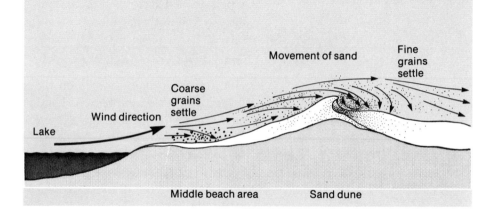

Fig. 4-3 Sand grass is especially adapted to the harsh dune environment. What are its adaptations?

Fig. 4-4 This juniper, an evergreen, often invades dunes around the Great Lakes. How is it adapted to this environment?

The Pioneer Stage

As time passes, some dead organic matter (leaves, twigs, fish) is sure to be swept onto the dune. This small amount of organic matter enriches the sand. Now patches of sand grass, a pioneer plant, begin to grow around you (Fig. 4-3). This hardy plant is well-adapted to the dry conditions of a sand dune. It has an extensive root system that absorbs the small amount of water available. This root system also anchors the plant in the shifting sand. The plant's narrow leaves bend against the force of wind-driven sand. The sand grass stabilizes the dune with its large branching root system. Also, it traps drifting sand, making the dune even larger.

The Shrub Stage

As sand grass dies, humus is added to the soil. This changed soil can now support plants which need more nutrients and water. A shrub called sand cherry often becomes established at this stage. You may even notice evergreen shrubs such as junipers around you (Fig. 4-4). Like sand grass, junipers have large branching roots. As well, they hug the ground as protection from the winds.

The Cottonwood Stage

Next, cottonwood trees (poplars) begin to shoot upward among the shrubs. These trees soon become the dominant plants in the area. As a result, they are called the index plants of this stage in succession. The shade cast by the shrubs and cottonwoods provides welcome relief to you from the scorching sun. It also helps the soil hold its moisture longer. Decaying leaves add further organic matter to the soil. Ants and beetles move busily among the sand grass plants. Birds feed on sand cherries and juniper berries. The digger wasp, an index animal of the cottonwood stage, burrows into the sand at your feet. You notice that the sand's colour is darker. This is because of the added organic matter.

The Pine Stage

The enriched soil now enables pine seedlings to become established in the area. Eventually they become the dominant plants. Thus they are the index plants of this stage in succession. As the pine trees develop, they drop needles about you. The soil becomes still richer. But now, a strange thing happens. Pine trees are sun-loving plants but the large pine trees cast a dense shade on the soil. As a result young pine trees do not receive enough light to develop. The pine trees have changed the environment so much that their own species cannot become established in the area. As adult trees mature and die, no young pines replace them.

The Oak Stage

Black oak seedlings grow well in the environment created by the pines. They need the added shade, moisture, and soil nutrients. They also need the protection from strong winds that the pines offer. Therefore, if a squirrel or blue jay drops an acorn from a black oak into the pine forest, it will germinate and grow. Eventually black oaks dominate the area. However, the trees are not very large nor are they closely spaced. This is because nutrients and water are still in short supply. This stage may remain for centuries while the black oaks slowly add humus to the soil through fallen leaves, bark, and branches (Fig. 4-5).

As further humus accumulates, red and white oaks invade the area. They grow well in the shade of black oak trees, whereas young black oaks do not. After many years, still more shade-tolerant trees invade the area—ash, basswood, and hickory.

Fig. 4-5   Oak leaves from the oak stage and pine needles from remaining pines slowly add humus to the soil.

Fig. 4-6 The climax forest in much of the Great Lakes region is dominated by maple and beech trees.

The Climax Stage

Oak, ash, basswood, and hickory cast a shade too dense for their young to survive. But young maple and beech trees are very shade-tolerant. They thrive in this environment. After a long period of time, they dominate the area (Fig. 4-6).

Unlike other species, young maple and beech trees can develop in the shade of the parent trees. As a result, the community becomes self-perpetuating. This means young trees are always ready to replace dead ones *of the same species*. Such a self-perpetuating community is called a climax community.

A climax forest seldom consists of just maple and beech. Occasional oaks, basswoods, and even pines may tower among the maples and beeches. Other species such as black cherry and ironwood may be present. And, in moist areas, hemlock, an evergreen, joins the climax community.

What Is Succession?

You have seen a hot, dry, bright environment change to a cool, moist, shady environment. You have also seen a plant succession occur from pioneer grasses to climax forest. An animal succession accompanied the plant succession. The ants and digger wasps of earlier stages were gradually replaced by earthworms, new insect species, millipedes, centipedes, and snails. Toads, salamanders, and a host of mammals and birds appeared.

Now, let us return to the original questions: What is succession? Why does it occur? In summary, living things change their environment. In doing so, they sometimes make the environment less favourable for themselves. But they also make it more favourable for another community of plants and animals. Each stage in succession, except the climax, brings about its own downfall. Succession, then, is the gradual replacement of one community of living things by another.

As succession continues, species diversity, population numbers, and niche availability increase. Also, total biomass and organic matter increase. All of these add to the complexity of the ecosystem. This complexity makes the ecosystem more stable. Many plant and animal species mean more food webs will be formed. Thus there is less chance of the entire community collapsing if one species disappears.

Obviously you cannot wait in one spot for hundreds of years to observe succession. But you don't have to. You can see all the stages in a few minutes. Simply start at the water's edge and walk inland (Fig. 4-7).

As a dune enlarges and becomes covered with plants, a new dune forms closer to the water. Then, as it becomes covered with plants, a still younger dune forms between the second dune and the water. Meanwhile the original dune has advanced further in succession. This process can happen again and again. As a result, a young dune with few or no plants exists closest to the water. The next dune inland will be further on in succession. And the next dune will be still further on. Thus you can see all the stages of succession by walking from the water's edge inland.

Fig. 4-7 Succession on a sand dune in the Great Lakes Region.

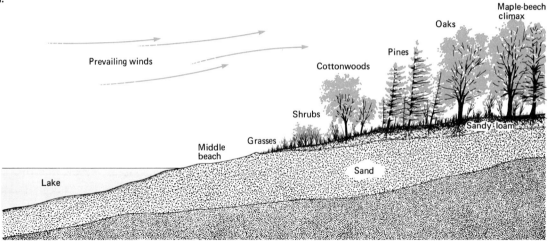

Protecting Sand Dunes

Some of the communities on the dunes around the Great Lakes took thousands of years to become established. But thoughtless humans can destroy them in minutes. Sand dune communities are very fragile because the topsoil is not very thick. If it is disturbed, it is quickly blown away by the strong winds (Fig. 4-8). Or, the dune may be washed away by a heavy storm. It may be fun to drive a trail bike, dune buggy, or other off-road vehicle over sand dunes. But this is certain to destroy the dune communities. Even climbing up through a dune community can destroy it. You should always stay on the trails when you are walking among sand dune communities.

Fig. 4-8 A "blowout" destroyed a community on this dune. The community was several thousand years in the making. Note, though, that sand grass has already colonized the dune. Thus, in hundreds of years, a forest may again cover this dune.

1. Describe how a sand dune forms.
2. List the seven harsh conditions found in the sand dune environment.
3. Give the meanings of these terms: pioneer plant, index plant, index animal, climax community
4. List, in order, the index plants of a sand dune succession.
5. Why does plant succession occur on dunes?
6. Define succession.
7. **a)** What is a blowout?
   b) How could we help prevent blowouts?

4.2 Types of Succession

Primary Succession

Succession that begins in an area that has not supported life within recent geological times is called primary succession. A sand dune succession is of this type. So too is the succession that occurs on bare rock. You have probably seen rocks covered with plants. You will see in Section 4.3 just how those plants got established on the rocks.

Secondary Succession

Succession that begins in an area that once supported life is called secondary succession. An abandoned field or a forest destroyed by fire or lumbering will undergo this type of succession. Secondary succession is generally more rapid than primary succession because soil is already present. Also, some forms of life are already in the area. Section 4.4 describes a typical secondary succession.

Autotrophic and Heterotrophic Succession

You may recall from Section 2.2 that autotrophic organisms make their own food. That is, they are plants and algae. Heterotrophic organisms, on the other hand, feed on other organisms. They do not make their own food. The following discussion shows how a parallel situation exists in autotrophic and heterotrophic succession.

Both primary and secondary succession are examples of autotrophic succession. In both cases succession is dominated by plants. These plants are largely responsible for changing the environment. That is, they direct the succession. They are the main source of energy for organisms in the area.

Plants do not, however, dominate heterotrophic succession. Further, the main source of energy in this type of succession is usually non-living organic matter, not plants. For example, a fallen log undergoes heterotrophic succes-

Fig. 4-9 The bracket fungus is often a pioneer in a fallen log succession.

sion. The energy source is the dead wood. As the log decays, it passes through a number of stages before it decays completely and becomes part of the soil.

- Beetles make tunnels in the wood and bracket fungi attack the bark (Fig. 4-9).
- Other animals and fungi enter the tunnels.
- The action of the animals and fungi loosens the bark and softens the wood.
- Slugs, snails, millipedes and other animals become established under the loose bark. Salamanders and snakes might make a home under the log.
- When the bark is all gone, many of these animals leave because their shelter is gone.
- Fungi such as moulds, and beetles which can bore into soft wood now dominate the succession. The log soon becomes a pulpy mass.
- Moulds and bacteria work on this mass and change it into humus. Earthworms, ants, millipedes and centipedes abound at this stage. These organisms help mix the humus into the soil.

Each stage in this succession has a special community of living things. These organisms use up their food or otherwise change their environment. Then they can no longer live there. But they are succeeded by other organisms that can live in the changed environment. In this way succession, or a gradual change in the communities, takes place.

A rotting carcass also undergoes heterotrophic succession. Bacteria are the first to colonize the carcass. Worms are next and, in turn, are followed by other invertebrates such as flies, beetles, and wasps. They complete the decomposition of the carcass.

Section Review

1. **a)** What is primary succession?
   b) Give two examples of environments in which it occurs.
2. **a)** What is secondary succession?
   b) Give two examples of environments in which it occurs.
3. What is the difference between autotrophic and heterotrophic succession?
4. Classify each of the following as autotrophic or heterotrophic succession:
   a) succession on bare rock
   b) succession on a sand dune
   c) a rotting carcass succession
   d) a fallen log succession
   e) succession in an old field

4.3 Succession on Rocky Surfaces

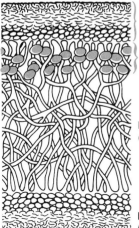

Fungal hyphae
(tightly woven)

Algal layer

Fungal hyphae
(loosely woven)

Fungal hyphae
(tightly woven)

Fig. 4-10 Structure of a lichen. The hair-like fungal hyphae are wrapped tightly around the algae. Thus the lichen seems to be one organism. You can see the fungus and alga if you break a lichen into tiny pieces and look at it under a microscope.

Lichens: The Pioneer Organisms

The pioneers of succession on bare rock are lichens. A lichen is not a single type of organism (Fig. 4-10). Instead, it is an alga and a fungus living together in a symbiotic relationship called mutualism. (You may recall that mutualism is a symbiotic relationship in which both organisms benefit.) The alga is autotrophic. That is, it can make foods by photosynthesis. It then shares these foods with the fungus which cannot make its own food. The fungus, in turn, provides the alga with water, mineral nutrients, and support.

Succession From Bare Rock to Forest

The first lichens to colonize a rocky surface are crustose lichens (Fig. 4-11, A). They usually appear as finely textured coloured patches that are difficult to remove by hand. These lichens send hyphae several millimetres into the rocky surface to obtain nutrients. They do this by secreting acid onto the rock. This action starts the breakdown of the rock.

Foliose lichens often join the crustose lichens (Fig. 4-11, B). These leaf-like lichens are not so firmly attached. In fact, large pieces can be easily pulled off the rocks. The crustose and foliose lichens weaken the rock. The weakened rock crumbles, forming parent soil material. Weathering (the freeze-thaw cycle) helps break up the rock.

Fig. 4-11 The three general types of lichens: crustose (A), foliose (B), and fruticose (C).

Pioneer mosses usually invade the area at this stage. They grow in clumps which help develop the soil by trapping wind-blown earth and organic matter. Soil continues to build as mosses and lichens die and decay.

Fruticose lichens like *Cladonia*, reindeer moss, may now appear (Fig. 4-11, C). These lichens are accompanied by larger mosses. These larger plants trap still more wind-blown material. Also, their great bulk quickly builds up the organic portion of the soil. Ferns often appear at this stage if the area is moist. Then seed-bearing plants, usually hardy annual weeds and grasses, begin to grow in the area. Biennials and perennials follow. Among the perennials are grasses. By now the soil can be up to 30 cm deep on the rock. Sun-loving shrubs like the sumac can grow in this soil. They provide the environment needed by the seedlings of sun-loving trees such as poplars and white birch.

Once sun-loving trees have become established, a succession of trees follows (Fig. 4-12). In the Great Lakes region this succession often resembles that of sand dunes. It may not, however, reach the maple-beech climax stage. That's because maple and beech are not native species in those parts of the country where succession begins on bare rock.

Fig. 4-12   Succession from bare rock to forest.

Ferns (if moist)

Fruticose lichens
Larger mosses

Small mosses

Annual weeds and grasses

Foliose lichens

Biennial plants
Perennial plants and grasses

Bare rock

Crustose lichens

Sun-loving shrubs

Poplar; Birch   Pine   Oak   Maple-Beech

1. What is a lichen?
2. Why are lichens able to colonize bare rock?
3. Explain how lichens and mosses make soil on rocky surfaces.
4. Make a summary of the stages in succession that occur on bare rock.

Succession from Bare Soil to Woodlot

4.4

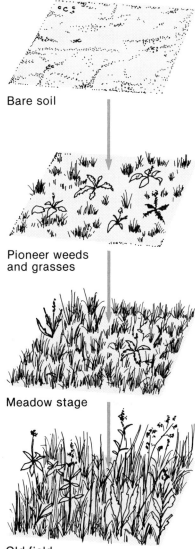

Bare soil

Pioneer weeds and grasses

Meadow stage

Old-field community

The succession which occurs in bare rock or sand is a primary succession. It begins where there has been little life in recent times. Such areas have no soil. Therefore succession moves slowly in the early stages as soil is developed. In old fields and meadows, however, soil is already present. Therefore succession usually proceeds much more quickly. Let's see how this secondary succession proceeds.

Succession in the Great Lakes and mid-Atlantic Regions

Imagine that you have just cultivated a garden or field. It is completely weedfree. Then suppose you decided not to plant this garden or field after all. You are just going to let it sit untouched. What will happen?

All of us know that, in a matter of weeks, or just days, weeds will invade the garden. These pioneers are usually grasses and annual plants such as pigweed, ragweed, sow thistle, and lamb's quarters. Later in the season these will be joined by biennial and perennial plants such as dandelions and thistles. Often perennial grasses such as quack grass dominate the area. The area could stay in this grassy or meadow stage for two or three years. Usually, though, it quickly moves into a stage called an old-field community (Fig. 4-13). This community is dominated by biennials and perennials such as goldenrod, milkweed, asters, fireweed, cinquefoil, yarrow, and wild carrot.

Sun-loving shrubs appear in the old-field community as soon as the tall plants provide the needed environment, usually a year or so after the old-field community is established. Among the sun-loving shrubs are sumac, red osier, dogwood, and ninebark. Then sun-loving trees invade the area. Hawthorn, a shrubby tree, and apple often dominate. Soon after, however, poplars and birches move in. Then the succession follows a path similar to that on sand dunes or bare rocks and a climax forest of maple and beech stands where once there was a field or garden.

Fig. 4-13 Formation of an old-field community.

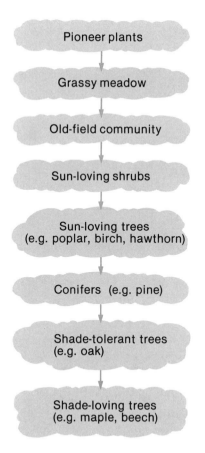

Pioneer plants

↓

Grassy meadow

↓

Old-field community

↓

Sun-loving shrubs

↓

Sun-loving trees
(e.g. poplar, birch, hawthorn)

↓

Conifers (e.g. pine)

↓

Shade-tolerant trees
(e.g. oak)

↓

Shade-loving trees
(e.g. maple, beech)

Fig. 4-14 The general path of succession. In your area, the succession may not go all the way to maple-beech climax forest because of temperature and rainfall differences.

Succession Where You Live

Secondary succession where you live may not be the same as that in the Great Lakes Region. It will probably, however, proceed along the same general path (Fig. 4-14). Just how far it goes on this path depends on where you live. In other words, climax communities may differ from place to place. Therefore the species at each stage may also differ.

If you live in the prairies, succession usually stops at the grassy meadow or old-field community stage. In wetter places, however, it may proceed to the shrub or even the poplar stage. In the St. Lawrence River valley, the climax community consists largely of white spruce and balsam fir. Minnesota has a climax community of maple and basswood. The tops of the Smoky Mountains in Tennessee and North Carolina have a climax community of red spruce and Frasier fir. The rest of those states have a pine-oak climax. Giant redwoods dominate the climax forest of California. Douglas firs and sitka spruce dominate the climax forest of British Columbia. (Douglas fir only dominates where forest fires occur frequently.) And black spruce make up the climax forest in the northern boreal forest of the United States and Canada.

All of these climax communities developed from a primary or secondary succession and all followed the same general path. Wherever you live, you are never far from an example of succession.

Section Review

1. Why does secondary succession proceed more quickly than primary succession?
2. Make a summary of secondary succession in the Great Lakes region. Begin with bare soil.
3. List the general steps in succession.

4.5   FIELD TRIP   Investigating Secondary Succession

In this activity your class will study five sites. Each site is at a different stage in succession. You will note the main biotic and abiotic factors of each site. When you have finished, you will see how the biotic and abiotic factors change as succession proceeds.

In preparation for this study your teacher has staked out five plots. Each plot is 10 m by 10 m in size. And each plot from 1 to 5 is at a stage further on in succession than the preceding number. The sites may be along a line as shown in Figure 4-15 or they may be scattered.

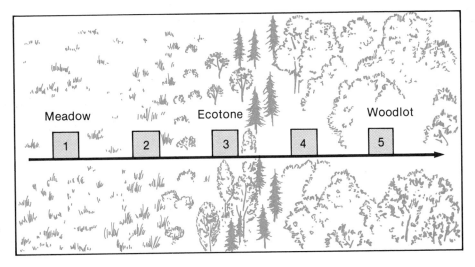

Fig. 4-15 Selection of plots for a study of secondary succession. If you can find an undisturbed meadow next to a woodlot, the plots may be located on a straight line. Put one plot in the ecotone, the region between the two communities.

Problem

How do the biotic and abiotic factors change as succession proceeds?

Materials

soil sampler	white tray
soil thermometer	probe
soil pH kit	air thermometer
plastic collecting jars for soil (5)	sweep net
trowel	hand lens
sling psychrometer	petri dishes (2)
light meter	identification guides for trees,
wind speed meter	shrubs, wildflowers, and insects
compass	plastic jars for animals (5)
clinometer	

Procedure

a. Prepare a copy of Table 4-1 that fills an entire page.

b. Prepare a copy of Table 4-2 that fills an entire page.

c. Prepare five full-page copies of Table 4-3.

d. Proceed with your team to the site designated by your teacher. Record all data in your tables as you perform the following studies.

e. Measure the air temperature. If the sun is shining, use your hand to shield the thermometer bulb from the direct rays of the sun.

f. Note the attitude of the site. Is it flat or does it face in some direction?

g. Use the clinometer to measure the slope of the site.

h. Measure the light intensity. Follow the directions supplied with the light meter.

i. Measure the wind speed using the wind speed meter.

j. Note the direction of the wind with a moistened finger. Then use the compass to find that direction.

k. Measure the relative humidity. Follow the directions supplied with the sling psychrometer.

l. Measure the soil temperature at depths of 2 cm, 5 cm, and 10 cm.

m. Find the percolation rate by following the description in Unit 4 of *Investigating Natural Resources.*

n. Find the soil pH. Follow the directions supplied with the kit.

o. Study the upper soil profile as follows: Note the average depth of the undecomposed litter. Then note the average depth of the decomposing litter. Now use the soil sampler to find the depth of the humus layer (black soil).

p. Collect a trowelful of soil from 5 places in the plot. Put these samples in a collecting jar and mix them. The mixture represents the average soil at your site.

q. Record in Table 4-3 the name, relative abundance, and adaptations of the plants in the plot. Use a four-category scale for relative abundance: abundant, frequent, occasional, rare.

r. Sweep the vegetation with the sweep net (see Figure 2-10, page 27). Transfer the animals to jars. Watch them with the hand lens. Record their names, relative abundance, and adaptations in Table 4-3. Then release the animals.

s. Use the trowel to collect some litter, decomposing litter, and humus. Put this in the tray. Spread it out and search for animals. Record their names, relative abundance, and adaptations in Table 4-3. Then release the animals.

t. Repeat steps (e) to (r) for at least one more study site.

u. Back in the classroom, find the water content, water-holding capacity, organic content, texture, particle size, and macronutrient content (nitrogen, phosphorus, and potassium) of the soil samples from your sites. See Unit 4 of *Investigating Natural Resources* for procedures and materials.

v. Back in the classroom, complete the fourth column in Table 4-3, "Advantages to the Organism".

w. Make sure you have a complete set of data from all five sites by comparing your findings with those of your classmates.

Discussion

1. Describe and account for the change in each abiotic factor from plot 1 to plot 5.

2. Describe and account for any changes in relative abundance of organisms from plot 1 to plot 5. Make reference to the adaptations you noted.

3. In Section 4.1 there is a subsection called "What is Succession?" Read it again. Do your results agree with what is said there? In what ways?

Table 4-1 Secondary Succession: Abiotic Factors (Field) General Comments (Sky; Weather)_____

Factor		Sample	Plot 1	Plot 2	Plot 3	Plot 4	Plot 5
Name and description							
Attitude		Southfacing					
Slope		18°					
Percolation rate		0.2 L/min					
Air temperature		24°C					
Light intensity		64 hlx					
Wind	Speed	10 km/h					
	Direction	NW					
Relative humidity		62%					
Soil temperature	2 cm	29°C					
	5 cm	26°C					
	10 cm	25°C					
Soil pH		8.0					
Upper soil profile	Undecomposed litter	6 cm					
	Decomposing litter	3.5 cm					
	Humus	14 cm					

Table 4-2 Secondary Succession: Abiotic Factors (Lab)

Factor		Sample	Plot 1	Plot 2	Plot 3	Plot 4	Plot 5
Soil water content		26%					
Soil water-holding capacity		42%					
Soil organic content		4%					
Soil texture	% sand	35%					
	% silt	32%					
	% clay	33%					
Soil particle size	1st sieve	7%					
	2nd sieve	11%					
	3rd sieve	20%					
	4th sieve	29%					
	bottom pan	33%					
Nitrogen		High					
Phosphorus		Low					
Potassium		Medium					

Table 4-3　Secondary Succession: Biotic Factors

Plot Number ___1___

Organism	Relative abundance (a,f,o,r)	Adaptations	Advantages to organism
Grasshoppers	a	biting & chewing mouth parts; hard exoskeleton; wings; jumping legs; greenish-brown	can feed on vegetation; moves freely in open spaces for defence; camouflage; protected against dessication
Grasses	a	narrow leaves; waxy cuticle; flexible; fibrous roots	resists wind damage; can survive high temperature and low moisture

4.6　CASE STUDY　Secondary Succession

A class of students studied a secondary succession as described in Section 4.5. If you have not done that field trip, read the procedure to find out what was done.

All five sites were studied on the same day. It was late spring and the sky was clear. Some of the data from the field trip are recorded in Table 4-4. A numeral in brackets indicates the height off the ground or in the ground at which the measurement was made. Study the data carefully. Then answer the questions.

Questions

1. Account for the changes in air temperature, relative humidity, wind speed, and light intensity from plot 1 to plot 5.
2. Why did the percolation rate increase from plot 1 to plot 5?
3. The soil gradually became more acidic from plot 1 to plot 5. What could have caused this change?

Table 4-4 Secondary Succession

Factor	Plot 1	Plot 2	Plot 3	Plot 4	Plot 5
Air temperature (1.5 m)	26°C	26°C	25°C	22°C	22°C
Relative humidity (1.5 m)	42%	44%	51%	72%	81%
Wind speed (1.5 m)	9.5 km/h	8.5 km/h	7.0 km/h	2.2 km/h	1.8 km/h
Light intensity (1.0 m)	1300 hlx	800 hlx	180 hlx	70 hlx	51 hlx
Soil pH	7.9	7.9	7.2	7.1	7.3
Percolation rate	0.2 L/min	0.3 L/min	0.4 L/min	0.9 L/min	1.2 L/min
Undecomposed litter	3.0 cm	5.0 cm	7.5 cm	11.0 cm	15.0 cm
Decomposing litter	0.0 cm	0.5 cm	2.5 cm	3.5 cm	5.0 cm
Humus	15 cm	17 cm	20 cm	29 cm	32 cm
Soil temperature (2 cm)	31°C	31°C	26°C	22°C	22°C
Soil organic content	3.0%	3.2%	3.8%	4.2%	4.8%
Grass plants/m^2	38	19	2	0	0
Aster plants/m^2	0	3	0	0	0
Goldenrod plants/m^2	1	5	1	0	0
Cottonwood trees/100 m^2	0	0	4	0	0
Pine trees/100 m^2	0	0	2	3	0
Bracken ferns/100 m^2	2	35	3	0	0
Oak ferns/100 m^2	0	0	0	10	14
Maple trees/100 m^2	0	0	0	0	4
Earthworms/m^2	81	90	61	50	135
Sow bugs/m^2	0	0	2	18	31
Millipedes/m^2	0	0	1	6	17
Web-building spiders/10 m^2	1	3	5	8	12

4. Why do the woodlot plots contain more undecomposed litter than the meadow plots?

5. a) Why does plot 1 contain no decomposing litter? (*Hint:* Look at the soil temperature.)

   b) Why does the depth of decomposing litter increase from plot 1 to plot 5?

   c) Why does the depth of humus increase from plot 1 to plot 5?

6. Account for the increase in soil organic content from plot 1 to plot 5.

7. Compare the environments in which bracken ferns and oak ferns live.
8. Which one of the following do sow bugs appear to feed upon: grass, asters, goldenrod, decomposing litter? Give evidence to support your answer.
9. Sow bugs breathe with gills. Gills only work when they are moist. How does the sow bug's habitat help keep the gills moist?
10. Account for the distribution of web-building spiders.
11. Name a fern that might colonize a clear-cut area of a forest like the one in this study.
12. a) Name two old-field community plants found in this study.
    b) Name three adaptations to their environment you would expect these plants to have.
13. What might happen to the millipede population if a maple bush were clear-cut? How do you know?
14. a) Pine needles tend to make soil acidic. What soil conditions, acidic or basic, do earthworms seem to prefer?
    b) What other environmental factors may be responsible for the distribution of earthworms? (*Hint:* Earthworms must have a moist cuticle ("skin") at all times.)

4.7   The Quadrat Method

In Sections 4.8, 4.9, and 4.10 you will use your knowledge of succession to help evaluate uses of a woodlot. To do this, you need data on the woodlot. It would take a long time to study every tree in a forest. Fortunately, you can simply sample the area at several sites using quadrats (plots). If these quadrats are set up properly, they give a reliable measure of the properties of the trees over the total area. This section describes the shape, size, number, and arrangement of quadrats you should use. The emphasis here is upon quadrats for woodlot studies. Similar methods can, however, be applied to all types of vegetation.

Fig. 4-16   Forming a right angle at the corner of a quadrat.

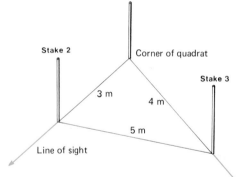

Stake 1

Stake 2

Corner of quadrat

Stake 3

3 m

4 m

5 m

Line of sight

Shape

Quadrats can be circular, rectangular or square. For the woodlot study in Section 4.9, you will use square quadrats.

The first step in laying out a square quadrat is to form a right angle for one of the corners. If you are good at using a compass, you will know how to use the compass to form a right angle. Without a compass, you can do this with stakes and a tape measure. Simply follow these steps:

1. Place 2 stakes in the ground 3 m apart.
2. Use a tape measure to find a point that is 4 m from Stake 1 and 5 m from Stake 2. Drive in Stake 3 at this point (Fig. 4-16). These 3 stakes have formed a right angle at Stake 1. It is one corner of the quadrat.

3. Find a second corner as follows: Lay the tape measure along the line of sight from Stake 1 to Stake 3. Move Stake 3 to mark the position of the second corner. If, for example, you are laying out a 10 m x 10 m quadrat, move it to the 10 m mark.

4. Find the third corner by repeating step 3 using Stake 2 instead of Stake 3.

5. Find the fourth corner by running lines out from Stakes 2 and 3 equal in length to the other 2 sides (10 m in our example). You can use tape measures or string to do this. Drive in Stake 4 where the two lines meet.

Table 4-5   Size of Quadrat

Stratum of vegetation	Area of quadrat
mosses and lichens	0.1 m^2
herbs, grasses, tree seedlings	1.0 m^2
shrubs and tree saplings (up to 3 m tall)	10-20 m^2
trees	100 m^2

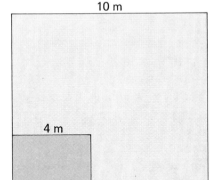

Fig. 4-17   Nested quadrats for sampling the vegetation in the main strata of a woodlot.

Size

Table 4-5 gives the area used to sample different sizes of vegetation. If all these strata of vegetation are being studied at once, you can save time in setting up the quadrats by "nesting" them as shown in Figure 4-17.

Number

Ecologists have discovered that the quadrats need only make up 10% of the total area of the site being studied. For example, suppose you are studying a woodlot with an area of 2 ha (20 000 m^2). To obtain reliable information, the total area of the quadrats must equal 10% of 20 000 m^2, or 2000 m^2. Since each quadrat is 100 m^2 (see Table 4-5), you need 20 quadrats.

Arrangement

Ecologists often use quadrats whose locations are selected randomly. In many cases this gives more valid results. A systematic arrangement of quadrats is, however, easier to plan and use. In such an arrangement the quadrats are spaced as widely and evenly as possible throughout the study site. Figure 4-18 shows how they could be arranged for a woodlot study.

A base line is laid out just outside the woodlot. Next several evenly spaced transect lines are laid out perpendicular to the base line. Then the required number of quadrats is laid out, evenly spaced along each transect line.

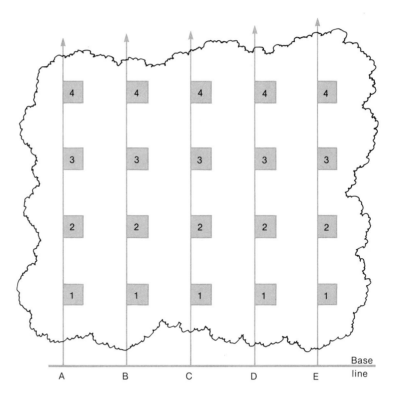

Fig. 4-18 Distribution of quadrats in a woodlot.

Base line

A   B   C   D   E

Section Review

1. What is a quadrat?
2. Why are quadrats used?
3. Describe how you would set up a 100 m² (10 m x 10 m) quadrat in a woodlot.
4. What area and shape of quadrat are used for sampling trees in a woodlot?
5. How many quadrats should be used to sample the trees in a 3 ha (30 000 m²) woodlot? Explain how you arrived at your answer.
6. Look at Figure 4-18. This woodlot has an area of 2 ha. What spacing should be used between the transect lines? between the quadrats (10 m x 10 m) on each transect line?

4.8   Importance Values

In Sections 4.9 and 4.10 you will use the importance values of tree species to help you decide whether or not trees should be harvested from a woodlot. This section explains what importance values are. It also shows you how to calculate them.

What Are Importance Values?

The importance value of a tree species is a number which gives the relative importance of that species in a woodlot. That is, it indicates how dominant that species is in the woodlot. The importance of a species is determined by three factors:

- its frequency (how widely distributed the species is in the woodlot)
- its density (how close together the trees of that species are)
- its cover (how large the trees of that species are)

Calculating Importance Values

To calculate the importance value of a species, you must first calculate its frequency, density, and cover.

a) *Frequency*

The frequency of a species is the percentage of the quadrats which contain that species.

$$\text{Frequency} = \frac{\text{Number of quadrats in which species occurs}}{\text{Total number of quadrats}} \times 100\%$$

Example: Suppose 20 quadrats were used and beech trees occurred in 10 of them. The frequency of beech trees is:

$$F_b = \frac{10}{20} \times 100\% = 50\%$$

This means that beech trees occurred in 50% of the quadrats. But, more important, it means that if you set up a quadrat *anywhere* in the woodlot, you have a 50% chance of finding one or more beech trees in it.

In general, the higher the frequency, the more important the tree is in the woodlot. Can you explain why?

b) *Density*

The density of a species is the average number of trees of that species per quadrat.

$$\text{Density} = \frac{\text{Number of trees of a certain species}}{\text{Total number of quadrats}}$$

Example: Suppose 20 quadrats were used and a total of 40 beech trees grew in them. Then the density of beech trees is:

$$D_b = \frac{40 \text{ beech trees}}{20 \text{ quadrats}} = 2 \text{ beech trees per quadrat}$$

This means that an average of 2 beech trees occurred in each of the 20 quadrats studied. But, more important, it means that, if you set up a quadrat *anywhere* in the woodlot, it will on the average have 2 beech trees in it.

In general, the higher the density, the more important the tree is in the woodlot. Can you explain why?

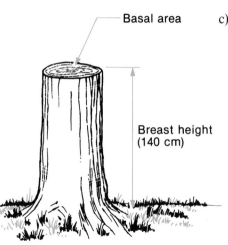

Basal area

Breast height
(140 cm)

Fig. 4-19   The meaning of basal area.

c) *Cover*

The cover of a species is the proportion of the average quadrat which is covered by that species.

$$\text{Cover} = \frac{\text{Total area covered by the species}}{\text{Total number of quadrats}}$$

You can get the cover of a tree by using the downward projection of the crown. That is, you can calculate the area of the ground shaded by that tree when the sun is directly overhead. But there is an easier method. Foresters have discovered that the basal area of the trunk gives a good measure of the *relative* cover. The basal area is the cross-section area of the trunk at breast height. Breast height is about 140 cm off the ground (Fig. 4-19). To get the basal area, you measure the diameter at breast height (d.b.h.). Then you use the formula $A = \pi r^2$ to calculate the basal area.

Example: Suppose 20 quadrats were used and 7 beech trees occurred in them. Table 4-6 shows the d.b.h. of each tree and the basal area calculated from it. The cover of the beech trees is:

Table 4-6   Calculating Basal Areas

Tree	d.b.h. (cm)	basal area (cm²)
1	14	154
2	21	346
3	37	1075
4	19	283
5	20	314
6	33	855
7	40	1256
Total basal area of beech = 4283 cm²		

$$C_b = \frac{4283 \text{ cm}^2}{20 \text{ quadrats}} = 214 \text{ cm}^2/\text{per quadrat}$$

This means that the basal area of the beech trees covered on average 214 cm² of each quadrat. But, more important, it means that, if you set up a quadrat *anywhere* in the woodlot, it will on average have beech trees in it with a total cover (total basal area) of 214 cm².

In general, the higher the cover, the more important the tree is in the woodlot. Can you explain why?

d) **Relative Frequency**

You can get a better idea of the importance of a species by comparing the frequency of that species with the total frequency of all species. The result is called the relative frequency.

$$\text{Relative frequency of a species} = \frac{\text{Frequency of that species}}{\text{Sum of frequencies of all species}} \times 100$$

Example: Suppose that a field study gave the frequencies listed in Table 4-7. The relative frequency of maple is:

$$RF_m = \frac{F_m}{F_m + F_b + F_a + F_o + F_p} \times 100$$

$$= \frac{50}{50 + 20 + 25 + 10 + 5} \times 100$$

$$= \frac{50}{110} \times 100 = 45$$

The relative frequency of a species cannot exceed 100. Under what circumstances would it be 100?

Table 4-7 Calculating Relative Frequency

Species	Frequency	Relative frequency
maple	$F_m = 50\%$	45
beech	$F_b = 20\%$	18
white ash	$F_a = 25\%$	23
red oak	$F_o = 10\%$	9
white pine	$F_p = 5\%$	5

e) **Relative Density**

You can also get a better idea of the importance of a species by calculating its relative density. It is calculated just like relative frequency.

$$\text{Relative density of a species} = \frac{\text{Density of that species}}{\text{Sum of densities of all species}} \times 100$$

Example: Suppose that a field study gave the densities listed in Table 4-8. The relative density of maple is:

$$RD_m = \frac{D_m}{D_m + D_b + D_a + D_o + D_p} \times 100$$

$$= \frac{2.1}{2.1 + 2.0 + 1.8 + 1.5 + 0.8} \times 100$$

$$= \frac{2.1}{8.2} \times 100 = 27$$

The relative density of a species cannot exceed 100. Under what circumstances would it be 100?

Table 4-8 Calculating Relative Density

Species	Density (trees/quadrat)	Relative density
maple	2.1	27
beech	2.0	24
white ash	1.8	22
red oak	1.5	18
white pine	0.8	10

f) **Relative Cover**

A better idea of the importance of a species can also be obtained by calculating its relative cover. It is calculated just like relative frequency and relative density.

$$\text{Relative cover of a species} = \frac{\text{Cover of that species}}{\text{Sum of covers of all species}} \times 100$$

Example: Suppose that a field study gave the covers listed in Table 4-9. The relative cover of maple is:

$$RC_m = \frac{C_m}{C_m + C_b + C_a + C_o + C_p} \times 100$$

$$= \frac{7100}{7100 + 6050 + 4800 + 3050 + 1500} \times 100$$

$$= \frac{7100}{22\,500} \times 100 = 32$$

The relative cover of a species cannot exceed 100. Under what circumstances would it be 100?

Table 4-9 Calculating Relative Cover

Species	Cover (cm²/quadrat)	Relative cover
maple	7100	32
beech	6050	27
white ash	4800	21
red oak	3050	14
white pine	1500	7

g) *Importance Value*

Relative frequency, relative density, and relative cover each indicates a different aspect of the importance of a species in the woodlot. Therefore, the sum of these three factors gives the best estimate of the importance of a species. This sum is called the importance value.

Importance value = Relative frequency + Relative density + Relative cover

What is the maximum importance value a species can have? Under what circumstances will it have this value?

Using Importance Values to Make Harvesting Decisions

Before any trees are removed from a woodlot, the harvester should know how their removal will affect the ecology of the woodlot. A sign of a healthy ecosystem is a wide diversity (large number) of species. Thus a healthy woodlot should have a wide diversity of species of trees. A harvesting plan should include a description of how the harvesting will affect species diversity.

You can predict the effect of harvesting on species diversity if you have two pieces of information:

- the importance values of the species
- the relative abundance of the species in the sapling stratum (trees with a d.b.h. < 10 cm). Relative abundance is expressed as abundant (a), frequent (f), occasional (o), rare (r), absent (ab).

Table 4-10 gives this information for a woodlot.

Table 4-10   Importance Values and Relative Abundance

Species	Importance Value	Relative abundance in sapling stratum
maple	91	a
beech	84	a
white ash	52	o
red oak	26	ab
white pine	15	ab

Clearly this woodlot is in an advanced stage of succession. Climax species (maple and beech) dominate the woodlot and they are abundant in the sapling layer. Therefore marketable maple and beech trees could be selectively cut without upsetting species diversity. The cut trees would simply be replaced by maple and beech from the sapling stratum.

The same reasoning does not apply to red oak and white pine, however. These species are absent in the sapling stratum. And, in a climax forest, there is little chance that they could survive, even if seedlings germinated in the future. Therefore, if any of these trees are removed, they will probably be replaced by maple and beech rather than their own species. Then species diversity would be reduced which means, of course, that animal diversity would also be reduced. For example, mammals and birds which feed on acorns and pine seeds would have to leave the area. And you would probably never see them or oak and pine trees again in that woodlot.

Summary

Importance values can help you decide at what stage in succession the woodlot is. You can then predict the path succession will likely follow, particularly if you have data on the sapling stratum. And, finally, you can predict the likely changes in species diversity if the marketable trees are harvested. Importance values help you answer two basic questions:
- Will harvesting eliminate certain species from the woodlot?
- Could certain species be harvested on a sustained yield basis (cut trees are replaced by trees of the same species)?

Section Review

1. Give a formula for finding each of the following:
   a) frequency
   b) density
   c) cover
   d) relative frequency
   e) relative density
   f) relative cover
   g) importance value
2. Refer to Figure 4-20 as you answer this question.
   Legend: m = maple tree   a = ash tree   p = pine tree
             b = beech tree   o = oak tree
   a) What is the frequency of maple trees in this woodlot?
   b) What is the density of maple trees in this woodlot?
   c) What information do you need to calculate the cover of the maple trees?
   d) Which species has the higher frequency, beech or oak?
   e) Which species has the higher density, pine or oak?
3. What is the basal area of a tree which has a d.b.h. of 30 cm?
4. The relative frequency of pitch pine in a woodlot is 100. What does this woodlot look like?
5. Under what circumstances will the density of lodgepole pine in a forest be 100?

Fig. 4-20   A quadrat study of a woodlot.

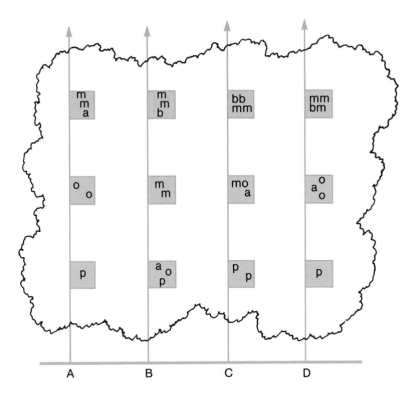

4.9   FIELD TRIP   **Evaluation of a Woodlot**

Uses of Woodlots

Everyone knows that we need wood for fuel, paper-making, lumber, and a variety of wood products. Much of this wood comes from the woodlots which dot the countryside in many areas. With proper management, these woodlots can produce a reasonable income for the owners. But woodlots have more than monetary value. First, they have ecological worth. That is, they help maintain ecological balance in an area. For example, they are the habitats for many plants and animals as well as helping to control erosion of the soil by wind and water. Second, woodlots are used by humans for recreational activities such as camping, hiking, and bird-watching. Further, most people enjoy simply looking at large trees.

To Cut or Not to Cut?

Because a woodlot has many values, some questions should arise when an owner is thinking about harvesting it.
- How much money are the marketable trees worth?
- How will the removal of these trees affect the animal and plant ecology of the area?

- Will the cutting upset the balance of tree species in the woodlot?
- What will be the future of the woodlot after cutting? How will succession proceed?
- Will the cutting eliminate forever certain tree species from the woodlot?
- How will other possible human uses of the woodlot be affected by the cutting?
- Does the owner have a moral obligation to leave some large trees for future generations to use and enjoy?

Purpose of this Field Trip

On this field trip you will collect the information needed to decide whether or not the marketable trees in a woodlot should be harvested. Study Figure 4-21 carefully. It summarizes the four things you will do on the field trip. Your teacher has selected part of a woodlot (about two hectares) for this study.

Materials (for a group of 6 students)

tree calipers	markers (4)
30 m measuring tape	Biltmore stick
compass	binoculars (optional)
coloured ribbons (4)	identification guides for trees,
strong cord or rope (two 10 m pieces)	other plants, mammals, insects, and birds

Fig. 4-21 Evaluation of a woodlot.

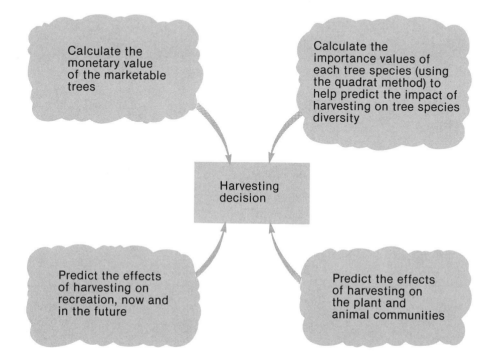

Calculate the monetary value of the marketable trees

Calculate the importance values of each tree species (using the quadrat method) to help predict the impact of harvesting on tree species diversity

Harvesting decision

Predict the effects of harvesting on recreation, now and in the future

Predict the effects of harvesting on the plant and animal communities

Table 4-11 Monetary Value of Marketable Trees

d.b.h. (cm)	Species	Number of board feet	Market value per board foot	Standing value per board foot	Standing value of tree
51 cm	maple	560	$1.50	$0.15	$84.00

Fig. 4-22 The d.b.h. of a tree can be measured with tree calipers. The measurement is made at breast height (about 140 cm off the ground).

Procedure A: Monetary Value of Marketable Trees

In this procedure you will calculate how much money you could get by harvesting and selling the trees which are large enough to be legally sold.

a. Prepare a full-page copy of Table 4-11. (Do not copy the example.)

b. Go to the section of the woodlot assigned by your teacher.

c. Find a tree which looks large enough to be legally marketable. Most areas have tree-cutting laws which prohibit the cutting of trees smaller than a certain d.b.h. (diameter at breast height). The d.b.h. is usually about 45 cm.

d. Find the d.b.h. of the tree. If it exceeds 45 cm, put the d.b.h. and the name of the tree species in your table (Fig. 4-22).

e. Use the Biltmore stick to find the number of board feet in the tree. Follow the directions on the stick. (*Note:* A metric equivalent of a board foot is not yet in use. A board foot is one foot square and one inch thick.)

f. Repeat steps (d) and (e) for all other marketable trees in your section of the woodlot.

g. Obtain from a lumber yard the market value per board foot of the species you found.

h. Buyers will usually pay about one-tenth of the market value for the standing trees. Therefore, calculate the standing value per board foot for each tree by dividing the market value by 10.

i. Calculate the standing value of each tree by multiplying the number of board feet by the standing value per board foot.

j. Share your results with your classmates. Then calculate the monetary value of all the marketable trees of each species.

Procedure B: Effects of Harvesting on Plant and Animal Communities

a. Make a full-page copy of Table 4-12. (Do not copy the examples.)

b. Visit the area beneath each of the trees you selected for harvesting in Procedure A. Using your copy of Table 4-12, make notes as shown on the species of organisms which may be affected by the harvesting.

Table 4-12 Species Affected by Harvesting

Name of organism	How harvesting may affect it
Gray squirrel	Harvesting of oak trees decreases food supply and nesting sites
Christmas fern	Harvesting of large trees reduces shade and moisture which this fern requires

Procedure C: Effects of Harvesting on Recreational Uses

The term "recreation" includes active pursuits such as camping, hiking, and bird-watching. It also includes the enjoyment many people get by simply being among large trees. Keep in mind, too, that we may have an obligation to provide future generations with such recreational opportunities.

a. Walk slowly through the entire woodlot. Sit down and listen and observe from time to time. Try to imagine how harvesting of the large trees would change the experience you are having. What positive changes might happen? What negative changes might happen?

b. Make a list of your thoughts. Discuss them with two or three other students.

c. Also make a list of ways in which harvesting might affect recreational opportunities for future generations, for example, 20 years from now.

Procedure D: Importance Values of Tree Species

Before the Field Trip:

a. Make sure you understand how to find importance values and how they can be used in making harvesting decisions (see Section 4.8).

b. Make a full page copy of Tables 4-13 and 4-14. Allow room for about 10 species. (Do not copy the examples.)

c. Your teacher will tell you the total area of the woodlot. (If the woodlot is quite large, your teacher will select just 2 ha of it as the area to be studied.) Use the given area to calculate the number of quadrats required. Then decide on the number of transect lines, the distance between lines, the number of quadrats per line, and the distance between the quadrats.

d. Make a diagram like Figure 4-18 on page 72. Then mark the information from part (c) on it.

e. Form a team with about five classmates. Discuss the following "Field Procedure". Then decide which tasks each team member will perform.

Table 4-13   Data Table for Quadrat Study Quadrat number

Tree species	1	2	3	4
red oak	14 22	18		33 20 16

Table 4-14   Relative Abundance in Sapling Layer

Species	a	f	o	r
red oak				
sugar maple				
white pine				

Field Procedure

a. Proceed to the point on the base line (A, B, C, D, or E) assigned to your team by your teacher.

b. Use the compass to find the direction of your transect line. It should be perpendicular to the base line.

c. Tie ribbons to trees along the line. Then you won't need to use the compass again.

d. Walk along your transect line until you are well within the woodlot. (The edge of a woodlot is not typical. Therefore do not include it in one of your quadrats.)

e. Set up quadrat 1 as described in Section 4.7.

f. Identify and measure the d.b.h. of each tree in the quadrat. *Note:* To be a tree, the d.b.h. must exceed 10 cm; anything less is a sapling. Record your results in Table 4-13. (In the example, quadrat 1 contains two red oak trees with d.b.h. of 14 cm and 22 cm.)

g. Note and record in Table 4-14 the relative abundance of each species in the sapling layer.

h. Repeat steps (f) and (g) for the remaining quadrats on your transect line.

Back in the Classroom

a. Share your data with the other teams.

b. Work with all teams to calculate the importance values of all species in the woodlot. Record them in a copy of Table 4-15.

c. Make a table like Table 4-10 on page 77. Rank the trees according to importance values in this table. Record also the relative abundance of each species in the sapling stratum.

Table 4-15 Calculating Importance Values

Tree species	Frequency	Density	Cover	Relative frequency	Relative density	Relative cover	Importance value

Discussion

During this field trip you collected data on:
- the monetary value of the marketable trees
- the effects of harvesting on plant and animal species
- the effects of harvesting on recreational uses
- the importance values

Use your data to develop a harvesting plan for the woodlot. Be sure to use your data to defend your harvesting decisions. For example, if you propose that there be no cutting of certain species, give evidence to support your decision. Or, if you propose sustained yield harvesting of one or two species, give evidence to show that this will not affect species diversity.

4.10   CASE STUDY   Using Importance Values

A class of students carried out a field trip to a woodlot as described in Section 4.9. If you have not done that field trip, read the procedure to find out what was done.

Table 4-16 contains the importance values calculated from data collected during Procedure D. It also contains data on relative abundance collected during Procedure D.

Questions

1. At what stage in succession is the woodlot? How do you know?
2. Of what significance are the lines drawn across Table 4-16?
3. **a)** Predict the future of the woodlot if it is left in its present unmanaged state with no human interference.
   b) Explain how you arrived at this prediction.
4. Some of the maple, beech, and hemlock trees are over 45 cm in d.b.h. Thus they can be legally cut. Will harvesting these trees affect species diversity? Explain your answer.
5. All the ash, basswood, oak, and hickory trees are over 45 cm in d.b.h. Make a list of the possible consequences of harvesting all these trees.
6. Could red oak trees be harvested on a sustained yield basis? Explain your answer.

Table 4-16   Importance Values and Relative Abundance

Species	Importance value of species	Relative abundance in sapling stratum
sugar maple	95	a
American beech	90	a
eastern hemlock	82	a
white ash	69	o
basswood	60	r
red oak	58	ab
bitternut hickory	42	ab
white pine	21	ab
trembling aspen	13	ab
white birch	10	ab
hawthorn	7	ab
apple	4	ab

7. Why are saplings of pine absent from the woodlot?
8. Which species could likely be harvested on a sustained yield basis?
9. **a)** What would have to be done if you wanted to bring white birch and white pine back into one part of this woodlot?
   b) Give two reasons why this probably should not be attempted.
   c) Give two reasons why some people might do this.

Main Ideas

1. Succession is the replacement of one community of living things by another.
2. Each stage in succession can be recognized by its index plants and animals.
3. A climax community is self-perpetuating.
4. Primary succession occurs in areas which have not supported life within recent geological times.
5. Secondary succession occurs in areas which have supported life within recent geological times.

Key Terms

autotrophic succession
climax community
cover density

frequency
heterotrophic succession
importance value

index organism   secondary succession
pioneer plant   succession
primary succession   sustained yield
quadrat

Chapter Review

A. True or False

Decide whether each of the following statements is true or false. If the sentence is false, rewrite it to make it true. (Do not write in this book.)

1. Secondary succession can start on a bare sand dune.
2. Sand grass is a pioneer plant of dune succession.
3. A climax community is self-perpetuating.
4. Primary succession is usually faster than secondary succession.
5. Quadrats are always 10 m x 10 m in size.
6. The density of a species is the percentage of the quadrats containing the species.
7. A Biltmore stick is used to calculate the number of board feet in a tree.

B. Completion

Complete each of the following sentences with a word or phrase that will make the sentence correct. (Do not write in this book.)

1. In a sand dune succession, pine trees are gradually replaced by ▓▓▓▓ trees.
2. In the Great Lakes region, the climax forest often consists of ▓▓▓▓ and ▓▓▓▓ trees.
3. A rotting carcass goes through ▓▓▓▓ succession.
4. The pioneers of succession on bare rock are ▓▓▓▓ .
5. To calculate importance value you need the frequency, density, and ▓▓▓▓ .

C. Multiple Choice

Each of the following statements or questions is followed by four responses. Choose the correct response in each case. (Do not write in this book.)

1. Where is primary succession likely to begin?
   a) in an abandoned field
   b) on volcanic lava
   c) where a forest has just been burned
   d) in a freshly dug garden
2. A sun-loving tree which is the first tree in many successions is
   a) maple b) cottonwood c) oak d) hemlock
3. An old-field community is usually dominated by
   a) trees   c) grasses and annual plants
   b) shrubs   d) biennial and perennial plants

4. A tree has a d.b.h. of 50 cm. Its basal area is
   a) 1963 cm² b) 2500 cm² c) 157 cm² d) 7850 cm²
5. A woodlot contains just three species. Their densities are: maple = 2.2; beech = 1.8; ash = 1.1. The relative density of the beech is
   a) 3.5 b) 18 c) 35 d) 180

Using Your Knowledge

1. List, in order, the stages in a secondary succession in your area.
2. Why do earthworms and other invertebrates become more abundant as succession approaches the climax stage?
3. Foresters use their knowledge of succession when they reforest a sand dune area which has lost its trees due to fire, wind, or lumbering. Figure 4-23 shows an area that has been replanted. What tree species do you think have been planted here? Why did the foresters select them?
4. Why do signs in many beach and dune areas prohibit the removal of grasses?
5. Many operators of trail bikes, dune buggies, and four-wheel-drive trucks like to drive over sand dunes. It's a challenge to see if you can get over the dunes without getting stuck. What do you think of this? Why?
6. Study Table 4-17 and then answer the following question. What species are probably growing as saplings under the oak and ash trees? How do you know?

Fig. 4-23 What species have been used to reforest this dune? Why?

Table 4-17 Importance Values

Species	Importance value
red oak	95
white ash	90
maple	40
beech	32

Investigations

1. Read Section 4.2 again, paying particular attention to the fallen log succession. Now visit a woodlot and study the stages of succession in a fallen log. Make careful notes regarding each stage. Take photographs if you can. **Important**: Leave things much as you found them. The logs are homes of many organisms. Don't tear their homes apart. Also, if you turn a log over, return it to its original position to protect the homes of any organisms that live under it.

2. Collect two or three samples of lichen. Do a microscopic study of the structure of these lichens. You can find instructions in many biology books. Write a report on your findings. Include sketches.

3. Walk through a woodlot. Make notes in a table on the numbers and sizes of the trees of each species. Note also the relative abundance of each species in the sapling layer. Now prepare a preliminary harvesting plan for the woodlot. Explain your choices of trees to be harvested. Do you feel that a detailed study like the one in Section 4.9 should be done? Give your reasons.

UNIT TWO

Terrestrial Ecosystems

Terrestrial ecosystems are those ecosystems that are based on land. They may be as small as a classroom terrarium. Or they may be as large as the Sahara Desert or the Arctic tundra. This unit begins with a study of small terrestrial ecosystems near your school. It then introduces factors such as weather and climate. After you have finished this unit, you will be able to explore and understand the material on biomes in Unit 3.

Fig. 5-0   This park is a terrestrial ecosystem. Its biotic (living) and abiotic (non-living) components interact with and affect one another.

5 Adaptations of Organisms to Temperature, Moisture, and Wind

The cactus and woodchuck in Figure 5-1 live in terrestrial (land) ecosystems. Like all organisms, they have adapted to their abiotic environments. The cactus, for example, shows structural adaptations. Its abiotic environment is hot and dry. Thus a cactus must have structural adaptations which make it possible for it to live in its environment. Can you think of some?

Fig. 5-1 The cactus shows structural adaptations; the woodchuck shows behavioural adaptations.

The woodchuck shows behavioural adaptations. It generally lives in open meadows and fields. Such areas get quite hot during mid-day. To escape the heat, woodchucks retire to their burrows. This is a behavioural adaptation.

In this chapter you will look at three abiotic factors and see how organisms have adapted to them.

5.1   Five Factors that Affect Organisms

Five main abiotic factors affect organisms in terrestrial ecosystems. They are temperature, moisture, wind, light and soil conditions (Fig. 5-2). Each organism has a range of tolerance for each factor. This range depends on the abiotic factor and on the organism. When the range is exceeded, in either direction, the organism suffers.

Within each range of tolerance there is an optimum point at which the organism lives best. Obviously conditions cannot be at the optimum all the time for all organisms. In fact, most organisms spend most of their lifetimes at conditions which are less than the optimum. Therefore those organisms with the broadest tolerance to all factors generally survive best and have the widest distribution. We say that these organisms have the best adaptations to their environments.

Fig. 5-2 How is this plant affected by the five abiotic factors? How has it adapted to them?

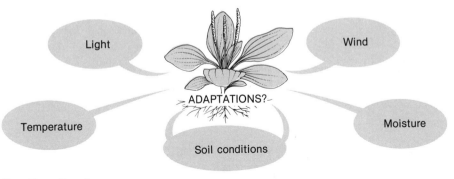

Light   Wind

ADAPTATIONS?

Temperature   Moisture

Soil conditions

Section Review

1. Name five abiotic factors which affect terrestrial organisms.
2. What is meant by the following terms: range of tolerance, optimum point?

5.2   Temperature

Optimum Temperature

Each species of organism has a different ability to tolerate extremes in temperature. For example, nematode eggs can withstand temperatures well below -200°C. But bird eggs are destroyed by such temperatures. Some

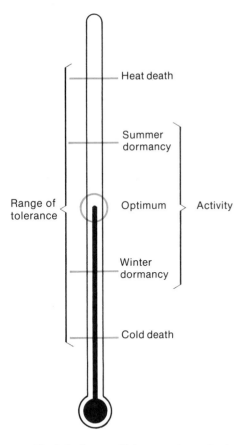

Fig. 5-3 Range of tolerance of an animal to temperature. Note that the animal goes dormant (inactive) if its environment gets too hot or too cold. Why is this?

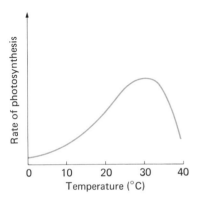

Fig. 5-4 Up to 30° C, the rate of photosynthesis increases as the temperature increases. Beyond 30° C, it decreases rapidly. Can you explain this sudden decrease?

pollen grains, fern spores, seeds, and bacteria spores can survive temperatures as low as -100° C. But most of these same organisms die at a temperature of 150° C. Many fungus spores, however, can survive such a high temperature.

Wide variations exist, then, in the high and low temperatures organisms can withstand. However, for each species there are temperatures below and above which it cannot live. Figure 5-3 calls these points "heat death" and "cold death". The temperature range between these extremes is called the range of tolerance to temperature.

Although a species can survive anywhere within its range of tolerance, it prefers a certain smaller range in which it is active. And the organism lives best at an optimum temperature in this range.

Temperature and Plants

Environmental temperature controls the temperature in a plant. Therefore it controls the rates of the metabolic processes in plants. For example, the rate of photosynthesis increases as the temperature is raised from 0° C to 30° C (Fig. 5-4).

In temperate climates, germination of many types of seeds is triggered by lower than average temperatures. The seeds of some pines will not germinate until they have been frozen. Spinach germinates and grows well only in early spring or late fall. So summer plantings are usually unsuccessful. Chilling is also an important factor for flower and fruit development in some species. For example, best growth, flowering, and fruiting in tomato plants occur when warm days (26° C) are followed by cool nights (10° C).

In desert and prairie regions, plants have adapted to high temperatures. Cacti have a thick outer coating. It helps prevent water loss due to the heat of the day.

Temperatures also vary by season. Thus plants must be able to adapt to changing temperatures. To survive freezing winter temperatures, many species of plants become dormant.

Section 2.8, page 33, is an activity dealing with the effects of temperature on seed germination and seedling growth. Review the results of that activity.

Temperature and Animals

Environmental temperature also affects animals. Some animals have body temperatures which vary with the environmental temperature. These species are called poikilotherms (poikilo means "various" and therm means "heat"). Among the poikilotherms are fish, amphibians, reptiles, arthropods, and all the animals simpler than these. Some people call these animals "cold-blooded". But a snake sunning itself on a 40° C rock will have a body temperature of close to 40° C, hardly cold-blooded! In fact, the snake's blood will be warmer than yours.

Mammals and birds have a constant body temperature. Yours is about 37.5° C. These animals have a temperature-regulating mechanism. It keeps the body temperature constant, regardless of the environmental temperature. Such animals are called **homeotherms** (**homeo** means "alike"). They are commonly called "warm-blooded". The fox in Figure 5-5 is a homeotherm. When the environmental temperature begins to drop, the fox produces more heat to maintain a constant body temperature. To supply this heat without wasting away, it must eat more food. The fox can also help maintain a constant body temperature by remaining inactive in its warm burrow.

Fig. 5-5 The red fox is a homeotherm. What does it do in the winter to keep its body temperature from dropping? And what does it do on a hot summer day to keep its body temperature from rising?

Section Review

1. Copy Figure 5-3 into your notebook. Then write an explanation of it.
2. Describe how temperature affects the germination of seeds.
3. Describe one way in which cacti have adapted to high desert temperatures.
4. How do some plants survive freezing winter temperatures?
5. Distinguish between poikilotherms and homeotherms.

5.3   Moisture

All organisms need water since it is part of their protoplasm. They also need water for many other life processes. Plants, for example, need water for the process of photosynthesis. There are two forms of moisture to which organisms must be adapted to survive. They are **precipitation** and **relative humidity**.

Just as organisms have optimum temperature conditions, they have **optimum moisture** conditions. They can, of course, live within a range of moisture conditions. Depending on their ability to adapt, the range may be narrow or wide. In all cases an overall water balance must be maintained between organisms and their environments. Too little water can cause the death of terrestrial plants and animals through dehydration. And too much water may drown many species of animals. It may even drown plants by preventing sufficient oxygen from reaching the roots. Birds often die as a result of chilling from long exposure to excess moisture.

Precipitation

Importance Rain, snow, and other forms of precipitation provide terrestrial organisms with much of their water. As a result, the distribution of precipitation over the surface of the earth plays an important role in deciding the distribution of organisms. However, precipitation does not act alone in determining the distribution of organisms. Temperature is equally important. Precipitation and temperature together are largely responsible for the **climate**

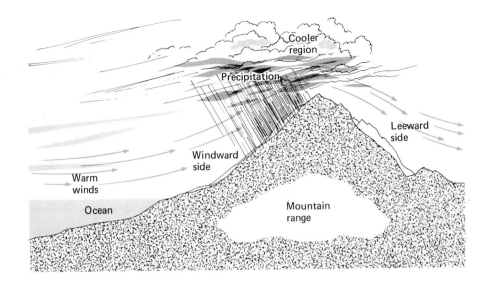

Fig. 5-6 Winds that hit a mountain are forced up into a cooler region of the atmosphere. The moisture in the winds condenses into precipitation and falls on the windward side. What might the valley on the leeward side be like?

of a region. The climate determines the distribution of organisms by making an area a tropical rain forest, a desert, a boreal forest, or another type of community.

The *total* amount of precipitation is not nearly as important to organisms as its *distribution* over the year. If you live in an area that has snowfall, you know that rain during the growing season is of greater value to plants than snow during the winter. We usually think of the tropics as being continuously wet. Yet many tropical regions have unequal distribution of rainfall over a year. That is, they have wet and dry seasons. In such regions the plants are largely deciduous—the leaves drop off during the dry season. Other tropical regions have precipitation that is spread more or less equally over the year. The vegetation in such regions is largely evergreen—the leaves do not all drop off at any one time.

Factors Affecting Precipitation   Three main factors affect precipitation:
- the direction of the prevailing winds
- the topography (shape) of the land
- the temperature

If the prevailing winds blow over large expanses of water, precipitation on nearby land masses is usually high. A high mountain range usually causes heavy precipitation on the windward side of the mountains. Temperature also affects prevailing winds because warm winds can pick up and hold more moisture than can cool winds. Figure 5-6 shows how these factors act together. Can you name regions of North America where this occurs?

Relative Humidity

Water vapour in the air is another form of moisture that affects organisms. For example, if the air is too dry, some organisms dry out and die. Other organisms adapt to the dry conditions.

Fig. 5-7 Many plants, like this spruce, have narrow waxy leaves to reduce water loss.

The amount of water vapour in the air is usually expressed as the relative humidity. The relative humidity is the ratio of the mass of water in a certain volume of air to the mass of water needed to saturate the same volume of air at the same temperature. It is expressed as a percentage. Thus a relative humidity of 80% means that the air contains 80% of the water it is capable of holding at that particular temperature.

Plants give off water vapour through pores in their leaves. This process is called transpiration and is needed by plants. It helps cool plant leaves on hot days, much as perspiration cools your body. More important though is its role in transporting minerals from the roots to the leaves of plants. Without transpiration, not enough water would pass through a plant to carry needed minerals to the leaves.

You know that on a humid day, sweat builds up on your skin. This happens because sweat cannot evaporate as quickly when the relative humidity is high. In general, plants are affected in a similar way. When the relative humidity is high, the transpiration rate is low. And when the relative humidity is low, the transpiration rate is high. Fortunately, most plants have adaptations that help prevent excessive transpiration that could kill them. Evergreens like pines and spruces have their pores (stomata) located in a groove on the underside of their leaves (needles). And they have narrow waxy leaves (Fig. 5-7). Cacti have very few pores and a thick epidermis (skin). What does a house plant do when it is not watered enough? How does this adaptation reduce water loss by transpiration?

Water Content of the Soil

You have likely seen areas close to one another which have quite different plants growing in them. Think, for example, of a hill with a pond at its base. The plants growing on the hill will likely be quite different from those growing around the pond. One reason for this difference is the water content of the soil. Both areas receive the same amount of precipitation. But, because of its location, the soil at the base of the hill contains more water. Also, organic matter tends to build up in lower areas. This organic matter will further help such areas hold the water that drains from the hillside.

Fig. 5-8 A pond community. What adaptations do the hydrophytes around this pond have? Why do they need them?

Hydrophytes In some areas the soil stays wet all year round. Only plants that have adapted to this extreme moisture condition can survive in these areas. Such plants are called hydrophytes. Communities of hydrophytes are found around ponds and lakes. They also occur along the banks of rivers and streams. Most marsh plants are hydrophytes.

Most hydrophytes grow with their roots in the mud below the water. Their leaves either float on the water or extend into the air above. Pond lilies, cattails, and bulrushes are examples (Fig. 5-8). Other hydrophytes grow totally submerged in water. Aquarium plants such as *Elodea* and *Cabomba* are examples. Still others, such as duckweed, float on the surface. In fact, they often cover the pond with a carpet of green.

Fig. 5-9 This desert has several species of xerophytes. What are some of their adaptations?

Xerophytes Some soils are not able to hold much water. Such a condition may result from a low organic content. If such soils are in an area of low precipitation and low relative humidity, a very dry environment results. Only specially adapted plants called xerophytes can live in such areas. A desert is an extreme example of a xerophytic area (Fig. 5-9). Less extreme xerophytic conditions occur on sand dunes and on rocky slopes.

Cacti are the most familiar xerophytes of deserts. Sage brush dominates the xerophytes of many dry prairies. Lichens which grow on rocks are xerophytes. And the sand grass which colonizes sand dunes is a xerophyte. Pine trees which grow on sandy soil and in rocky sites are xerophytes. The evergreens of our northern forest are usually considered xerophytes. Water may be plentiful in the northern forest. But during the winter this water is frozen and cannot be absorbed by plants.

All xerophytes have adapted to lessen the loss of water from leaves through transpiration. The leaves and stems of many xerophytes are thick and fleshy to allow space to store water. The leaves of xerophytes are usually small. For example, the spines of cacti are all that remain of their leaves. The leaves also have very few pores (stomata). And most of these are located on the underside of the leaves. Why is this? Some xerophytes have long tap roots that extend deep into the ground to reach moisture. Others, like sand grass, have large branched fibrous roots to gather the little available moisture (Fig. 5-10).

Fig. 5-10 Adaptations of the roots of xerophytes. Tap roots (A) reach deep into the soil to get water. Fibrous roots (B) spread widely through the soil to gather water.

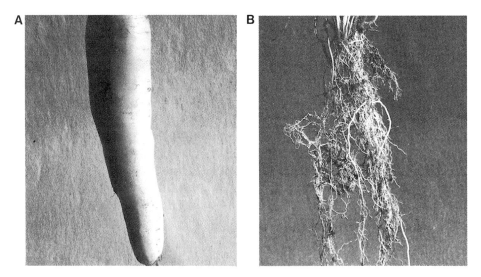

Mesophytes These plants prefer moisture conditions between those of xerophytes and hydrophytes. The trees and other plants of a mature deciduous forest are mainly mesophytes (Fig. 5-11). So too are the common plants of a grassy meadow—orchard grass, buttercups, and goldenrod. Mesophytes grow best when moderate amounts of moisture are available throughout most of their growing seasons.

Fig. 5-11 A forest dominated by deciduous trees usually contains mainly mesophytic plants.

Adaptations to Moisture Conditions Adaptation to *changes* in moisture conditions is one key to survival of a species. A certain species may prefer certain moisture conditions. But it won't last long unless it can tolerate extremes from time to time. For example, most mesophytic areas have periods in which xerophytic conditions occur. The organisms of such areas have adaptations that permit them to survive through the dry periods. Deciduous trees drop their leaves during the winter (a xerophytic period). Alfalfa plants develop long tap roots to obtain water in midsummer. Annual plants (plants that live only one year) survive long periods of drought as seeds. The seeds germinate only when favourable moisture conditions return. Desert animals conserve moisture by staying in their burrows during the day. They are active only at night when it is cooler and the relative humidity is higher. Many animals enter a period of dormancy during dry periods. Grasshoppers have an exoskeleton (a thick body covering) that aids in water retention. And the spittlebug surrounds itself with juices from the plant on which it lives. In this way it can live in dry meadows without suffering from water loss (Fig. 5-12).

Fig. 5-12 The grasshopper has a structural adaptation to xerophytic conditions. The spittlebug has a behavioural adaptation.

Section Review

1. Name the two forms of moisture to which organisms must adapt.
2. Why is the distribution of precipitation over the year usually more important than the total amount of precipitation?
3. List three factors which affect precipitation.
4. Copy Figure 5-6 into your notebook. Then write an explanation of what the figure shows.
5. What does "a relative humidity of 60%" mean?
6. Give two reasons why transpiration is important to plants.
7. Why is transpiration faster when the relative humidity is low?
8. How have evergreens and cacti adapted to prevent excessive transpiration?
9. What is a hydrophyte?

10. **a)** What is a xerophyte?
    b) List three ways in which xerophytes have adapted to conserve water.
11. What is a mesophyte?
12. **a)** List three ways in which mesophytic plants have adapted to periods of xerophytic conditions.
    b) Describe four adaptations of animals to xerophytic conditions.

5.4   *ACTIVITY*   Effects of Soil Moisture on Plant Growth

Each species of plant has an optimum soil moisture content at which it grows best. It also has a range of tolerance to soil moisture content. In this range the plant will grow but not as well as at the optimum. Beyond the range of tolerance the plant dies. The soil is either too wet or too dry for the plant to stay alive. In this activity you will study how soil moisture content affects the growth of various plants.

Problem

How does soil moisture content affect the growth of various species of plants?

Materials

3 sets of potted plants of various   3 trays
   species   ruler

Procedure

a. Prepare 3 sets of equally developed plants. Each set should contain the same species. All plants should be healthy and growing in ideal situations. Figure 5-13 shows an example of a set. Include plants you think need different soil moisture conditions.

Fig. 5-13   An example of a set of plants. You need three identical sets.

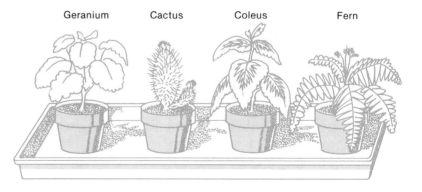

Geranium   Cactus   Coleus   Fern

b. Place all 3 trays in the same conditions of light and temperature.
c. Water the plants in the first tray according to the schedule recommended in books on the care of house plants.
d. Add 3-4 cm of water to the second tray. Add water when necessary to keep the level the same throughout the experiment.
e. Water all the plants in the third tray much more lightly than you did in step (c).
f. Continue the experiment for several weeks. Measure the heights of the plants every few days. Record your results in a table.
g. Make careful notes on how each species is affected by overwatering and underwatering.
h. Carefully knock the root ball from each pot. Examine the roots to see how the watering schedule affected them.

Discussion

1. State the optimum soil moisture conditions for each species of plant that you used.
2. Describe and explain the effects of overwatering on each species.
3. Describe and explain the effects of underwatering on each species.
4. Which species has the widest range of tolerance to soil moisture content? Which species has the narrowest?

5.5   Wind

Desirable Effects

Wind has both desirable and undesirable effects on ecosystems. The most important among the desirable effects is bringing precipitation to an area. Winds blowing over large bodies of water become laden with water vapour. As these winds move inland, the vapour precipitates out, adding moisture to the land.

Hay fever sufferers are well aware that the pollen grains of many plants are transported by wind. In fact, without wind, many species of plants would not be pollinated at all. Thus seeds would not be produced and the species would vanish. Grasses depend largely on wind for pollination. Conifers such as the pine tree have pollen grains with wing-like attachments. This adaptation permits pine pollen to be carried many kilometres by wind.

Wind also plays an important role in increasing the distribution of plant species over a land mass. It carries spores from mushrooms and other fungi many kilometres. These spores land, germinate, and start new colonies. The wind also carries the seeds of many plants to new locations. How have the seeds of maple trees, ash trees, and dandelion plants adapted to being distributed by wind? Sometimes the wind moves an entire plant to help it disperse its seeds. For example, as the familiar tumbleweed is blown along,

Fig. 5-14 Wind helps the tumbleweed spread its seeds over the grasslands of the West.

Fig. 5-15 A blowout can destroy in hours a forest that took hundreds of years to develop. Blowouts are brought on by anything that disturbs too much of the vegetation on the ground—heavy rains, off-road vehicles, careless logging.

Fig. 5-16 This pine indicates, like a weather vane, the direction of the prevailing wind.

its seeds are gradually dislodged (Fig. 5-14). One original plant may seed a strip several kilometres long.

Undesirable Effects

Everyone is familiar with the eroding effects that strong winds have on soil. Clouds of dust often fill the air in farming regions where vast tracts of land are under intense cultivation. Much valuable farmland is lost due to careless agricultural practices that make dust storms possible. The causes of erosion are understood. Preventive measures have been developed but, nonetheless, three-quarters of the farmland in North America is still being mismanaged.

Figure 5-15 shows another example of the harmful effects of winds on ecosystems. A forest can develop on unstable soil, as it does in a sand dune area. But it can be destroyed overnight by a powerful wind.

Wind also affects the growth of plants. Strong winds blow away water vapour from the vicinity of plant leaves. The drier air outside the leaves encourages excessive transpiration. Some plants have special adaptations to counteract this drying action. But others either die or their growth is stunted. Thus trees such as spruces that are normally tall and slim become short and spreading when they grow in areas regularly exposed to strong winds. The delicate growing tips do not develop properly because of the drying action of the wind. Only those branches close to the ground, out of the full force of the wind, develop.

Strong winds alter the physical appearance of trees in other interesting ways (Fig. 5-16). The branches on the windward side of trees in exposed areas are often bent around. Eventually they permanently point in the direction of the prevailing wind. Also, cold dry winds often kill the twig-forming buds on the windward side of trees. The result is that no limbs grow on that side.

As well as deforming trees, strong winds can uproot them or break limbs from them. Such damage is most common in forests where humans have removed the larger trees, thereby exposing the smaller trees to the full force of the wind (Fig. 5-17). Since the smaller trees often have not developed extensive rooting systems, they are easily uprooted. Rooting systems are generally shallow and not very extensive in wet soils since the trees do not require large and deep roots to obtain moisture. Thus uprooting is particularly common in an area such as a cedar wetland where the larger trees have been logged.

Section Review

1. List three desirable effects of wind.
2. What is the most serious undesirable effect of wind?
3. a) Describe how wind affects the growth of plants.
   b) In what other ways can wind harm plants (particularly trees)?

Fig. 5-17 This tree was shallow-rooted. Logging exposed it to strong winds which uprooted it.

Main Ideas

1. Terrestrial ecosystems vary in size from a handful of soil to a biome.
2. Organisms show structural and behavioural adaptations to their abiotic environments.
3. Five main abiotic factors affect organisms: temperature, moisture, wind, light, and soil conditions.
4. Each organism has a range of tolerance to each of the five abiotic factors.
5. Temperature controls the metabolic rates of plants and poikilotherms.
6. Precipitation, humidity, and soil water content are three forms of moisture which affect plants.
7. Plants can be classified as hydrophytes, xerophytes, or mesophytes.
8. Wind pollinates some plants and disperses the seeds of others.

Key Terms

behavioural adaptation
deciduous
evergreen
homeotherm
hydrophyte
mesophyte

optimum temperature
poikilotherm
range of tolerance
relative humidity
structural adaptation
xerophyte

Chapter Review

A. True or False

Decide whether each of the following statements is true or false. If the sentence is false, rewrite it to make it true. (Do not write in this book.)

1. A field is a terrestrial ecosystem.
2. The optimum temperature is the temperature at which an organism lives best.
3. An increase in temperature always increases the rate of photosynthesis.
4. Strong winds can damage plants by causing excessive transpiration.

B. Completion

Complete each of the following sentences with a word or phrase that will make the sentence correct. (Do not write in this book.)

1. The temperature range between "heat death" and "cold death" is called the ▨▨▨▨ to temperature.
2. An animal with a constant body temperature is called a ▨▨▨▨ .
3. Cacti usually have a ▨▨▨▨ to protect them from water loss.
4. Strong winds blowing over bare soil can cause ▨▨▨▨ .

C. Multiple Choice

Each of the following statements or questions is followed by four responses. Choose the correct response in each case. (Do not write in this book.)

1. Look at Figure 5-4. Photosynthesis is fastest at
   a) $0°C$ b) $20°C$ c) $30°C$ d) $40°C$
2. All plants which have adapted to hot dry conditions are called
   a) cacti b) hydrophytes c) xerophytes d) mesophytes
3. A snake is best described as
   a) cold-blooded b) a poikilotherm c) a homeotherm d) a xerophyte
4. The narrow waxy leaves (needles) of a pine tree are an adaptation to
   a) high relative humidity
   b) mesophytic conditions
   c) hydrophytic conditions
   d) xerophytic conditions
5. In cold windy areas, limbs often do not form on the windward side of some trees because
   a) the relative humidity of the wind is too high
   b) the relative humidity of the wind is too low
   c) the twig-forming buds are killed by the cold
   d) the wind snaps new twigs off

Using Your Knowledge

1. Why do changes in the environmental temperature affect poikilotherms more than homeotherms?
2. a) Make a list of five poikilotherms. Explain how each of these animals protects itself from very high and very low temperatures.
   b) Repeat 2 (a) for five homeotherms.
3. A frog has trouble swimming in icy cold water. But a beaver does not. Why not?
4. What do you think would be the average relative humidity of a desert? Of a tropical rain forest?
5. Suppose that the relative humidity in a field was 80% in the late afternoon. The temperature was $25°C$ and the wind speed 0 km/h. By midnight the temperature was $10°C$ and the wind speed was still 0 km/h. What happens to the relative humidity? Why? What evidence might you see that supports your answer?
6. Which wind will dry out a terrestrial ecosystem more quickly: one with a relative humidity of 10% or one with a relative humidity of 70%? Explain your answer. (Assume that wind speed, wind direction and temperature are the same in both cases.)
7. A black spruce tree in a northern (boreal) forest may be standing in 2 m of snow. Yet ecologists say that its environment is xerophytic. Why?

8. Deciduous trees drop their leaves in the winter. Why is this adaptation an advantage to the trees?

9. Hydrophytic plants which grow in fast rivers usually have narrow leaves. Why is this adaptation important to the plants?

10. **a)** Where does a submerged hydrophyte get its oxygen?

    b) Submerged hydrophytes usually have thin cell walls. As well, they usually lack a cuticle (waxy skin) on their leaves. Why?

11. Why don't wind-pollinated plants such as pines and grass have colourful flowers?

12. Which do you think produces more pollen grains: a flower on a wind-pollinated plant or a flower of the same size on an insect-pollinated plant? Why?

13. **a)** Why is soil erosion a more serious problem now than it was 200 years ago?

    b) Why is soil erosion continuing, even though we know how harmful it is?

Investigations

1. The stomata (breathing pores) of pine and spruce trees are usually located in a groove on the underside of each needle.

   a) Look at one of these needles with a hand lens. Draw what you see.

   b) If possible, look at the needle with a dissecting microscope. Add further details to your drawing.

   c) How does this adaptation help the tree withstand xerophytic conditions?

2. Select a desert animal. Find out how it has adapted to xerophytic conditions.

3. Visit a park, the countryside, or any other greenbelt area. Sketch or photograph evidence of the effects of wind on that ecosystem.

4. **a)** Collect pollen grains from a number of wind-pollinated plants. (Put a thin coating of petroleum jelly on a microscope slide. Hold the flower above the slide and tap the flower.) Look at the pollen grains with a microscope. Sketch their shapes. Explain how each is adapted for wind pollination.

   b) Repeat 4 (a) for several insect-pollinated plants.

6 Adaptations of Organisms to Light and Soil

In Chapter 5 you found out how organisms have adapted to temperature, moisture, and wind conditions. This chapter explores adaptations to two other abiotic factors, light and soil. Most of this chapter deals with light adaptations. You can find out about soil adaptations in Unit 4 of *Investigating Natural Resources.*

6.1 Light

Three aspects of light affect organisms. These are intensity (brightness), duration (how long the light shines), and quality (colour). This section describes these three factors and their effects.

Light and Its Importance

What is Light?   The sun gives off electromagnetic waves which have a wide range of wave lengths. At one extreme are the very short gamma rays and X-rays. Fortunately for life on the earth, little of this dangerous radiation passes through the atmosphere. At the other extreme are the long radio waves. Most of these pass through the atmosphere easily. (What evidence do you have of this?) Between the two extremes are the ultraviolet, visible, and infrared bands of radiation (Fig. 6-1).

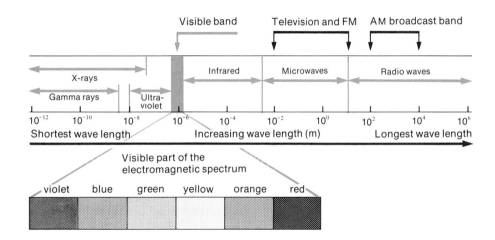

Fig. 6-1 The place of light (visible radiation) in the electromagnetic spectrum.

Light is the one form of energy the eye can detect. As you can see from Figure 6-1, the visible band makes up only a small part of the electromagnetic spectrum. Most peoples' eyes cannot detect radiation that has a wave length longer than 770 nm (red light). Nor can they detect radiation that has a wave length shorter than 390 nm (violet light). (Wave lengths of light are usually given in nanometres. A nanometre is 10^{-9} m, or 0.000 000 001 m.)

Ultraviolet radiation has wave lengths shorter than 390 nm. Some ultraviolet light reaches the surface of the earth. It has both helpful and harmful effects on organisms. For example, certain wave lengths of these invisible rays cause tanning of human skin and help make Vitamin D. But other wave lengths cause sunburn and, possibly, skin cancer.

Infrared radiation has wave lengths longer than 770 nm. These invisible rays are largely responsible for the transmission of heat through space. Some infrared radiation gets through the earth's atmosphere. When it strikes the surface of the earth, it warms the soil, water, and air.

Importance of Light Provided atmospheric conditions are normal, the visible band of radiation passes through the atmosphere easily. Its effects on organisms are many and varied.

Most organisms depend on sunlight for survival. Plants (producers) obtain their energy requirements by converting light energy to chemical energy through photosynthesis. Consumers indirectly obtain their energy from the sun by eating producers or other consumers. Light is, therefore, of unquestionable value to an ecosystem. Yet too much light kills most organisms. For example, the chlorophyll vital to green plants is destroyed by excessive light. Thus light is both an essential factor and a limiting factor; it must be present, but too much or too little can be harmful. This creates a real problem for plants and animals. They must somehow seek out or create an environment that offers the right amount of light. Many of the structural features and behaviour patterns of organisms are related to solving this problem. Can you think of some examples?

Within certain ecosystems such as forests, the light conditions are not uniform. The light may vary in intensity, duration, and quality from place to place and from time to time. For example, the light is not as bright (intense) on the forest floor as it is at the top of the leaf canopy. The sun does not shine on the forest for as many hours per day in March as it does in June. The light does not have the same colour (quality) in the depths of the forest as it does in more open areas. It is important, therefore, to study the effects of light on organisms under these three headings—intensity, duration, and quality.

Intensity

Many factors affect light intensity. Among these are latitude, altitude, topography, time of year, time of day, and cloud cover. Over any community, provided it is not too large, these factors are fairly uniform. But within a community, the stratum in which the organism lives can greatly affect the intensity of the light that reaches it. For example, an organism in the upper or tree stratum in a forest will probably receive much brighter light than an organism in the lower or ground stratum.

A combination of a thick canopy of leaves and long cloudy periods can often reduce the light intensity to the compensation intensity for some plants. Compensation intensity is the intensity at which the light is just bright enough to make it possible for photosynthesis to replace the sugars as fast as respiration uses them. If the intensity is below this level for too long, some plant species will die. Most plants have a compensation intensity of about 10 hlx (hectolux). That is, they will eventually die if the intensity stays below 10 hlx. The intensity on your desk top in your classroom is likely between 5 and 10 hlx.

Light intensity has a controlling influence on any ecosystem. It determines, to a large extent, the degree of primary production in the ecosystem. (Primary production is the rate at which energy is stored by producers through the process of photosynthesis.) Up to a certain point, the rate of photosynthesis increases as the light intensity increases. But a saturation intensity exists. Beyond the saturation intensity, the rate of photosynthesis decreases (Fig. 6-2). For shade-tolerant plants, the maximum rate of photosynthesis occurs at very low intensities. This adaptation helps make it possible for many plants—ferns, mosses, trilliums, maple seedlings—to live in the dense shade of the forest floor.

Light intensity also plays a role in determining the orientation of plants and animals. That is, it helps determine the direction of growth and movement of plants and the direction of movement of animals. Plants exhibit tropisms (from the Greek trope which means "turn"). First, plants exhibit geotropism, or response to gravity. You can plant a seed any way you like. But the root will always turn down and the stem up. Second, plants exhibit phototropism, or response to light. The growing tips of plants will head up toward the light. This is positive phototropism. Foresters make use of positive phototropism and crowding to ensure tall erect growth of trees that

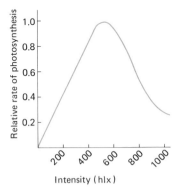

Fig. 6-2 **The relationship between light intensity and rate of photosynthesis for a forest community. In this community, photosynthesis starts to slow down when the light intensity reaches about 500 hlx (hectolux).**

Fig. 6-3 These pine trees grow straight and tall, with little lateral growth, as they compete for light and space.

are to be used as lumber (Fig. 6-3). Sun-tolerant plants such as geraniums turn their leaves toward the sun to obtain maximum exposure. Sunflowers follow the movement of the sun across the sky each day so they can present the broad sides of their leaves continuously to the sun. In areas where the light intensity is excessive most of the time, many plants exhibit negative phototropism. They turn their leaves so that the edges face the sun. Why do they behave like this?

Many animal species also orient themselves using light intensity. With animals, this orientation is not called a tropism but, instead, a taxis. You exhibit geotaxis. That is, you use gravity to keep yourself vertical as you walk around. Many animals exhibit phototaxis. Moths and other insects often move to a porch light at night. The honeybee determines its path from its hive to a nectar source by the angle between the path and the sun. What does it do when the sun is covered with clouds? All a bee needs is a small patch of blue sky. It then orients itself by using the angle of polarization of the light in this patch of sky.

The migration of birds over long distances is just as amazing as the ability of bees to find their food supply. Birds may use landmarks, prevailing wind direction, and even the earth's magnetic field to help orient themselves during migration. Many species of birds also use the direction of the sunlight for the same purpose. Furthermore, they can compensate for changes in the position of the sun during the day.

Duration

You probably know that seasonal changes occur in the behaviour of plants and animals. At a certain time of year a particular plant flowers; at a certain time of year a particular bird migrates. What causes these seasonal changes in behaviour? You might think they are associated with how light intensity changes over the course of a year. Scientists believe, however, that seasonal behaviour has more to do with changes in *length of exposure*, or duration, than with changes in intensity. This response of organisms to the length of day is called photoperiodism.

Photoperiod and Plants Plants can be classified as long-day, short-day, or day-neutral. The flowering of day-neutral plants is not affected by the length of day. On the other hand, long-day plants will only flower when the length of day exceeds a certain critical value. This value is different for each species of plant. It usually exceeds 12 h and is commonly about 14 h. Such periods of long days and short nights occur in middle and upper latitudes in the late spring and summer. You probably know some of these long-day plants: red clover, spinach, timothy grass, oats, and radish. If the daily period of light is less than the critical value, flowering will be poor and, frequently, growth will be stunted.

Short-day plants flower naturally only under conditions of short days and long nights. The critical length of day for these plants is less than 12 h and commonly about 10 h. In the middle and upper latitudes, days of this length occur in the early spring and in the late summer or early autumn. Trilliums, Jack-in-the-pulpits, and other spring flowers are short-day plants. Most of these plants are perennials. Their roots and buds were formed the previous year. You may have noticed that in deciduous woods these plants flower before the leaves of the trees have fully developed. Why do you think this happens?

Other short-day plants require a long period of growth before they are mature enough to flower. These plants develop during the bright sunny days of the summer. Then flowering is triggered by the shortened days of late summer or early autumn. Chrysanthemum, tobacco, goldenrod, cosmos, dahlia, ragweed, and aster are common plants in this category.

Since the duration of light controls flowering, it determines the season in which a particular plant flowers. Furthermore, it influences the geographical distribution of a plant species. Consider, for example, a long-day plant that has a photoperiod of 14 h. This plant could flower early in July in parts of the United States having the same latitude as Virginia. In Northern Ontario, Vermont, and places of similar latitude the length of day is 14 h in May and again in August. The plant could theoretically flower at either of those two times. In practice, however, it can flower only in August because the temperature is too low in May to permit flowering. Yet August flowering can mean that seed development is not completed before frost kills the plant. In this way, therefore, plants are restricted to certain geographical areas. Plants that live in the Arctic must be able to tolerate long days, since the duration of daylight is very long there during the growing season. On the other hand, tropical plants are adapted to short days since the photoperiod near the equator is about 12 h.

Photoperiod and Animals   The duration of light also controls the life cycles of many animals. The long days of late spring induce some mammals such as ferrets to breed. The shorter days of autumn are necessary before the same process is initiated in deer. Photoperiodism plays a role in the migration of birds. If you live in Canada or the northern United States, you know that birds arrive in the spring at about the same time every year. They may even leave their winter homes during a cold spell and arrive during a blizzard. Thus temperature does not appear to be a major factor in determining migration times. Instead, the photoperiod is the underlying cause. The length of day controls the reproductive cycle which, in turn, determines the times of migration. Birds need long periods of daylight for nest building and collecting food for their ever-hungry young. Under periods of long daylight, the process of raising young can be completed more quickly and, as a result, more successfully. Birds migrate north to breed because the length of day is longer there during the summer. At the same time, food supply and temperature also favour reproduction. Birds migrate south in the fall to escape the killing cold and limited food supply of northern areas in winter. Remember that although photoperiodism plays a role in migration it does not explain how birds find their way during migration. Nor does it explain why this behaviour evolved in the first place.

Quality

Quality is used when referring to the colour or wave length of light. As an ecological factor it is less important than intensity or duration. It is in photosynthesis that light quality plays its most important ecological role. Not all wave lengths of the visible spectrum are used in photosynthesis. Only the violet and red ends of the spectrum are absorbed. The green portion is reflected (Fig. 6-4). This is why chlorophyll-bearing plants appear green when exposed to daylight or its equivalent.

In general, quality is affected by the same factors that affect intensity—altitude, latitude, time of year, time of day, and atmospheric conditions. For example, smog cuts down light intensity. It also disperses blue light so less blue light reaches the earth. These factors are relatively constant over large areas. Therefore they are not as important ecologically as local variations such as the stratum in which the organism lives. For example, the ground stratum in a forest receives less red and blue light than the tree stratum. The chlorophyll in the leaves of the tree stratum has absorbed much of this light before it reaches the ground stratum plants. However, many species of plants have adapted to light of different qualities. In fact, the reduction in intensity appears to be more of a limiting factor in the ground stratum than does the change in quality.

The quality of light affects mainly those animals that have colour vision. Certain species of arthropods, fish, birds, and mammals have well-developed colour vision. Other species in the same groups do not. For example, primates are the only mammals that have well-developed colour vision. What advantages do you think colour vision gives to an animal?

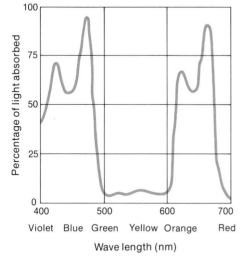

Fig. 6-4 The absorption curve of chlorophyll.

Section Review

1. Name the three aspects of light that affect organisms.
2. Define light.
3. Why is light important to all organisms (to both producers *and* consumers)?
4. Give the meanings of the following terms: compensation intensity, primary production, saturation intensity.
5. **a)** What is phototropism?
   b) What is phototaxis?
   c) Describe an example of positive phototropism you have seen.
6. **a)** Give the meanings of the following terms: long-day plant, short-day plant, day-neutral plant.
   b) Explain how the duration of light determines the season in which a plant will flower.

c) Explain how the duration of light determines the geographical distribution of a plant species.

7. Describe the role of photoperiodism in the migration of birds.
8. **a)** What is light quality?
   b) What factors affect light quality?
   c) Which colours are most important in photosynthesis?
   d) What makes a leaf look green in daylight?
   e) What animals are most affected by light quality?

6.2 ACTIVITY Response of Arthropods to Light Intensity

You read in Section 6.1 that many animals exhibit phototaxis. That is, they respond to light intensity. Some animals are positively phototactic; they *move toward* bright light. Others are negatively phototactic; they *move away* from bright light. In this activity you offer an arthropod a choice between bright and dark conditions. Then, by observing its behaviour, you can decide if it is positively or negatively phototactic.

Problem

How does the arthropod respond to choices in light intensity? How does its response relate to its choice of natural habitat?

Materials

large petri dish with one half
  covered with black tape
25 W bulb
10 sow bugs

Optional:
10 flour beetles, 10 ants, 10 fruit
  flies, 10 houseflies, 10 millipedes, 10 earwigs, or 10 of any
  other small arthropod

Fig. 6-5 Does the arthropod prefer a high or low light intensity?

Procedure

a. Place the 25 W bulb about 25 cm above the petri dish (Fig. 6-5).
b. Place 10 sow bugs in the petri dish.
c. Let the dish stand undisturbed for 5 min. While you are waiting, make two copies of Table 6-1 in your notebook.
d. Count the number of sow bugs in the uncovered part of the dish at 2-min intervals for 10 min. Record your results in one of your tables.
e. Turn the lid through 180°. The part that was dark before should now be bright. Repeat steps (c) and (d). Record your results in your other table.
f. Share your findings with two or three other groups. Then calculate the percentage of sow bugs found, on the average, in the bright side of the dish.
g. If possible, repeat the experiment with one or more other arthropods.

Table 6-1 Response of Arthropods to Light Intensity

Arthropod	Natural habitat	Predicted response	Actual Response						
			0 min	2 min	4 min	6 min	8 min	10 min	Average
Sow bugs									
Flour beetles									
Ants									
Fruit flies									
etc.									

Discussion

1. Are sow bugs positively or negatively phototactic? How do you know?
2. Why do all sow bugs not respond in the same way at the same time?
3. **a)** In what natural habitats have you seen sow bugs?
   b) Describe the light intensity of these habitats.
4. Why do sow bugs seek out such habitats?
5. Answer questions 1 to 4 for any other arthropods you study.

Adaptations of Plants to Light Intensity

6.3 ACTIVITY

Within a community, light intensity often varies from place to place. For example, it will be low beneath a dense stand of trees in a woodlot. But it will be high in a clearing in the same woodlot. It is easy to spot adaptations of plants to light intensity. Plants that are always exposed to low intensity may have broad dark green leaves. These two adaptations help the leaves trap more of the little light that is available. In this activity you look for such adaptations in a community near your school or home.

Problem

In what ways have plants adapted to high and low light intensity?

Materials

light meter (optional)

Table 6-2   Adaptations to Light Intensity

Plant	Light intensity	Adaptations	Advantages to the plant

Fig. 6-6   This light meter is indicating a light intensity of 3 hlx (hectolux).

Procedure

a. Make a full-page copy of Table 6-2.

b. Find a plant community which has variations in light intensity within it. Two examples are a woodlot and a grassy area which is partly shaded.

c. Find a site in the community where the light intensity is higher than average for the community throughout most of the day. Record the light intensity in your table as very bright, bright, moderate, low, or very low. If you have a light meter, record the intensity in hectolux (Fig. 6-6). *Note:* Take readings at different spots and average them. Place the meter among the plants and point it upward so it will record the light intensity the plants receive.

d. Study the plants in the site carefully. Look for adaptations to light intensity. Shape, size, colour, thickness, arrangement, and orientation of leaves are some factors to study. Record your findings in your table.

e. Repeat steps (c) and (d) at a site where the light intensity is lower than average for the community throughout most of the day.

f. Repeat the experiment at two or three other sites in the community.

Discussion

1. Complete the last column "Advantages to the Plant". Why, for example, are narrow leaves an advantage to a plant which is usually exposed to bright light? And why do some plants in dull areas turn their leaves toward the sun?

6.4   *ACTIVITY*   Photoperiod and Plant Development

In Section 6.1 you learned that the photoperiod, the daily length of exposure to light, affects flowering in many plants. In this activity you will observe the effects of photoperiod on long-day, short-day, and day-neutral plants.

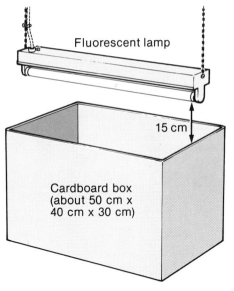

Fluorescent lamp

15 cm

Cardboard box
(about 50 cm x
40 cm x 30 cm)

Fig. 6-7 A growing chamber for studying the effects of photoperiod on plant development. Place the chamber in a location where daylight will help the lamp provide light.

Problem

How does the photoperiod affect flowering of long-day, short-day, and day-neutral plants?

Materials

2 growing chambers with covers
2 fluorescent light sources (40 W)
4 long-day plants (*e.g.* radish)

4 short-day plants (*e.g.* chrysanthemum)
4 day-neutral plants (*e.g.* tomato)

Procedure

a. Prepare two growing chambers, shown in Figure 6-7. The boxes must be tall enough to hold mature plants (at least 40 cm).

b. Buy or grow 4 radish plants, 4 chrysanthemum plants, and 4 tomato plants. The plants should be 20-30 d old at the start of the experiment. They must be mature but not in flower.

c. Put 2 of each kind of plant in each growing chamber. Maintain the same environmental conditions (soil, moisture, temperature) in both growing chambers. Only the photoperiod is to be different.

d. Expose one growing chamber to 8 h of light and 16 h of darkness. Cover the chamber with a lid and opaque cloth so that *no light* can enter during the dark period.

e. Expose the other growing chamber to 16 h of light and 8 h of darkness.

f. Continue these light-dark cycles until the plants flower or you are sure that they are not going to flower.

Discussion

1. Why were radish, chrysanthemum, and tomato plants selected for this experiment?
2. Describe the effects of "short days" on each species of plant.
3. Describe the effects of "long days" on each species of plant.
4. How does this experiment illustrate the terms long-day, short-day, and day-neutral?
5. Would chrysanthemums flower best outdoors in the early summer or early fall? Why?
6. Would radishes flower best in Ontario or in Georgia in June? Why?

6.5   Soil

Up to this point you have studied how four abiotic factors affect organisms: temperature, moisture, wind, and light. The fifth and final factor is soil. It is the most complex factor affecting life in terrestrial ecosystems. If you have studied Unit 4 of *Investigating Natural Resources*, you know the soil characteristics which affect organisms. The main ones are listed below. If you have not studied them, read about them before you do Activity 6.7.

Geophysical Factors
- temperature
- profile
- texture
- structure
- particle size
- percolation rate
- capillarity
- water content
- water-holding capacity

Chemical Factors
- organic content
- macronutrients
- micronutrients
- pH

6.6 Microenvironments

Fig. 6-8 Why will the air temperature and relative humidity be higher in the ferns than in the open nearby?

Abiotic factors such as temperature, moisture, wind, light, and soil conditions act together to create the overall environment over a broad region of land. The overall environment in turn determines the biotic nature of the region. Yet, within any region, abiotic factors vary greatly from place to place. That is, microenvironments exist within the larger region. For example, the soil may contain more organic matter in a hollow than on a nearby hill. The relative humidity is higher in tall grass than it is a metre above the grass. The air temperature in the summer is higher at ground level than one metre above the ground. The light intensity will likely be higher under a pine tree than under a maple tree in the same woodlot.

The temperature and moisture conditions of a microenvironment act together to create a microclimate. It usually differs greatly from the overall climate of the area. For example, the microclimate among the ferns in Figure 6-8 is similar to the climate of a tropical rain forest.

When you are doing a field study such as Activity 6-7, remember that microenvironments exist. For example, suppose you want to measure the *overall* temperature and relative humidity of a region. You must keep your instruments at least 1.5 m from the ground. If you don't, you may get readings from microenvironments instead of the overall environment.

There are, of course, times when you will want to make measurements of the microenvironment. Suppose, for example, that you want to find out what conditions are most suitable for the growth of seedlings. In this case you would make all environmental measurements near the ground. The overall environment is not nearly as important to the seedlings as is the microenvironment around them.

1. What is a microenvironment?
2. What is a microclimate?
3. Use an example to illustrate a case in which the microenvironment is more important than the overall environment.

6.7 *FIELD TRIP* Comparing Two Terrestrial Ecosystems

Everything in nature is interdependent. Change the environment and you change the organisms present. Change the organisms and you change the environment. See if you can prove this by comparing two terrestrial ecosystems.

Problem

Can you show that all parts of an ecosystem are interdependent?

Some Suggested Sites

a) area dominated by long grass versus area dominated by cut grass
b) wooded area versus meadow (grassy area)
c) coniferous tree area versus deciduous tree area
d) low wet area versus sunny area of the schoolyard
e) area with organically rich soil versus area with sandy soil
f) sheltered area versus windy area
g) south-facing slope of a hill versus north-facing slope of a hill

Materials

The following is an ideal list. If your school does not have a certain piece of equipment, you can find substitutes. For example, a camera light meter can take the place of the light meter. Or you can simply rate the light intensity on a relative scale: very light, bright, moderate, dim, very dim.

light meter	tape measure (10 m)
sling psychrometer (for humidity)	sweep net
air thermometer	white tray
soil thermometer	hand lens
soil test kit for pH	jars (plastic) for soil (2)
compass	probe
soil sampler (or small shovel)	petri dishes (2)
trowel	jars (plastic) for animals (5)
wind speed meter	identification guides for trees,
clinometer	shrubs, wildflowers, and insects

Procedure

a. Make one copy of Table 6-3, two copies of Table 6-4, and one copy of Table 6-5 in your notebook. Make each table a full page in size. *Record all data in these tables as soon as you get the data.*

b. Select two ecosystems for the comparison. They must differ in at least one obvious way. They need not be large.

c. Stake out a study plot of identical size and shape at each of the two ecosystems. An area of 100 m² for each study plot is more than adequate.

For each ecosystem, do the following:

d. Name and describe the ecosystem.

e. Note the attitude of the site. Is it flat or does it face in some direction?

f. Use the clinometer to measure the slope of the site.

g. Measure the air temperature. If the sun is shining, use your hand to shield the thermometer bulb from the direct rays of the sun.

h. Measure the light intensity. Follow the directions supplied with the light meter.

i. Measure the wind speed using the wind speed meter.

j. Note the direction of the wind with a moistened finger. Then use the compass to find that direction.

k. Measure the relative humidity. Follow the directions supplied with the sling psychrometer.

l. Measure the soil temperature at depths of 2 cm, 5 cm, and 10 cm.

m. Find the percolation rate by following the description in Unit 4 of *Investigating Natural Resources.*

n. Find the soil pH. Follow the directions supplied with the kit.

o. Study the upper soil profile. First, note the average depth of the undecomposed litter. Then note the average depth of the decomposing litter. Now use the soil sampler to find the depth of the humus layer (black soil).

p. Collect a trowelful of soil from 5 sites in the plot. Put these samples in a collecting jar.

q. Record the name, relative abundance, and adaptations of the plants in the plot. Use a four-category scale for relative abundance: abundant, frequent, occasional, rare.

r. Sweep the vegetation with the sweep net (see Figure 2-10, page 27). Transfer the animals to jars. Watch them with the hand lens. Record their names, relative abundance, and adaptations. Then release the animals.

s. Use the trowel to collect some litter, decomposing litter, and humus. Put everything in the tray. Spread it out, then search for animals. Record their names, relative abundance, and adaptations. Then release the animals.

t. Back in the classroom, find the water content, water-holding capacity, organic content, texture, particle size, and macronutrient content (nitrogen, phosphorus, and potassium) of the soil samples from your sites. See Unit 4 of *Investigating Natural Resources* for procedures and materials.

u. Back in the classroom, complete the fourth column in Table 6-4, "Advantages to Organism".

Table 6-3   Terrestrial Ecosystems: Abiotic Factors (Field)

Factor		Sample	Ecosystem #1	Ecosystem #2
Name and description				
Attitude		south-facing		
Slope		18°		
Percolation rate		0.2 L/min		
Air temperature		24° C		
Light intensity		64 hlx		
Wind	Speed	10 km/h		
	Direction	NW		
Relative humidity		62%		
Soil temperature	2 cm	29° C		
	5 cm	26° C		
	10 cm	25° C		
Soil pH		8.0		
Upper soil profile	Undecomposed litter	6 cm		
	Decomposing litter	3.5 cm		
	Humus	14 cm		

Table 6-4 Terrestrial Ecosystems: Biotic Factors

Ecosystem # _____

Organism	Relative abundance (a,f,o,r)	Adaptations	Advantages to organism
Grasshoppers	a	biting & chewing mouthparts; hard exoskeleton; wings; jumping legs; greenish-brown	can feed on vegetation; moves freely in open spaces for defence; camouflage; protected against dessication
Grasses	a	narrow leaves; waxy cuticle; flexible; fibrous roots	resists wind damage; can survive high temperature and low moisture

Discussion

1. Write a paper which supports the ecological principle that everything in nature is interdependent. Use the data from this field study to illustrate your ideas. Pay particular attention to the differences in the biotic and abiotic factors at the two sites.

6.8   CASE STUDY   Comparison of Two Terrestrial Ecosystems

A group of students investigated the ecology of a grassy field community (Fig. 6-9). This area had not been mowed for 2 years. The students then repeated their investigations in an old field community. It had not been mowed for 6 years.

Both studies were conducted on the same day. It was early autumn and the sky was clear. Some of the data from the investigations are recorded in Table 6-6. A numeral in brackets indicates the height off the ground at which the measurement was made. Study the data carefully. Then answer the questions that follow.

Table 6-5   Terrestrial Ecosystems: Abiotic Factors (Lab)

Factor		Sample	Ecosystem #1	Ecosystem #2
Soil water content		26%		
Soil water-holding capacity		42%		
Soil organic content		3%		
Soil texture	% sand	35%		
	% silt	32%		
	% clay	33%		
Soil particle size	1st sieve	7%		
	2nd sieve	11%		
	3rd sieve	20%		
	4th sieve	29%		
	bottom pan	33%		
Nitrogen		High		
Phosphorus		Low		
Potassium		Medium		

Fig. 6-9   A grassy field (2-year stage of succession) and an old field community (6-year stage of succession) are compared in this study.

Table 6-6 Comparing Two Terrestrial Ecosystems

Factor	Grassy field	Old field
Air temperature (1.5 m)	26°C	26°C
Air temperature (0.5 m)	27°C	30°C
Relative humidity (0.5 m)	65%	78%
Wind speed (0.5 m)	9.5 km/h	8.0 km/h
Percolation rate	0.2 L/min	0.3 L/min
Soil pH	6.9	6.7
Undecomposed litter	6 cm	8 cm
Decomposing litter	0 cm	2 cm
Humus	14 cm	17 cm
Soil temperature (2 cm)	38°C	31°C
Soil organic content	3.2%	4.5%
Number of plant species	10	19
Number of arthropod species	20	32
Number of earthworms	95/m^2	113/m^2
Number of bird species	4	7
Cottonwood (poplar) trees	0/1000 m^2	7/1000 m^2

Questions

1. Account for the differences between the two ecosystems at 0.5 m in the following factors.
   a) air temperature
   b) relative humidity
   c) wind speed
2. Why is the percolation rate lower in the grassy field?
3. What could be responsible for the difference in pH?
4. Why can the old field support a larger earthworm population?
5. Why is arthropod diversity higher in the old field?
6. Why does the grassy field contain no decomposing litter? (*Hint:* Look at the soil temperature.)
7. Why does the old field contain a greater depth of humus?
8. Why can the old field support a larger number of bird species?
9. Which ecosystem do you think is more stable? That is, which one will be least disturbed, overall, by environmental stresses? Why?

Main Ideas

1. Most organisms depend on sunlight, directly or indirectly, for survival.
2. Three light factors affect organisms: intensity, duration, and quality.
3. Many microenvironments exist within an ecosystem.

Key Terms

day-neutral plant
infrared
intensity
long-day plant
microenvironment

photoperiod
phototaxis
phototropism
short-day plant
ultraviolet

Chapter Review

A. True or False

Decide whether each of the following statements is true or false. If the sentence is false, rewrite it to make it true. (Do not write in this book.)

1. Excessive light can kill a plant.
2. Light intensity is influenced by latitude.
3. Sun-loving plants such as geraniums will show negative phototropism if they are placed in a window.
4. A short-day plant will likely flower in early summer.

B. Completion

Complete each of the following sentences with a word or phrase that will make the sentence correct. (Do not write in this book.)

1. The response of a plant to light intensity is called ▨▨▨ .
2. The quality of light could also be called its ▨▨▨ .
3. The length of day has no effect on the flowering of tomato plants. Thus they are called ▨▨▨ plants.

C. Multiple Choice

Each of the following statements or questions is followed by four responses. Choose the correct response in each case. (Do not write in this book.)

1. A sow bug crawls under a rock to escape bright light. This behaviour is best called
   a) negative phototaxis
   b) positive phototaxis
   c) negative phototropism
   d) positive phototropism

2. Timothy grass is a long-day plant. In middle latitudes it will likely flower in
   a) late April
   b) mid-June
   c) mid-September
   d) late October
3. The migration of birds is often triggered by changes in
   a) light intensity
   b) temperature
   c) the direction of the prevailing winds
   d) the photoperiod

Using Your Knowledge

1. Trees growing under street lights in Detroit, Toronto, and Chicago are often damaged by frosts in the fall. But the same species growing nearby but away from the lights are not. Why?
2. The chrysanthemum is a short-day plant. It blooms naturally in the fall. Yet florists sell these plants in full bloom during the long days of June. How do you suppose florists get these plants to bloom then?
3. a) Why is a "green" plant green in daylight?
   b) What colour would the plant be if you shone only green light on it? Why?
   c) What colour would it be if you shone only red light on it? Why?
   d) You have likely seen the special fluorescent "growing lamps" which give off a pinkish-blue colour. They emit light mainly from the red and violet ends of the spectrum. Does it make sense to use these lamps? Why?
4. How do the trees of a forest help determine the microenvironments of the small communities on the forest floor?
5. How will the microclimate in a cornfield differ from the overall climate around the cornfield? Why? (Corn plants are up to 3 m tall and are planted close together.)

Investigations

1. The leaves of most maples and oaks become brightly coloured in the fall. Find out what role, if any, in this colour change is played by environmental factors.
2. Find out how organic matter (dead plants and animal wastes) helps prevent soil erosion on farmland.
3. Grow or buy a *Mimosa* (sensitive) plant. Use this plant to study thigmotropism (response to touch). What causes thigmotropism in *Mimosa*?

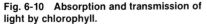

Fig. 6-10 Absorption and transmission of light by chlorophyll.

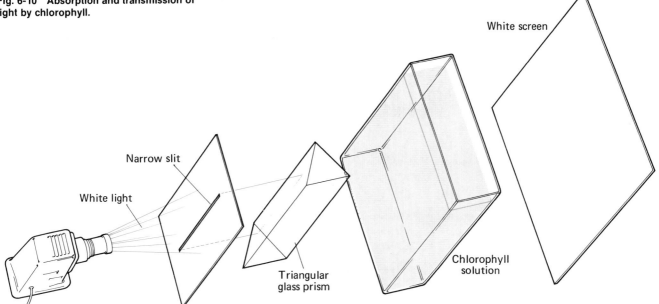

White screen

Narrow slit

White light

Triangular glass prism

Chlorophyll solution

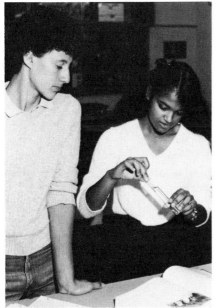

Will temperature, light intensity, or soil moisture affect either how the plant responds or its rate of recovery?

4. Design and complete an experiment to determine the compensation intensity of a certain species of plant. You will need a light meter.

5. Ask your teacher for a piece of polarized glass. Go outside and look at blue sky through the filter. Look in various directions. Always keep the same side of the filter upward. Describe your results. How could a bee use what you saw to orient itself in flight?

6. Visit a greenhouse or flower shop. Discuss the use of photoperiodism in horticulture with the manager. Write a report of about 500 words on your findings.

7. Design and complete an experiment to illustrate your answer to 3(c) of "Using Your Knowledge" on page 122.

8. With your teacher's permission and help, study the absorption and transmission of light by chlorophyll. Tear up a few green leaves. Place them in a beaker. Cover them with ethyl alcohol. Boil the alcohol until it is deep green. Use a hotplate or water bath. *Do not expose the alcohol to an open flame!* Adjust the positions of a prism, light source, and screen until a spectrum appears on the screen (Fig. 6-10). Insert a rectangular tank in the path of the beam of light. Pour the chlorophyll solution into the tank. Describe and explain the results.

9. Design and conduct an experiment to show how the growth of plants is affected by different colours of light.

10. Design and conduct an experiment to find out if seeds can germinate without light. Include endive seeds in your study.

Chapter Review 123

7

Weather, Climate, and Biomes

North America has a wide variety of biomes—tundra, forests, grasslands, deserts, and mountains. All these biomes differ greatly from one another. Why? Why, for example, is the area shown in Figure 7-1 a grassland instead of a forest or a desert? And why do Saskatchewan and Montana have grasslands while Québec, Ontario, and New York State do not?

To understand the nature and location of biomes, you first need to understand what climate is. What makes up the climate of an area? Is weather the same thing as climate? How does climate affect the nature and location of a biome?

Fig. 7-1 Why is this area a grassland?

7.1 Weather

"What's the weather going to be like today?" How many times have you asked that question first thing in the morning? Think, for a moment, about what you mean when you use the word "weather". Then think about what the people in the weather forecasting office mean when they use the same word.

What is Weather?

The word "weather" is used in two different ways. When you ask about the weather, you probably want to know whether it will be hot or cold, sunny or cloudy, or whether it will rain or snow. This use of the word is the most common. To scientists, however, weather is much more than that. Meteorologists (scientists who study weather) define it this way: **Weather** is all aspects of the state and movement of the atmosphere which can be seen or experienced, and which affect life and human activity. In short, it is the day-to-day change in atmospheric conditions.

The Weather Factors

Four main factors make up the weather: temperature, wind, moisture, and sky conditions. As you read about them, think about how they relate to one another.

Wind   Wind is the main weather factor. Its effects on the weather depend on three things:

- its speed (how fast the air is moving)
- its direction (where the moving air has come from)
- how long the air has taken to move to its present location

Many instruments are available for measuring wind speed. Figure 7-2 shows one. If you don't have a wind meter, you can still get a good idea of the speed of the wind by using the **Beaufort Scale** in Table 7-1.

Section 5.1 describes the effects of wind direction on precipitation, another important aspect of weather. And Section 5.5 describes other effects of wind. Read these sections again. Then see if you can answer the following questions.

- In what ways does wind speed affect weather?
- Why does wind direction affect weather?
- Why might the weather be affected by the time the wind takes to get to its present location?

Fig. 7-2   This simple wind meter is one of many instruments that are used to measure wind speed.

Temperature   Temperature is another important weather factor. You read about its effects on life in Section 5.2. And you are, no doubt, well aware of its effects on human activities.

The temperature of a region is governed, in part, by the wind. Depending on its direction and speed, the wind can bring either cool or warm air into most regions of the continent.

Table 7-1   Beaufort Scale on Land

Code number	Speed (km/h)	Description	Effects
0	0–1.6	calm	smoke rises vertically
1	1.6–5	light air	smoke drift shows direction of wind; most wind vanes won't
2	6–12	light breeze	wind felt on face; leaves rustle; wind vanes work
3	13–19	gentle breeze	leaves and small twigs move constantly; small flags are extended
4	20–29	moderate breeze	blows dust and loose paper; small branches move
5	30–39	fresh breeze	small trees sway; small crested waves appear on inland waters
6	40–49	strong breeze	large tree branches move; hydro wires whistle; umbrellas hard to hold
7	50–61	moderate gale	whole trees in motion; inconvenient to walk against the wind
8	62–74	fresh gale	twigs break off trees; walking against the wind is difficult
9	75–87	strong gale	slight structural damages; shingles may go
10	88–101	storm	trees uprooted; roofs damaged; other structures damaged
11	102–120	violent storm	widespread damage to structures and trees
12	over 120	hurricane	damage is disastrous

Fig. 7-3 A wet-and-dry bulb hygrometer can be used to measure relative humidity.

Moisture The third weather factor is moisture. It occurs in two forms which affect the weather. It occurs as precipitation—rain, snow, hail, or fog. And it occurs as humidity—water vapour in the air. You read about these two factors and their effects on organisms in Section 5.1. Read that section if you have not yet done so.

You have probably heard the weather report state the relative humidity. This numeral tells us how close the air is to being saturated with water. For example, if the relative humidity is 50%, the air is holding half the water it is able to hold at that temperature.

The relative humidity is calculated using the formula below:

$$\text{Relative humidity} = \frac{\text{Mass of water vapour in 1 m}^3 \text{ of air}}{\text{Mass of water vapour needed to saturate 1 m}^3 \text{ of air at the same temperature}} \times 100\%$$

Example: Suppose a meteorologist found 4.3 g/m³ of water vapour in the air at 20°C. He or she can look up the saturation point in tables of data. It is 17.1 g/m³ at 20°C. Therefore, the relative humidity is

$$\frac{4.3 \text{ g/m}^3}{17.1 \text{ g/m}^3} \times 100\% = 25\%$$

The air is holding 25% as much water vapour as it can at 20°C.

Relative humidity can be measured with a wet-and-dry bulb hygrometer. Figure 7-3 shows one you can buy and Figure 7-4 shows one you can make. When water on the wet bulb evaporates, it cools the bulb and lowers the temperature to below that of the dry bulb. If the air has a high relative humidity, little moisture evaporates from the wet bulb. Thus it will have a reading only slightly lower than that of the dry bulb. But if the air has a low relative humidity, much evaporation occurs from the wet bulb. It will now have a reading several degrees lower than that of the dry bulb. If you know both the wet and dry bulb temperatures, you can use Table 7-2 to find the relative humidity. A wet-and-dry bulb hygrometer should be fanned for 2 min before taking the temperature readings. This ensures maximum evaporation.

Figure 7-5 shows a sling psychrometer. This device is simply a wet-and-dry bulb hygrometer which can be whirled through the air. Whirling for 2 min allows maximum evaporation better than fanning does.

Sky Conditions This final weather factor is the one most of us note first when we want to predict the weather. It includes cloud cover—the type, amount, height above ground, rate of formation, and rate of breakdown. It also includes visibility, or the clarity of the air—the amount of fog, its rate of formation and disappearance. In what ways do sky conditions affect temperature and moisture? And how do temperature, moisture, and wind affect sky conditions?

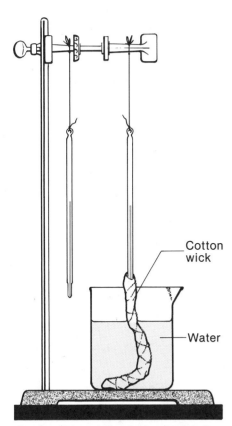

Cotton wick

Water

Fig. 7-4 A home-made wet-and-dry bulb hygrometer. The thermometers must be fanned for 2 min before a reading is taken.

Fig. 7-5 A sling psychrometer is a wet-and-dry bulb hygrometer which can be whirled.

Table 7-2 Relative Humidity

Wet bulb temperature (°C) \ Dry bulb temperature (°C)	10	11	12	13	14	15	16	17	18	19	20	21	22	23	24	25	26	27	28	29	30
1	10																				
2	15	9																			
3	24	18	12	7																	
4	34	27	21	15	10	6															
5	44	36	29	23	18	13	8														
6	55	46	39	32	26	20	15	11	7												
7	66	56	48	41	34	27	23	18	14	10	6										
8	77	67	58	50	42	36	30	25	20	16	12	9	6								
9	88	78	68	59	51	44	38	32	27	22	18	14	11	8	5						
10	100	91	78	69	60	53	46	40	34	29	24	20	17	13	10	8					
11		100	89	79	70	61	54	47	41	36	31	26	22	19	15	12	10				
12			100	89	79	71	63	55	49	43	37	32	28	24	20	17	14	12	5		
13				100	90	80	71	64	57	50	44	39	34	30	26	22	19	16	13	7	
14					100	90	81	72	65	58	51	46	40	36	31	28	24	21	18	15	9
15						100	90	81	73	65	59	53	47	42	37	33	29	26	22	19	17
16							100	90	82	74	66	60	54	48	43	39	34	31	27	24	21
17								100	91	82	74	67	61	55	49	44	40	36	32	28	25
18									100	91	83	75	68	62	56	50	46	41	37	33	30
19										100	91	83	76	69	62	57	51	47	42	38	35
20											100	91	83	76	69	63	58	52	48	43	39
21												100	92	84	77	70	64	58	53	49	44
22													100	92	84	77	71	65	59	54	50
23														100	92	84	78	71	65	60	55
24															100	92	85	78	72	66	61
25																100	92	85	78	72	67
26																	100	92	85	79	73
27																		100	93	86	79
28																			100	93	86
29																				100	93
30																					100

Section Review

1. What is the scientific meaning of weather?
2. Name the four main weather factors.
3. What three aspects of wind affect the weather?
4. How is air temperature influenced by the wind?
5. Define relative humidity.
6. **a)** What does a relative humidity of 70% mean?
   b) The dry bulb on a wet-and-dry bulb hygrometer reads 26°C and the wet bulb reads 17°C. What is the relative humidity?
7. **a)** How might cloud cover affect temperature and relative humidity?
   b) How might sky conditions be affected by temperature, moisture, and wind?

7.2   *ACTIVITY* **Monitoring the Weather**

Weather is the day-to-day change in atmospheric conditions—wind, temperature, moisture, and sky conditions. In this activity you will monitor the weather for about 2 weeks. You will then write a paper which describes and explains how the weather factors are related.

Problem

How are the four main weather factors related?

Materials

wind meter (optional)
compass (optional)
thermometer
maximum-minimum thermometer (optional)

sling psychrometer (or homemade hygrometer)
rain gauge and ruler
cloud chart

Procedure

a. Make a copy of Table 7-3. Make enough "Day" columns for at least 2 weeks. Insert in the "time" columns the times at which you plan to do your studies. *You should perform each of the following steps at regular intervals for at least 2 weeks. If possible, do them two or three times a day. Record all measurements in your table.*

b. Use a compass if you have one to find the wind direction.

c. Use the wind meter or Beaufort scale to find the wind speed.

d. Use the thermometer to find the air temperature. Shield the bulb from the direct rays of the sun.

Table 7-3 Monitoring the Weather

Weather factor		Day 1 08:00	Day 1 18:00	Day 2 08:00	Day 2 18:00	Day 3 08:00	Day 3 18:00
Wind	Speed						
	Direction						
Temperature	Air						
	Max.-Min.						
Moisture	Precipitation						
	Relative Humidity						
Type of clouds							
Amount of cloud							
Height of clouds							
Rate of formation							
Rate of breakdown							
Visibility							

e. If you have a maximum-minimum thermometer, record the daily maximum and minimum temperatures.

f. Set up a rain gauge in an open area. Any straight-sided glass container will do. You can measure the collected rain with a ruler. Note the depth of rain in the gauge.

g. Use the cloud chart to determine the type of clouds.

h. Estimate the percentage of the sky which is covered by clouds. This percentage is the amount of cloud.

i. Estimate the height of the clouds above ground.

j. Note whether clouds are forming and breaking down rapidly or slowly.

k. Describe the visibility by using one of these terms:
   • foggy (visibility less than 1 km)
   • misty (visibility greater than 1 km but still restricted)
   • hazy (a general lack of clarity in the atmosphere, but long distance visibility is fair)
   • clear (no noticeable material in the air)

l. Find the relative humidity using the sling psychrometer. Follow the directions that come with the instrument.

Discussion

Write a paper of about 500 words which describes and explains how the four main weather factors are related. You may wish to consult encyclopedias and books on weather to learn more about the formation and effects of various types of clouds.

7.3   Climates of the World

Fig. 7-6 In the summer, the climate in this alpine meadow is usually quite moderate. However, this hiker found that a change in wind direction brought cold Arctic air to the region. And the weather for the day was not like the average weather, or climate.

Weather and Climate

Weather is the day-to-day or short-term change in atmospheric conditions. That is, it is the wind, temperature, moisture, and sky conditions which we observe daily. In contrast, climate is the average weather in a region over a long period of time, usually two or three decades (Fig. 7-6).

Suppose you are planning a holiday in Mexico in January. You will probably want to know what the "weather" will be like when you get there. If you look up the climate of Mexico, you will find that it should be quite warm and pleasant. You may, however, arrive in Mexico and find the weather much different than you expected. The atmospheric conditions on a particular day (the weather) are not always the same as the average weather over a long period of time (the climate).

Classification of World Climates

The climate of a region is determined by many factors. But the two basic factors are the temperature and precipitation patterns over the past few decades. Scientists have studied the average temperature and precipitation in all regions of the world for many decades. They have also studied how temperature and precipitation change with the seasons in those regions. Based on such studies, they have classified the climates of the world into six major types (Fig. 7-7).

1. *Cold Polar Climates*   These climates are, as the name suggests, near the poles. Closest to the poles is an icecap climate. Here the temperature averages below 0°C even in the warmest month of the year. Almost all precipitation falls as snow. The total accumulation is less than 25 cm a year. And the annual accumulation of snow and ice exceeds the amount that melts. Icecap climates occur on the glaciers which cover Greenland, Antarctica, and the northernmost islands of Canada.

   A tundra climate occurs on the land masses of North America, Asia, and Europe which border on the icecap region. Though not as cold as the icecap climate, the tundra climate still stays below 0°C most of the time (Fig. 7-8). The low temperature keeps the relative humidity high. So the sky is usually cloudy. Precipitation is frequent though total accumulation is low (less than 25 cm a year). The soil is frozen most of the year. In fact, the deeper soil never thaws. As a result, it is called permafrost. The Antarctic has no tundra climate, since land masses do not occur next to the Antarctic icecap.

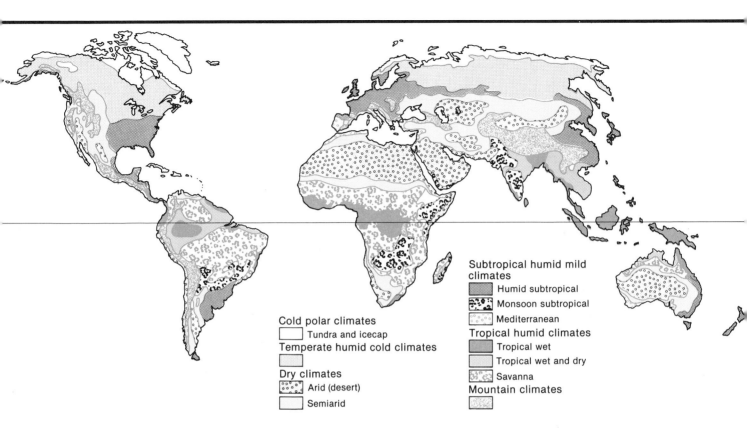

Subtropical humid mild climates
- Humid subtropical
- Monsoon subtropical
- Mediterranean

Tropical humid climates
- Tropical wet
- Tropical wet and dry
- Savanna

Mountain climates

Cold polar climates
- Tundra and icecap

Temperate humid cold climates

Dry climates
- Arid (desert)
- Semiarid

Fig. 7-7   The main climates of the world.

Fig. 7-8   Auyuittuq National Park on Baffin Island in northern Canada has a tundra climate. A parka is required on most days in July. And the relative humidity is so high that rain or snow falls almost every day in July. The total amount, however, is low.

2. ***Temperate Humid Cold Climates***   South of the tundra and stretching across North America, Europe, and Asia is a wide belt of land with a temperate humid cold climate. Here the average annual precipitation is from 50-125 cm. Winters are very cold. But summers can be surprisingly warm at times, due to the long periods of sunlight. As a result, dense forests of coniferous trees cover much of this area.

3. ***Subtropical Humid Mild Climates***   Three types of subtropical humid mild climate exist on earth. As Figure 7-7 shows, a humid subtropical climate dominates much of the southeastern United States and Europe. A monsoon subtropical climate occurs in parts of India, Pakistan, Africa, and central South America. And a Mediterranean climate occurs around the Mediterranean Sea and along the northwest coast of the United States.

All these climates have moderate temperatures, warm long summers, and ample precipitation (from a low of 75 cm a year in parts of the southeast United States to over 600 cm in the northwest United States). The humid subtropical climate has no dry season. The monsoon subtropical climate has a dry winter and a very wet summer. The Mediterranean climate has a dry summer and a very wet winter.

4. *Dry Climates*   Two main types of dry climate occur on earth. An arid (desert) climate occurs in large areas of Africa, Asia, and Australia. Smaller areas exist in the United States and South America. The total annual precipitation is less than 25 cm. In fact, some years no precipitation falls at all. The relative humidity is very low. Thus the sky is usually clear, allowing very high daytime temperatures to develop. The clear sky, however, also speeds up cooling at night. In fact, night temperatures can drop to the freezing point. An arid climate has no definite winter period.

A semiarid climate usually occurs next to an arid climate. Here precipitation is from 25-75 cm per year. It is enough to permit grasses to grow. As a result, lands with a semiarid climate are used across the earth to grow grasses such as wheat which feed millions of people (Fig. 7-9). Note where these wheat-growing regions are in North America, South America, Africa, Asia, and Australia. Which countries on earth are the major producers of wheat?

5. *Tropical Humid Climates*   Three types of tropical humid climate exist on earth. A tropical wet climate occurs along the equator. Large areas with this climate occur in the Amazon Basin of South America, the Congo area of Africa, in parts of Central America, and in Indonesia and the Malaysian peninsula of Asia. This climate is very warm and precipitation is abundant (over 250 cm a year). As well, both temperature and precipitation change little between the various seasons. As a result, there is no dry season. In fact, seasons are often not recognizable. This constant warm humid climate produces the lush evergreen vegetation known as the rain forest.

Bordering the tropical wet climate is a tropical wet and dry climate. Large sections of South America and Asia have this climate. In a tropical wet and dry climate precipitation is lower but still abundant. And there is a short but definite dry season. As a result, the tropical rain forests in regions with this climate have many deciduous trees.

Large tracts of land with a savanna climate occur in South America, Africa, and Australia. This climate is quite warm, but precipitation is low (13-25 cm a year). Further, a savanna climate has a dry winter with warm days and cool nights. This combination of temperature and moisture conditions favours the growth of tall grasses and scattered shrubs and trees.

6. *Mountain Climates*   Mountain climates occur in western North America, western South America, parts of Europe (Spain and Switzerland), parts of east-central Africa, and in a large portion of southeast Asia. Mountain climates differ greatly from the climates of nearby lowlands. Such climates may vary from a tropical or subtropical humid climate at the bottom of the mountains to a cold polar climate at the top.

Fig. 7-9 These wheat fields in Saskatchewan have a semiarid climate. They barely get enough precipitation to grow the wheat.

1. What is the difference between weather and climate?
2. What are the two basic factors which determine the climate of a region?
3. Copy Table 7-4 into your notebook. Complete it as you read "Classification of World Climates".

Table 7-4 Classification of World Climates

Climate	Sub-climate	Description	Location
Cold polar	icecap		
	tundra		
Temperate humid cold	—		
Subtropical humid mild	humid subtropical		
	monsoon subtropical		
	Mediterranean		
Dry	arid (desert)		
	semiarid		
Tropical humid	tropical wet		
	tropical wet and dry		
	savanna		
Mountain	—		

7.4 Climates of Canada and the United States

Factors which Determine the Climates

Three main factors determine the major climates of Canada and the United States:

- the position of the continent
- the locations of mountains on the continent
- the nature of ocean currents along the shores of the continent

Position   North America stretches from the cold polar climate of northern Canada and Alaska to the tropical humid climate of southern Florida and

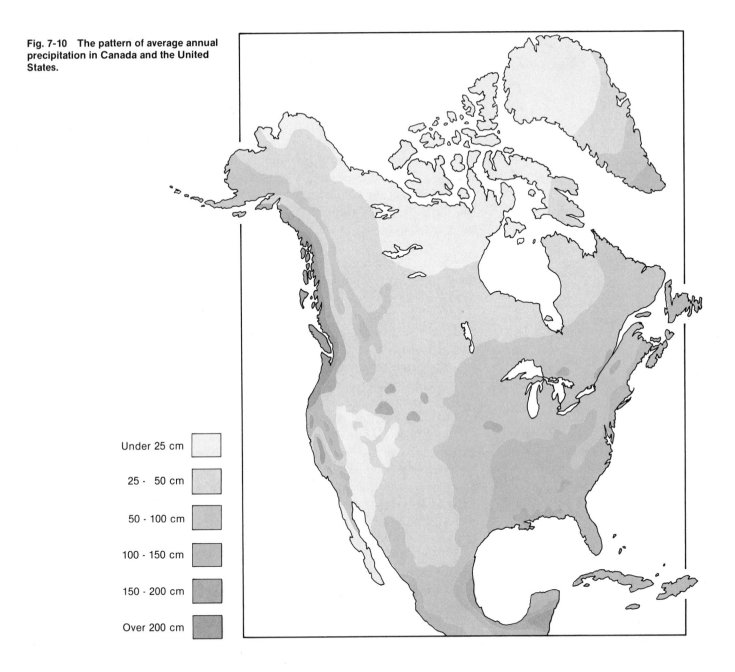

Fig. 7-10 The pattern of average annual precipitation in Canada and the United States.

Under 25 cm

25 - 50 cm

50 - 100 cm

100 - 150 cm

150 - 200 cm

Over 200 cm

parts of Mexico. As a result, the continent is exposed to both cold dry air masses and warm moist air masses. These air masses meet over the United States and Canada. Their meeting produces the storms which give us most of our precipitation.

As Figure 7-10 shows, this precipitation is not spread evenly over the continent. Much of the continent is in the paths of westerly winds coming in from the Pacific Ocean. Because these winds are laden with moisture from the ocean, the west coast receives heavy precipitation. The winds are much drier after they pass the mountains. As a result, little precipitation falls in the central part of the continent. However, warm tropical air brings moisture northward from the Gulf of Mexico. When this air meets the cooler dry air mass, storms result. Thus the eastern part of the continent receives ample rainfall.

Mountains   Two main sets of mountains occur in North America. One set consists of the large mountain ranges which run north to south along the western part of the continent. The other set consists of smaller ranges which run north to south along the eastern part of the continent. Between these mountains is a vast plain which covers most of the central part of the continent.

The western mountains force the moisture-laden Pacific winds to drop much of their moisture (see Figure 5-6, page 100). Thus heavy precipitation occurs on the windward (west) side of the mountains. The drier winds move over the mountains and across the plain. They are largely responsible for the arid and semiarid climates of the western part of the plains region.

North America has no mountains which cross the continent in an east-west direction. As a result, cold polar air from the Arctic can move freely as far as the southern United States. The polar air often meets warm tropical air coming from the south. This meeting causes the tornadoes and other unusual weather of the central part of the continent.

Ocean Currents   As you might expect, ocean currents have a great influence on the climates of coastal regions. Two main currents affect the western coast of the continent. The Alaska Current brings warm Pacific water north to the coast of British Columbia and southern Alaska. As a result, the climate in these regions is warmer and wetter than one might expect it to be. The California Current brings cool Pacific water to the west coast of the continental United States. As a result, the climate in places such as San Francisco is more moderate than that of inland cities at the same latitude.

Two main currents also affect the eastern coast of the continent. The Gulf Stream moves warm water northward along the southeast coast of the United States. And the Labrador Current brings cold Arctic water south along the east coast of Canada and the northeast coast of the United States. Cape Cod in Massachusetts often feels the Labrador current. In fact, the cold water often chills the beaches as far south as Cape Hatteras in North Carolina.

Major Climates of Canada and the United States

Table 7-5 summarizes some basic information about the major climates of the United States and Canada. As you study this table, look back to Figure 7-7 to see where the climates are located.

Table 7-5   Major Climates of Canada and the United States

Climate	Sub-climate	Location	Dominant vegetation
Cold polar	icecap	• most northerly islands of Canada	• none
	tundra	• northern Canada • northern Alaska	• mosses • lichens
Temperate humid cold	—	• coast to coast in central Canada • north-central and northeast U.S.	• coniferous trees
Subtropical humid mild	humid sub-tropical	• southeast U.S. • south coast of Alaska • northern coast of British Columbia	• hardwood trees and pines (in SE) • mixed conifers (in NW)
	Mediterranean	• southern coast of British Columbia • northwest coast of U.S.	• giant coniferous trees (redwood, Douglas fir, red cedar)
Dry	arid	• southwest U.S.	• cacti
	semiarid	• southwest U.S. • west-central U.S. and Canada	• grasses • shrubs
Tropical humid	tropical wet and dry	• tip of Florida	• evergreen trees and shrubs • some deciduous trees and shrubs
Mountain	—	• western Canada • western U.S.	• conifers at lower elevations • mosses, lichens, or none at higher elevations

Microclimates

As you have seen, there are six major climate regions in Canada and the United States. Within each of these, however, are many local climates. Local climates are often called **microclimates**. A woodlot, for example, usually has a lower wind speed and higher relative humidity than the open fields around it. In other words, its microclimate is different than the major climate of the area.

Cities also create their own microclimates. Buildings change wind speed and direction. And heat builds up in pavements and buildings. As a result, the microclimate of a city tends to be quite different than the major climate of the area (Fig. 7-11).

Fig. 7-11 These tall buildings in Toronto, Ontario help create strong winds at times. Overall, however, they, the pavement, Lake Ontario, and the air pollution form a microclimate in downtown Toronto which is like the subtropical humid climate found in North Carolina.

Fig. 7-12 This spruce tree has been stunted by the strong mountain winds. But it still provides a warmer and less windy microclimate on its leeward side.

A large body of water such as a lake can create a microclimate in an area. The lake tends to moderate the temperature. It cools hot summer winds and warms cold winter winds. It can also cause increased precipitation.

Finally, mountains create numerous microclimates. The highlands are cooler and more windy than the lowlands. The windward sides are usually wetter and cooler than the leeward sides. And sheltered valleys are warmer and less windy than nearby exposed ridges. Even a tree on an exposed mountain-top can create a microclimate on the leeward side (Fig. 7-12).

Section Review

1. Describe the effect of the position of the continent on the climate of North America.
2. Describe the effect of mountains on the climate of North America.
3. a) Describe the effect of the Alaska Current and California Current on the climate of the west coast of North America.
   b) Describe the effect of the Gulf Stream and the Labrador Current on the climate of the east coast of North America.
4. Use Table 7-5 and Figure 7-7 to find the names of the major climates in the following areas of North America:
   a) Florida
   b) southern shore of Hudson Bay
   c) north coast of Alaska
   d) south coast of Alaska
   e) Great Lakes region
   f) above the Arctic circle
   g) southwest United States
   h) most of Canada
   i) most of the eastern United States
   j) prairies of Saskatchewan and Montana
5. a) What is a microclimate?
   b) Describe how each of the following creates microclimates: a woodlot, a city, a lake, a mountain.

7.5   Major Biomes of the World

What Is a Biome?

A biome is a large region of the earth with a characteristic climate and climax community. The boreal coniferous forest is an example (Fig. 7-13). This biome extends across Canada and occurs in all provinces. It also covers

Fig. 7-13 The boreal coniferous forest is dominated by black spruce trees.

much of Alaska. And it occurs in parts of other northern states including Maine, New Hampshire, Vermont, New York, Michigan, and Minnesota. The boreal coniferous forest has a characteristic climate—cold and wet. This climate is determined by the long term patterns in temperature and precipitation. It, in turn, creates a certain climax community. This community is most easily recognized by its dominant vegetation. For example, the boreal coniferous forest is dominated by conifers (cone-bearing trees) like black spruce. They thrive in this cool moist climate.

Number and Location of Biomes

There are only 10 or 15 major biomes on earth (Fig. 7-14). The actual number depends on how one classifies the biomes. There are zones between biomes in which one biome blends into another. Some ecologists call these zones biomes. Others call them ecotones.

If you look carefully at Figure 7-14, you can easily spot the largest biomes on earth. The boreal coniferous forest biome circles the earth in a wide band just below the Arctic circle. The desert biome occurs in large parts of the southwest United States and Africa, and in smaller parts of Asia, Australia, and South America. The tropical evergreen and tropical deciduous rain forest biomes occur in a wide belt along the equator. The temperate deciduous forest occurs in the southeast United States, part of China, and much of Europe. The tundra biome circles the earth above the Arctic circle. The savanna biome covers large parts of Australia, Africa, and South America. And the grassland biome occurs in the central United States, western Canada, and in a wide belt across southern Asia. See if you can find the remaining major biomes: mountains, warm temperate evergreen forest, temperate rain forest, chaparral, and semi-desert shrubland.

Each biome occurs where it does because of a unique climate. And each biome has a characteristic climax community because of that climate.

Climate and Biomes

Limiting Factors   Life in an ecosystem such as a biome is determined by many factors acting together—temperature, moisture, wind, light, and soil conditions. In many cases, however, one of these factors may be the limiting factor. That is, it is present at such a low level that it alone controls which species can live in the ecosystem. For example, an ecosystem may have rich soil, abundant light, gentle winds, and a moderate temperature. But most organisms could not live there if moisture consisted of only 10 cm of rain a year. Moisture, then, limits life in this ecosystem. That's why it is called the limiting factor.

Precipitation as a Limiting Factor   Table 7-6 shows how precipitation is the limiting factor which determines whether a biome will be a desert, grassland, or forest. If the average annual precipitation is less than 25 cm, vegetation

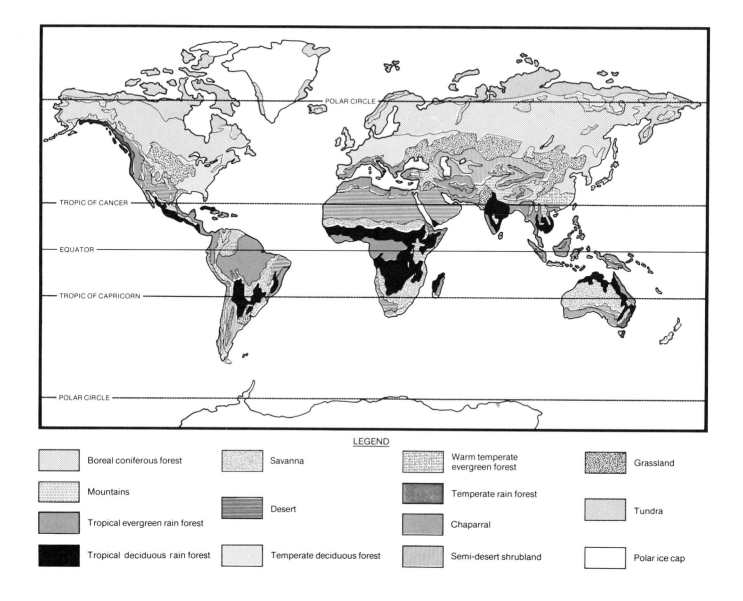

LEGEND

Boreal coniferous forest	Savanna	Warm temperate evergreen forest	Grassland
Mountains	Desert	Temperate rain forest	Tundra
Tropical evergreen rain forest		Chaparral	
Tropical deciduous rain forest	Temperate deciduous forest	Semi-desert shrubland	Polar ice cap

Fig. 7-14 A general guide to the major biomes of the world. How does this diagram compare to Figure 7-7?

cover is low. Cacti and other xerophytic plants are present. But they are far apart, reducing competition for the little available moisture. Much of the ground has no vegetation on it. In contrast, an average annual precipitation of 25-75 cm is sufficient to support the growth of grasses over most of the ground. An amount over 75 cm supports the growth of trees.

Temperature as a Limiting Factor The average annual precipitation determines whether a biome will be a desert, grassland, or forest. But it does not determine the *type* of desert, grassland, or forest. Temperature is the limiting factor in this instance. Figure 7-15 shows how temperature determines the type of desert, grassland, or forest at a certain precipitation level.

Table 7-6   Precipitation as a Limiting Factor

Average annual precipitation	Type of biome
less than 25 cm	desert
25–75 cm	grassland
over 75 cm	forest

Fig. 7-15 Average annual precipitation determines whether an area will be a desert, grassland or forest. Temperature acts with precipitation to determine the *type* of desert, grassland, or forest.

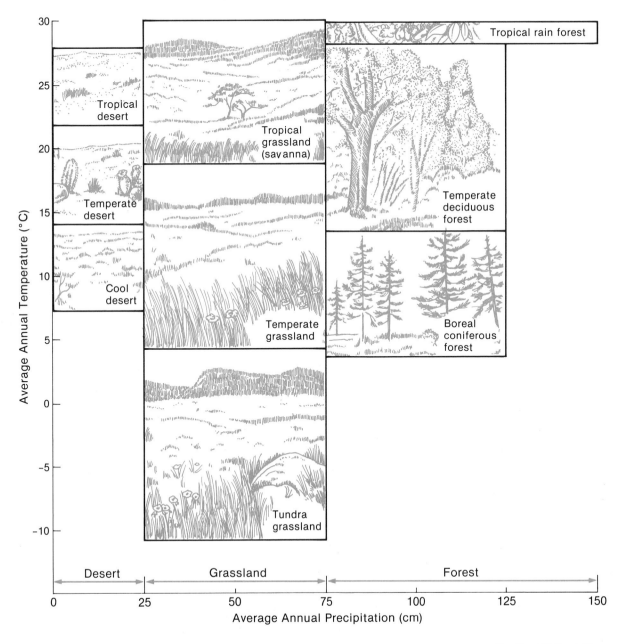

Summary   Temperature and precipitation act together to form the climate of an area. Then the climate determines the biotic nature of the biome. The biome can usually be recognized by its climax plant community.

Section Review

1. **a)** What is a biome?
    b) What is an ecotone?
2. Copy Table 7-7 into your notebook. Then complete it for the 13 biomes listed in this section.

Table 7-7   Major Biomes of the World

Name of biome	Location
boreal coniferous forest	• across Canada in all provinces • in Alaska and other northern states

3. What is a limiting factor?
4. Describe the role of precipitation as a limiting factor in biome formation.
5. Describe the role of temperature in biome formation.

7.6   *ACTIVITY*   Biomes of Canada and the United States

Canada has just seven major biomes—tundra, boreal coniferous forest, temperate deciduous forest, grassland, mountain, chaparral, and temperate rain forest. The United States has the same seven plus three more—warm temperate evergreen forest, desert, and semi-desert shrubland. In this activity you will try to figure out why these biomes are located where they are.

Problem

Why are the biomes of Canada and the United States located where they are?

Materials

Table 7-8   Biomes of Canada and the United States

Name of biome	Location of biome	Climate of biome	Climatic factors determining location and nature of biome
tundra	• northern Canada • north coast of Alaska	• cold and dry	• area is dominated by a cold, dry polar air mass
boreal coniferous forest			
temperate deciduous forest			
grassland			
mountain			
chapparal			
temperate rain forest			
warm temperate evergreen forest			
desert			
semi-desert shrubland			

Procedure

a. Make a full-page copy of Table 7-8 in your notebook.

b. Go back and reread Section 7-4, "Climates of Canada and the United States".

c. State the location of each biome in the second column of your table. Use Figure 7-16 to locate the biomes.

d. Summarize the climate of each biome in the third column of your table. You can find this information in Section 7-4.

e. Three factors determine the climate of Canada and the United States:
   - position of the continent
   - locations of mountains
   - nature of ocean currents

   Describe in the fourth column of your table how these factors determine the climate of each biome.

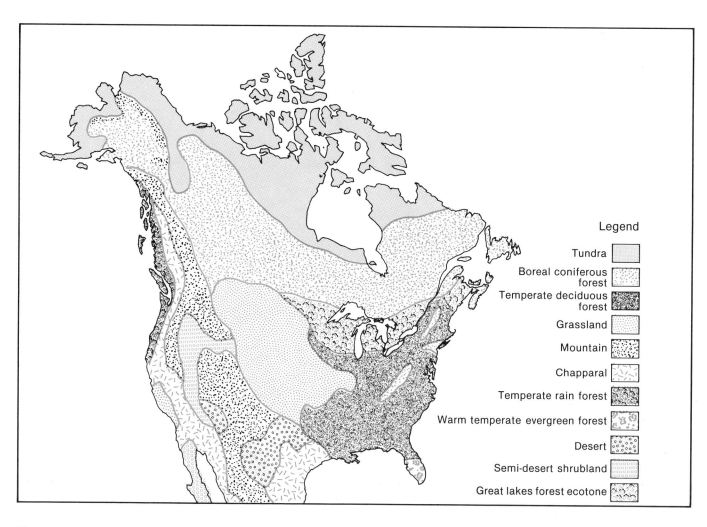

Legend

Tundra

Boreal coniferous forest

Temperate deciduous forest

Grassland

Mountain

Chapparal

Temperate rain forest

Warm temperate evergreen forest

Desert

Semi-desert shrubland

Great lakes forest ecotone

Fig. 7-16   The major biomes of Canada and the United States. Which biome do you live in? Which biomes have you visited?

Discussion

1. Your completed table is your report for this activity.
2. Which biome do you live in?
3. Which biomes have you visited?

7.7   Climatograms

Ecologists who study the distribution and adaptations of organisms in a biome need to know the past history of the climate of that biome. This history is often summarized in a climatogram. A **climatogram** summarizes in graphical form the monthly variations in temperature and precipitation for a year (Fig. 7-17).

A climatogram does not include information on wind and sky conditions, the two other major factors that affect climate. But temperature and precipi-

Fig. 7-17 Compare these two climatograms. The line graph gives the average monthly temperature (in degrees Celsius). The bar graph gives the average monthly precipitation (in centimetres). What do Cambridge Bay and El Paso have in common? How do they differ?

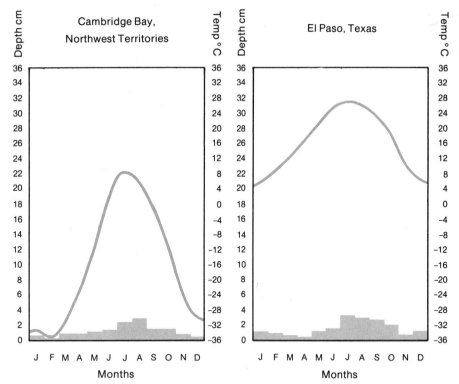

tation are clearly related to these other factors. And experience has shown that looking at temperature and precipitation is enough when accounting for the distribution and adaptations of the organisms in the biome. Therefore climatograms are drawn with only temperature and precipitation data.

Unit 3 of this book describes the major biomes of Canada and the United States. In each chapter, the abiotic factors (mainly climate) are discussed. Then the biotic factors (mainly plants and animals) are described, with emphasis on their adaptation to the abiotic factors. In many cases, climatograms are used to summarize the climate data. Be sure, therefore, that you can understand climatograms by answering the following questions.

Section Review

1. What is a climatogram?
2. How do you think scientists got the temperature data for the graphs in Figure 7-17?
3. How do you think scientists got the precipitation data for the graphs in Figure 7-17?
4. In which month is precipitation heaviest at Cambridge Bay? at El Paso?
5. Which month is coldest at Cambridge Bay? at El Paso?
6. On the average, how much warmer is El Paso than Cambridge Bay in July?

7.8

ACTIVITY **Drawing and Using Climatograms**

In this activity you are given the temperature and precipitation data for three biomes found in North America. You will first use the data to draw the climatograms for the three biomes. Then you will use the climatograms to deduce information about the biomes.

Problem

What can a climatogram tell us about a biome?

Materials

graph paper (3 sheets)
pencils (2 colours)

Procedure

a. On each sheet of graph paper, draw the axes for a climatogram. Use the same scales as those in Figure 7-17.
b. Plot the climatogram for Biome A on one sheet of graph paper. Use the data in Table 7-9. Give the climatogram a suitable title. Use a different colour for the temperature and precipitation graphs.
c. Repeat step (b) for Biome B and Biome C.

Table 7-9   Temperature-Precipitation Data for Three Biomes

T=Temperature (°C)   P=Precipitation (mm)

		Jan.	Feb.	Mar.	Apr.	May	June	July	Aug.	Sept.	Oct.	Nov.	Dec.
Biome A	T	26.7	26.9	26.7	26.7	26.4	25.8	25.3	26.1	26.7	26.7	27.2	26.7
(altitude 83 m)	P	262.0	196.0	254.0	269.0	305.0	234.0	224.0	183.0	150.0	175.0	183.0	264.0
Biome B	T	10.4	12.5	15.8	20.4	25.0	29.8	32.9	31.7	29.1	22.3	15.0	11.4
(altitude 330 m)	P	18.0	21.0	17.0	8.0	3.0	3.0	20.0	29.0	18.0	11.0	13.0	21.0
Biome C	T	-6.0	-5.6	-0.7	6.6	12.3	18.2	20.5	19.7	15.7	9.9	3.1	-3.6
(altitude 280 m)	P	76.0	65.0	72.0	78.0	75.0	81.0	81.0	73.0	79.0	74.0	83.0	87.0

Discussion

For each of the following descriptions, you are to do two things:
• State which biome best fits the description.
• Explain why you chose that biome.
1. lies closest to the equator
2. lies furthest from the equator

3. has seasonal changes in temperature
4. has the longest growing season
5. has the highest total annual precipitation
6. has a measurable snowfall
7. has the highest average relative humidity
8. has the driest soil
9. has the highest soil moisture content
10. has the fastest rate of decomposition of organic matter
11. has the greatest abundance of plant growth
12. has the greatest variety of plant species
13. has numerous plants adapted for storing water
14. has plants which enter a seasonal period of dormancy
15. has the greatest variety of animal species
16. has animals adapted to reduce loss of body moisture
17. has animals which enter a seasonal period of hibernation
18. most closely resembles the biome you live in

Now, name each of the three biomes.

Main Ideas

1. Weather is the day-to-day or short-term change in atmospheric conditions.
2. Climate is the average weather in a region over a long period of time (usually two or three decades).
3. The two basic factors which determine climate are temperature and precipitation patterns over the past few decades.
4. The world has six major climate types: cold polar, temperate humid cold, subtropical humid mild, dry, tropical humid, and mountain.
5. Three factors determine the major climates of Canada and the United States: position, mountains, and ocean currents.
6. A biome is a large region of the earth with a characteristic climate and climax community.
7. A climatogram summarizes in graphical form the monthly variations in temperature and precipitation for a region.

Key Terms

biome
climate
climatogram
ecotone
limiting factor

microclimate
precipitation
relative humidity
weather

Chapter Review

A. True or False

Decide whether each of the following statements is true or false. If the sentence is false, rewrite it to make it true. (Do not write in this book.)

1. Weather is the day-to-day change in atmospheric conditions.
2. The temperature of a region is governed, in part, by the wind direction.
3. The climate of an area can change in just a few days.
4. A tundra climate has heavy snowfall (over 150 cm a year).
5. The largest major climate in North America is the temperate humid cold climate.
6. A humid subtropical climate has a distinct dry season.
7. The arid climate of parts of the western plains in the United States is due mainly to the western mountains.
8. Part of Canada has a subtropical humid mild climate.
9. The *type* of forest in a region is determined by the temperature.

B. Completion

Complete each of the following sentences with a word or phrase that will make the sentence correct. (Do not write in this book.)

1. The two moisture factors which affect weather are ▓▓▓▓ and ▓▓▓▓ .
2. The weather factor "sky conditions" includes cloud cover and ▓▓▓▓ .
3. The climate of a region is determined by two basic factors: ▓▓▓▓ and ▓▓▓▓ .
4. Cold polar climates include the icecap climate and the ▓▓▓▓ climate.
5. Most of the wheat-growing regions of the world occur in areas with a ▓▓▓▓ climate.
6. ▓▓▓▓ determines whether an area will be a desert, grassland, or forest.

C. Multiple Choice

Each of the following statements or questions is followed by four responses. Choose the correct response in each case. (Do not write in this book.)

1. The wind breaks twigs off trees and walking is difficult. But no structural damage occurs. The wind speed is most likely
   a) 55 km/h   b) 70 km/h   c) 80 km/h   d) over 120 km/h
2. A sling psychrometer has a wet bulb reading of 14°C and a dry bulb reading of 24°C. The relative humidity is
   a) 5%   b) 100%   c) 37%   d) 31%

3. The vegetation in an area with a savanna climate will normally be
   a) tall grasses only
   b) tall grasses with scattered trees and shrubs
   c) cacti and other xerophytes
   d) deciduous trees
4. Cold polar air enters the central part of our continent largely because
   a) North America has no east-west mountains
   b) polar winds are very strong
   c) cold air tends to move along the ground
   d) polar air is cold and dry
5. The biome with the heaviest annual precipitation is
   a) the boreal coniferous forest   c) the tropical rain forest
   b) the tundra   d) the temperate deciduous forest
6. If precipitation increased twenty-fold in the savanna of Africa, this region would likely become a
   a) temperate deciduous forest   c) boreal coniferous forest
   b) grassland   d) tropical rain forest

Using Your Knowledge

1. a) In what ways does wind speed affect weather?
   b) Why does wind direction affect weather?
   c) Why might the weather be affected by the time taken for the wind to get to a new location?
2. a) Air at 20°C is saturated with water vapour when it contains 17.1 g/m³ of water vapour. What is the relative humidity of air at 20°C which contains 3.4 g/m³ of water vapour?
   b) Air at 0°C has a relative humidity of 100% when it contains 4.8 g/m³ of water vapour. What will the relative humidity of this air become when it enters a building and is warmed to 20°C?
3. a) Explain the difference between weather and climate.
   b) Why is it possible for an area to have bad weather but a good climate?
4. a) Explain why the largest trees in North America grow along the western coast of Canada and the United States.
   b) What environmental problems could arise if most of these trees are removed by logging operations?
5. If the earth's average temperature increased about 2°C, much of the semiarid climate of North America would become arid.
   a) Which parts of Canada and the United States would be affected?
   b) What would be the consequences of this change?
6. Why are the exact boundaries of each biome difficult to find?
7. a) Name the biome in which you live.
   b) Describe the climate of your biome.
   c) What is the dominant vegetation of your biome?

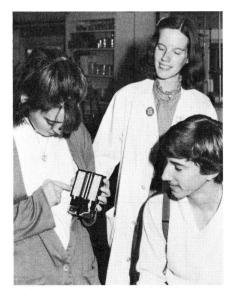

Investigations

1. Make a wet-and-dry bulb hygrometer. Monitor the relative humidity for one month. Then write a report on how relative humidity affected your comfort and the general weather.
2. Monitor the wind speed and direction for two weeks in the early morning, at noon, in the early evening, and before you go to bed. What was the pattern on most days? How did wind speed and direction relate to the general weather?
3. Prepare a table which shows names and sketches of cloud types in one column. Include in the other column a description of what those clouds forecast about the weather.
4. Many countries in Africa have had serious famines in recent years.
   a) Find the names of those countries.
   b) What biome(s) are they in?
   c) What are the climates which dominate these countries?
   d) Propose solutions for the famine problem.
5. Prepare a map which shows how the major ocean currents move along the west and east coasts of the United States and Canada.
6. The arid and semiarid regions of the United States need more water if farmers are to continue growing the crops they now grow. The main source of this water would be the Great Lakes. The governments of Ontario and most of the Great Lakes states are opposed to the transfer of water from the Great Lakes. Research this matter. Why are these governments opposed? Do the dry states have any alternatives? What may be the ecological consequences, in both the north and south, of such a water transfer scheme?

UNIT THREE

Biomes of North America

Fig. 8-0 This mountain biome is one of nine biomes in Canada and the United States. Like the other eight, it is a terrestrial ecosystem. Can you name some of the biotic and abiotic factors that interact in this ecosystem?

In Chapter 7 you saw that North America can be divided into ten biomes. Each biome is a large region with a characteristic climate and climax community. Each also contains a wide variety of organisms which show unique and interesting adaptations to their environments. Unfortunately, each biome is also suffering from human impact.

The main purpose of this unit is to prepare you to make informed decisions on how we should treat the various biomes. To achieve this end, each biome is dealt with under three main headings:

- abiotic factors
- biotic factors (plant and animal)
- human impact

You will enjoy reading about the adaptations of plants and animals to abiotic factors. We ask you though to give the sections on human impact your greatest attention.

8 The Tundra Biome

Stretching beyond the forests of the north to the edge of the Arctic icecap lies a vast, treeless plain. Figure 7-14 (page 140) shows that this biome, the Arctic tundra, is circumpolar. That is, it surrounds the north pole. Most of the earth's tundra occurs in Canada and the Soviet Union. But some also occurs in Alaska, Greenland, Iceland, and Norway.

A similar climate exists in the far southern hemisphere, north of the Antarctic icefields. However, no tundra biome occurs there. None exists because oceans cover the area which has the climate to support tundra. Isolated patches of tundra do occur, however, in the upper regions of mountains throughout the world. This Alpine tundra is described in Section 13.1 of Chapter 13. This chapter describes the Arctic tundra of Canada and Alaska (see Figure 7-16, page 144).

8.1 Abiotic Factors

Climate

The tundra climate is cold, windy, and dry. The temperature is below 0°C most of the year. And the long winters are extremely cold. Average January temperatures range from –22°C along the Labrador coast to –29°C in Barrow, Alaska. The soil is completely frozen. Thick fogs prevail wherever the icy land meets the sea. For 9 months, tundra lakes lie buried beneath a thick blanket of ice. Shallow ponds freeze to the bottom. When the warmth of springtime finally arrives to melt this frozen wasteland, the short Arctic summer is close upon its heels. In fact the entire growing season lasts only about 60 d.

Summer brings long hours of daylight. But the sun's rays do not generate much heat. June and July in the tundra are usually chilly and raw, much like

March or April in southern Ontario or January in Georgia. The warmest month is July. Then average temperatures range from a low of 0°C to a high of 10°C. Killing frost can occur at any time.

Precipitation is frequent in the tundra biome. However, the total annual precipitation is low. Most areas receive less than 25 cm of precipitation in a year. Even the wettest months, which occur in the summer, have only 2-3 cm of precipitation. In the winter there is little snowfall. But the snow is constantly blown around. Therefore one gets the impression that snowfall is heavy. Because of the light precipitation, the tundra is often called a frozen desert.

Light

Tundra areas north of the Arctic Circle lie in the "land of the midnight sun". Most of you would be startled to find the sun peeping through your window at midnight. But if you lived in this part of the world, you would be used to 24 h of daylight in midsummer. The summer sun never sets. But you must also endure 24 h of darkness during midwinter. Then the sun is too far south to rise above the Arctic horizon. Below the Arctic Circle the photoperiod depends on the latitude. Most of the tundra is north of 57°N.

The sun's rays strike the tundra at a very low angle. Thus the light received by the tundra is never very bright, even though summer days are long.

Soil

An aerial view of the tundra reveals unique land patterns. Note how they resemble a patchwork quilt (Fig. 8-1). These patterns are molded by the constant freezing and thawing of the soil. The finer soil particles (clays) retain high moisture levels. Each time the soil freezes, the particles move apart. (Water expands when it freezes.) Then they move together again during the next thaw. This continual process forces larger soil particles above the surface. The larger particles then form patterned ridges in the land. Large boulders can be splintered into rock fragments by similar frost action. The constant heaving and movement of earth greatly limits vegetation. Unstable soil and rocks tend to gradually creep down any slope which forms. Frost is more effective than water erosion in wearing down the surface features.

During the short spring and summer interval the surface of the soil thaws to a depth varying from a few centimetres in some places to half a metre in others. Below this depth lies the permafrost, soil which never thaws. This permanently frozen layer is 700 m deep in spots. It prevents proper drainage of the water produced by melting snow in the spring. Instead, the meltwater collects on the flat land surface. This produces vast marshy areas called muskeg, dotted with ponds and streams. This important water reservoir enables plants to grow despite the low rainfall.

Fig. 8-1 This aerial photograph shows the quilt-like pattern which occurs on much of the tundra. It is caused by repeated freezing and thawing of ice in the tundra soil.

1. a) Describe the temperature conditions of the tundra.
   b) Why are summer temperatures low, even when the sun shines 24 h each day?
2. a) Describe the precipitation conditions of the tundra.
   b) Why is the tundra often called a frozen desert?
3. a) Describe the photoperiod north of the Arctic Circle.
   b) Describe the photoperiod of that part of the tundra south of the Arctic Circle.
4. How long is the tundra growing season?
5. a) What is permafrost?
   b) Why is tundra soil unstable for plant growth?
6. a) What is muskeg?
   b) How does it form?
   c) Why is muskeg important to Arctic vegetation?

8.2   Biotic Factors: Vegetation

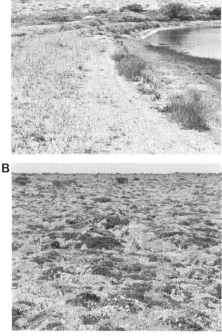

Fig. 8-2 Two views of the tundra in summer. Photograph A shows dwarf trees and shrubs in low areas. Photograph B shows mounds covered with lichens and mosses, with grasses, sedges, and herbs in lower areas. Note the absence of trees (other than dwarf ones).

The tundra may appear to be a rather barren region. However, its ecology is very important to scientists for two reasons. First, the Arctic contains resources that we need such as oil and natural gas. Therefore we must know how extraction of those resources will affect tundra plant and animal communities. Second, tundra ecology is rather simple. Temperature alone greatly limits the number of species which can adapt to and live in this biome. This makes basic ecological relationships such as food chains, food webs, and adaptations simple and easy to study. Such studies in the tundra may help scientists understand more complicated ecosystems in other parts of the world.

This section describes some of the common tundra vegetation. And, more important, it explains how this vegetation has adapted to the harsh abiotic factors. Adaptations in the tundra are striking. They are easy to spot and they are fascinating to study.

Types of Vegetation

During the Arctic summer, tundra vegetation flourishes. At first glance, the tundra in summer looks like a grassy plain. In fact, it is often called the tundra grassland (see Fig. 7-16, page 144). But a closer look reveals a complex pattern of vegetation. In some places, mounds of earth are covered by lichens and mosses (Fig. 8-2, A). Among them are blueberry shrubs and heaths such as Labrador tea (Fig. 8-3). The wetter hollows are filled with sedges and reeds, typical marsh plants.

In other places, exposed ridges have little vegetation (Fig. 8-2, B). But every sheltered nook and cranny is filled with vegetation, including lichens,

Fig. 8-3 Labrador tea is an evergreen. It does not drop its leaves in the fall. Instead, it slowly replaces them during the growing season. Of what advantage is this adaptation to a tundra plant? (*Hint*: Tundra plants cannot afford to waste energy.)

Fig. 8-4 Willow herb, a colourful plant of the tundra grassland.

Fig. 8-5 Tufts of "cotton" rise above other vegetation in wet areas of the tundra.

Fig. 8-6 This tundra dwarf willow is only 20 cm tall. Yet it is a mature tree several decades old.

mosses, grasses, sedges, and reeds. And colourful flowering plants such as the willow-herb abound (Fig. 8-4). Clumps of cotton grass rise above a carpet of sphagnum moss (Fig. 8-5). Dwarf trees, mainly willow and birch, stand just a few centimetres tall among the other plants. And a rich growth of taller shrubs, grasses, and other plants occurs on south slopes of hills and in river valleys.

You are familiar with the abiotic factors governing this biome. Therefore, before you read on, think about how plants have adapted to these factors. For instance, how is growth affected by the low summer temperatures? What type of root system can develop in the thin layer of shifting soil? How do these plants photosynthesize properly in the low light intensity of the Arctic? And how does tundra vegetation manage to propagate during the brief growing season? The answers to these and other related questions reveal the extent of plant adaptation to the tundra environment.

Adaptations to Low Temperatures

The low soil and air temperatures greatly retard plant growth in the Arctic. Plants tend to be small and stunted. A good example is the dwarf willow (Fig. 8-6). This plant cannot grow vertically like most willows. Any terminal buds which form (those at the ends of twigs) are quickly killed by the chilling winds. But some of the sun's radiant energy which strikes the ground is absorbed by the soil. Thus the soil temperature is generally much higher than that of the air above. In fact, soil temperatures in the tundra can change from 0°C to 40°C during a summer day. The rest of the heat energy is reflected back into the atmosphere. Therefore, the air temperature immediately next to the soil is higher than the air temperature 30 cm or more above the ground. This means that buds can grow on branches of the plant which spread laterally, close to the warmer soil surface.

Growth close to the ground also protects plants against the constant abrasion from soil and ice particles driven by the wind. As a result, the growth of the dwarf willow is greatly modified compared to related willow species in more southern areas of North America.

Winter survival for a tundra plant is often determined by the terrain. Tall shrubs growing in hollows are protected from icy winter gales by insulating snow drifts. Large snowbank formations usually nurture specialized snowbed plants. These receive water from the melting snowbank throughout the growing season.

Adaptations to Soil Conditions

Root systems trying to develop in the thin, unstable tundra soil face many of the problems associated with sand dunes. Thus you might expect to find similar plant species, namely grasses and shrubs. Have you ever tried to pull up a clump of grass? If you have, you know how firmly the shallow, branching root network grips the soil. By weaving around soil particles, the root mass can better absorb any available moisture. This is a critical factor in the dry portions of the tundra.

Mosses and lichens cling to the soil using hair-like rhizoids rather than true roots. Their ability to absorb and retain moisture enables them to grow on the driest surfaces. Yet they also thrive in bogs. These simple plants play an important role by retarding erosion. A dense growth of this vegetation tends to stabilize soil particles. A carpet of moss can slow the rapid runoff of rain water or melted snow. Such moss beds, with their reservoir of water, also provide growth sites for larger flowering plants.

If the carpet of mosses and lichens is disturbed, erosion can occur. Look back to Figure 8-1. Can you see a pair of vehicle tracks running from the lower right? This vehicle tore through the carpet of mosses and lichens. Then running water washed the soil away. Growth is slow in the Arctic. This damage may not be repaired for hundreds of years.

The cold climate and short summers greatly reduce the action of decomposers. Therefore, a layer of undecayed vegetation covers much of the tundra. The slow decomposition of organic matter leaves tundra soils deficient in nitrates, phosphates and other essential minerals. As well, water leaches minerals from the soil. But wherever animal wastes provide these nutrients, plant growth is better. Patches of lush green vegetation are signposts for animal burrows, bird cliffs, or the nesting sites of geese.

The small plants of the tundra wage a constant battle for existence in the shifting earth. They can rarely stabilize the ground surface long enough to change the soil. Studies of succession are limited to isolated plant communities. And these face continual upheaval from the action of frost. A true climax vegetation is unknown.

Adaptations to Light Conditions

During the short growing season, tundra plants must photosynthesize and store enough food to last the entire year. The production of flowers and seeds uses a great deal of energy. As a result, most tundra plants are perennials. They must grow for several seasons before they have stored enough energy to flower. To attract the limited number of insect and bird pollinating agents, flowers tend to bloom in clusters. These blossoms are very large compared to the tiny plants which produce them. Different species of herbs generally bloom in succession. This lessens competition among them. Yet even if pollination does occur, the resulting seeds have little chance of germinating in this hostile terrain. Thus vegetative propagation is predominant among plants of the Arctic tundra. That is, new plants grow from the rooting of leaves or branches.

Some tundra plants, such as Labrador tea, are evergreen. They do not drop their leaves all at once in the fall. Instead, they replace them one by one over the growing season. This adaptation helps the plants conserve valuable energy after the long winter. A great deal of energy would be needed to grow a new set of leaves in the spring. And this energy may not be available after the long winter.

The light intensity in the Arctic is low. But the days are long. Therefore, for about two months, Arctic plants can capture enough light to ensure adequate photosynthesis. Arctic plants are long-day plants. That is, flowering is stimulated by long days followed by short nights.

Section Review

1. State two reasons why the study of tundra ecology is important.
2. Why is the tundra called a grassland?
3. Give a general description of the tundra landscape. What shape is it? What vegetation dominates it? What patterns can be seen?
4. Why do many Arctic plants grow along the ground instead of vertically?
5. What is a snowbed plant?
6. How are tundra plants adapted to the thin unstable soil?
7. What kind of a microenvironment do mosses provide for flowering plants?
8. Describe how a vehicle can cause erosion damage on tundra soil.
9. Why is tundra soil low in nutrients?
10. Why are climax communities hard to find in the tundra?
11. Why is it an advantage for a tundra plant to be a perennial?
12. Why is vegetative propagation common among tundra plants?
13. Name two adaptations of flowering tundra plants which increase their chances of pollination.
14. Why is it an advantage for a tundra plant to be an evergreen?

8.3   Biotic Factors: Animals

Animals have adapted to the harsh environment of the tundra. In fact, they are quite abundant in the summer. This section describes some of the common animals and their adaptations.

Fig. 8-7 The tundra offers little protection from predators. Therefore animals like these ptarmigan rely on camouflage. They are brownish in the summer and white in the winter.

Some Adaptations

What kind of animal life would you expect to find in the Arctic tundra? Because they seldom see humans, most northern animals do not fear us. But you must search carefully. Several mammal species, both predator and prey, are white during winter to blend with the snow. These include the Arctic hare, grey wolf, collared lemming, and Arctic fox. Even a few bird species— willow and rock ptarmigans and the snowy owl—turn white in the winter. In the spring, many of these animals change back to darker colours. The darker colours provide better camouflage in the summer (Fig. 8-7).

How do animals of the tundra stand the severe cold of winter? The larger mammals and permanent bird residents develop an insulating layer of fat. They also have air pockets trapped within long, dense fur or feathers. Ptarmigans and snowy owls grow extra feathers on their legs and feet. Exposed body surfaces such as nostrils and feet are a special problem. A great deal of body heat can be lost from such surfaces. You, for example, could not stand about in the snow in your bare feet for long. But gulls have no trouble walking along an icy shoreline. These creatures avoid losing body heat by having two internal temperatures. The main body is kept at a normal temperature. But exposed extremities function at a temperature which varies with that of the surrounding environment (Fig. 8-8). Veins and arteries intermingle in a simple heat-exchange system. Blood from the heart, en route to the extremities, warms the returning cold blood. It, in turn, is cooled.

An animal's shape and size also affect its ability to retain body heat. A large animal has less surface area per unit volume. Therefore it loses heat more slowly. A spherical shape also helps conserve body heat. Thus polar animals tend to be larger and more rotund than their southern relatives. Extremities such as ears, tails, and legs are shorter to reduce heat loss further (Fig. 8-9).

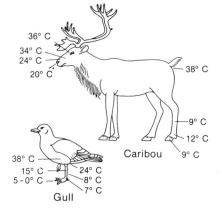

Fig. 8-8 Body extremities such as feet, legs, and nostrils have little protection against snow, ice, or cold water. Too much body heat would be lost if they were at the same temperature as the body. Therefore, in most polar animals, these extremities function at low temperatures.

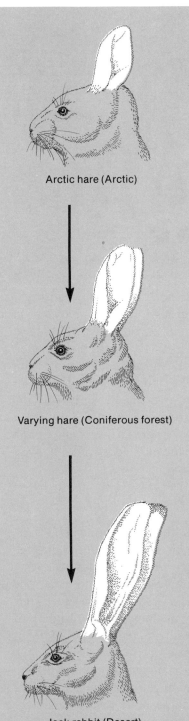

Fig. 8-9 Species in colder climates have smaller body extremities. This reduces heat loss.

Arctic hare (Arctic)

Varying hare (Coniferous forest)

Jack rabbit (Desert)

If you were to scan the Arctic landscape, you might discover a snowbank tunnel. A ptarmigan will sometimes roost here for days. At other times it is busy feeding on buds and tender shoots of shrubs which stick up through the snow. This winter food has a higher fat content than the ptarmigan's summer diet which is mainly leaves. Smaller animals such as lemmings and voles escape the cold and their predators by staying in runways. These runways connect nests beneath the snowdrifts in sheltered hollows. Here they feed on stored seed supplies or nibble at plant growth. Polar bears shelter in dens where the females give birth to cubs in midwinter. The only animal which actually hibernates is the Arctic ground squirrel. It builds a burrow in a sandbank or hilly mound. Here, unusual drainage has left a layer of unfrozen soil beneath the frosted surface.

How do invertebrates survive the winter? Most of them winter in a larval or pupal stage which resists freezing. Spiders, beetles, and a few other species survive in adult form. Aquatic organisms such as rotifers and midge fly larvas can be frozen in the ice for months or even years. Yet they become active as soon as they thaw!

Muskox

Shaggy muskox paw the snow to uncover vegetation which they can eat. Dense wool under a long hairy coat provides insulation. These heavy powerful animals have a mass of 350 to 400 kg (Fig. 8-10). They graze almost continuously in the summer. This builds up stores of fat for the winter. Yet they must still eat in the winter. In fact, some starve to death when sleet storms make the snow so hard they cannot paw through it. Sleet storms can also coat these animals with a thick layer of ice. Then they cannot escape predators such as wolves. The tundra environment is harsh. It kills many muskox but the worst enemy of this species is humans. We pushed this species to the brink of extinction in the recent past. Its numbers have, however, recovered due to laws which prevent overhunting. Yet the muskox head remains a highly prized addition to the trophy rooms of hunters from the south.

Barren Ground Caribou

Animals which cannot adjust to the cold and lack of food migrate south during the winter. Thousands of barren ground caribou seek shelter and vegetation below the tree line. The autumn skies are filled with departing birds. Only an occasional hawk, raven, or owl can be spotted in the winter. However, marine birds, such as gulls, are found near the open sea. The Arctic fox moves to the edge of the iceflows. There it scavenges on seal carcasses and the dung left by polar bears.

Barren ground caribou, or reindeer, are well adapted to the Arctic environment (Fig. 8-11). Those from the far north are almost white to blend with the snow. Their colour gradually darkens as they migrate south. Caribou

Fig. 8-10   The muskox has insulating wool under its hairy robe. The Inuit name for the muskox is oomingmak. This means "the bearded one".

Fig. 8-11   Caribou means "shoveller". It uses its splayed hooves to dig, or shovel, through the snow to find food.

have a light air-filled hairy coat. This provides good insulation against the cold. But it also serves as a life jacket! Barren ground caribou are always on the move. In the summer they migrate back and forth across the tundra. And, as winter approaches, they migrate south. In the Arctic, water often blocks these migration routes. The caribou's air-filled coat helps it swim across rivers, lakes, and other watery areas. In the summer, the caribou's foot pads are large and soft. And the edges of the hooves are badly worn. Thus the fleshy foot pads rest on the ground. But in the winter, the hooves grow much longer. The foot pads shrink and harden. Then hair grows from between the toes over the pads. Now the caribou walks on the hard edges of its hooves. And the fleshy pads do not touch the cold ground.

Spring Activity

Huge flocks of snow geese honk their way across the sky as spring heralds the return of many tundra species. Animal activity in the Arctic is geared to the short summer. For example, the ground squirrel surfaces only between May and September. It emerges from the hibernation burrow ready to mate. The young squirrels, born in June, are self-sufficient just a month later. They reach adult size and prepare for hibernation in late September. Certain bird species of the tundra also demonstrate an unusually rapid life cycle. Many of the returning birds have already mated. They begin to nest immediately. Others mate after arrival and loudly proclaim nesting territories from high in the air. There are no trees in the tundra large enough for nesting. Therefore eggs are easily stolen by predators. Thus northern birds tend to lay large clutches of eggs. The young birds also develop much faster than their southern counterparts.

Tundra food chains are remarkably short in winter. They lengthen during the productive summer period. But the total number of species involved remains low. Reptile and amphibian life is rare. Even the insect population is relatively limited. However, any tundra visitor will tell you that mosquitoes, black flies, and deer flies are the most common animals. Bumblebees are plentiful. Yet the highly adaptable ant is scarce. Songbirds live on seeds, insects, and the August berries. Larger birds of prey seek rodents. Waterfowl make up most of the tundra bird life. They live along the coast or take advantage of the many ideal nesting sites beside freshwater ponds and lakes. The limited period of thaw results in low productivity in these bodies of water, however. That is, they cannot support much life. Fish are largely migratory, and are most numerous in the rivers.

The Lemming: A Key Animal

The most critical link in the tundra food web is a little rodent called the lemming. Once each month from April to September, a female brown lemming can produce a litter of 3-11 offspring. The young are born in a grassy nursery lined with moss, feathers, and fox moult. The babies are weaned within two weeks. They soon reach a length of 15 cm. Their cousin, the collared lemming, is the only North American mouse to have a white winter robe. When fall arrives, lemmings are busy stocking their underground honeycomb of tunnels and runways with grass, willow catkins, moss, and sedges. Snow insulates the colony from the bitter cold of winter.

Life is full of hazards for lemmings. They are hunted by foxes, weasels, wolves, and bears. Birds of prey such as snowy owls deal death from the sky. Even browsing caribou occasionally abandon their normal lichen meal to munch lemmings crushed beneath their broad hooves. Lemmings attempting to swim streams fall prey to large trout. As the lemmings flourish, the predator population grows (Fig. 8-12). But nature seems aware of the dangers posed by unlimited animal activity in the fragile tundra ecosystem.

Fig. 8-12 The food supply of many tundra animals depends in some way on the lemming. Lemmings also change the soil and vegetation as they make burrows.

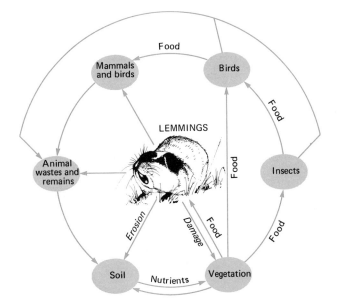

The growth cycle reaches a peak every 3-4 years. Then suddenly the balance is upset. Overcrowding takes its toll. Disease and death sweep through the lemming colonies. Sometimes hordes of these rodents make a mass migration across the tundra. They leave a trail of devastated vegetation behind. In their search for living space, the lemmings swim across small ponds and streams. But they cannot distinguish larger bodies of water like the sea. Countless thousands drown as they seek the other bank.

In the short tundra food chains a big change in any trophic level has a violent effect on other levels. Starvation now haunts the predators. Northern shrikes, rough-legged hawks, and other birds fly south. Snowy owls go as far south as Michigan. The Arctic fox becomes a scavenger, following the hunting polar bear. Wolf numbers drop. Caribou vanish from the ranges they overgrazed when relieved of attack from wolves. Trappers note the dwindling number of fur-bearing animals. Until the lemming population is renewed, many birds, particularly owls and hawks, will not breed. With fewer predators, lemmings begin to increase in numbers and the cycle begins again.

Section Review

1. Name six Arctic animals which turn white in the winter.
2. Describe six different ways in which Arctic animals have adapted to the cold.
3. **a)** How does a ptarmigan protect itself on very cold days?
   b) How do small rodents such as lemmings and voles escape the cold?
4. Describe two ways in which muskox have adapted to the cold Arctic environment.
5. **a)** What two advantages do barren ground caribou gain from their southward migration each fall?
   b) Describe the caribou's coat.
   c) Give two advantages of the special nature of this coat.
   d) How do caribou feet change as winter approaches? Of what advantage is this change?
6. **a)** What type of bird life finds the tundra most favourable? Why?
   b) State three special problems these birds encounter.
   c) Why do many Arctic birds lay a larger than average number of eggs?
7. Study Figure 8-12 carefully. Then describe the role of the lemming as shown by this figure.

8.4   Human Impact on the Tundra

For countless generations the Arctic has been inhabited by the Inuit. They have lived in harmony with the environment. Until recently the Arctic escaped the damage that "development" sometimes causes. That's because developers saw the Arctic as harsh and remote. Therefore they stayed away from it. Now its resources, particularly oil and gas, are needed. Exploration for and extraction of these resources has changed large parts of the Arctic. Roads, airstrips, pipelines, towns, pollution, and fires are common in many areas. Tourism has increased due to better services such as roads. Fly-in hunting and fishing trips take people to the most remote areas.

All these activities bring some positive benefits to the Arctic. But the tundra is a fragile ecosystem. It is easily damaged. And, due to the extreme cold, repair of even minor damage can take decades or even hundreds of years.

Permafrost

Permafrost, you may recall, is soil which never thaws (Fig.8-13). This permanently frozen layer is a major controlling factor in the tundra ecosystem. If it is changed in any way, the whole ecosystem is affected. Let's see how this happens.

What is Permafrost? Permafrost is quite common. It occurs in about half the land area of Canada. In fact, it underlies about one-fifth of the earth's land surface. It is likely to exist wherever the average annual temperature is $-1°C$ or lower.

In Canada's Arctic islands, 20 000 years of ice age conditions have formed permafrost as deep as 700 m. In Siberia, the permafrost is up to 1.5 km deep! You have likely heard of the woolly mammoths the Soviets have discovered preserved in this icy soil. The southern limit of the permafrost in North America runs in a broad arc from northwestern Alaska, through the Yukon and the Northwest Territories, to Québec. It drops to within 350 km of Winnipeg. And it lies under Moosonee, Ontario (see Fig. 7-16 page 144).

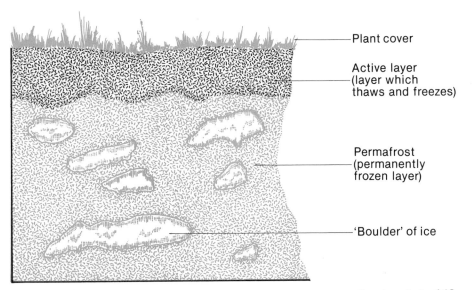

Fig. 8-13 The structure of tundra soil. The top layer is up to 0.5 m deep. It may thaw in the summer. But the layer below stays frozen all year.

Plant cover

Active layer (layer which thaws and freezes)

Permafrost (permanently frozen layer)

'Boulder' of ice

Permafrost appears to be frozen solid. But it is by no means one solid chunk. Small amounts of liquid water move slowly through it. This water turns to ice as it nears the surface. Sometimes it collects into giant "boulders" of ice up to 25 m thick. As these boulders form, they heave the soil and shift it around.

The Active Layer   Permafrost has a thin layer on it which is called the active layer. This layer thaws in the summer and freezes in the winter. It varies in depth from just 10-15 cm in the far north to an average of about 0.5 m in the rest of the tundra. It can reach 2-3 m deep at the southern edge of the tundra.

When the active layer thaws, water forms. This water cannot soak very far into the permafrost. Therefore it tends to collect in the active layer. Of course, it will gradually drain away to low areas. This forms vast stretches of waterlogged soil called muskeg. The water also collects in deep depressions to form ponds and lakes.

Vegetation on the Active Layer   The active layer supports the growth of several types of vegetation: lichens, mosses, grasses, sedges, and other plants. This mat of vegetation is very thin. But it forms an insulating blanket which prevents the summer thaw from going far into the ground.

Thermokarst

Even a slight disturbance of the vegetation cover greatly affects the depth of the active layer. In fact, if the vegetation is removed, the thaw may be up to three times its normal depth. Such deep thawing of the permafrost is called thermokarst

Natural Thermokarst   Thermokarst can occur because of natural causes. For example, lightning may start a fire which removes the vegetation cover. The permafrost now thaws much deeper. The whole area may sink, forming a pond where once there was dry land. Thermokarst also occurs naturally along the tree line. The trunk of a fallen tree stores heat from the sun. And this heat melts the permafrost. Also, the roots of a falling tree will rip large holes in the active layer. Thawing can now go deeper. Just one fallen tree can eventually result in a pond hundreds of metres across!

Human-made Thermokarst   Thermokarst caused by humans is widespread in the north. And it is likely to spread even more. Permafrost makes a good base upon which to build roads, buildings, and other structures. But only if it is kept from melting. Unfortunately, most human activities give off heat. Roads and airstrips absorb heat from the sun. Heat escapes through the floors of houses. And pipes in towns carry hot water and warm sewage. Oil pipelines carry oil heated to over 65°C so it will flow. And, unless care is taken, all these heat sources can cause serious thermokarst.

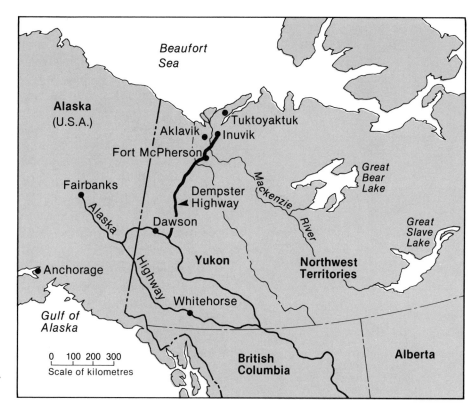

Fig. 8-14 The upper end of the Dempster Highway was built on permafrost.

Fig. 8-15 This building is in Pangnirtung on Baffin Island at the east of the Northwest Territories. Construction projects here must be designed to prevent thermokarst. What was done when this building was built?

In 1978 the Dempster Highway was built to connect Dawson City in the Yukon with Inuvik in the Mackenzie Delta of the Northwest Territories. This 750 km highway is the only public highway on the continent stretching north of the Arctic Circle (Fig. 8-14). Much of the upper end is built on permafrost. Special care was taken to protect the permafrost when this road was being built. But today, places where vehicles parked off the highway have turned to lakes. Vehicles destroyed the vegetation in the parking areas, resulting in thermokarst. And the soil collapsed and sunk.

About 50 years ago, some ground was dug in Dawson City to grow potatoes. A few years later the area was a boggy hole. It still is today.

In Pangnirtung, on Baffin Island in the Northwest Territories, the floor of a municipal garage dropped 0.5 m (Fig. 8-15). It had not been properly insulated. The building had to be torn down. Improperly insulated houses can sink, twist, crack, and warp.

Inuvik, NWT, was built in the 1950s as a supply centre for the western Arctic. It is now a main supply base for oil and gas exploration in the Beaufort Sea (see Fig. 8-14). It has become an active and fairly large town with a population of over 3000. The problems caused by thermokarst were well known when this town was built. Therefore steps were taken to prevent thermokarst. Thick layers of gravel were placed on the active layer when it was frozen. Then roads and parking lots were built on top of the gravel.

Section 8.4 165

Buildings were built on wooden piles to keep warm floors away from the ground. Water and sewer mains are in a "utility corridor". It is built above ground on wooden piles. The same corridor carries a hot water pipe that supplies central heating to buildings. This pipe also prevents water and sewer mains from freezing. Techniques learned at Inuvik are now in widespread use across Alaska and northern Canada.

Oil pipelines present special problems. Imagine, for example, a pipeline carrying 80°C oil and buried 2 m in the tundra. It would thaw permafrost around it to a diameter of 8-10 m in just a few years. In 20 years the permafrost would be thawed to a depth of 10-15 m. Even if the oil were heated to just 30°C, the thaw would only decrease by about 30%. Imagine what could happen to the pipeline when the melt occurred. Pipelines are built above ground to prevent thermokarst. But this can cause another problem. What is it?

People walking or driving on the tundra can also cause serious damage. A footpath used for just one summer may take decades to grow over. Wheel marks of vehicles can cause extensive erosion. For example, some trails were made on Alaska's north shore by Navy vehicles in the 1940s. They are now gullies 4-5 m deep, up to 7 m wide, and several kilometres long. This damage will not repair itself for centuries, if ever. Even a fencepost in a backyard can warm the soil and cause thermokarst.

Impact on Wildlife

Human activities in the Arctic can have serious effects on wildlife. Roads, pipelines, and railways can disturb migration routes of caribou. If a pipeline breaks, the oil can affect both terrestrial and aquatic life. Increased tourism, with its accompanying hunting and fishing, could threaten some animal populations. Mineral exploitation can cause widespread thermokarst. And hydroelectric power development projects can flood vast tracts of tundra. This can destroy the nesting sites of birds. It can destroy the spawning grounds of fish which used the rivers before they were dammed. It can also affect migration routes of caribou. In 1984, for example, about 10 000 migrating caribou drowned in northern Québec. They were attempting to swim the Caniapiscau River. Many people believe that too much water was released from a reservoir used to generate power. The river became so deep and fast that the caribou could not swim across it.

Increased human activity means more fires. Fires have already destroyed vast tracts of lichens, a major food of caribou. Serious drops in caribou numbers have been noted in burned areas. Burned-out areas are very slow to grow lichens again.

Canadian scientists and engineers are known throughout the world for their research on permafrost problems. But much more research needs to be done if the Arctic is to be developed without destroying its fragile ecology.

Section Review

1. a) What is permafrost?
   b) What temperature conditions make it possible?
   c) How extensive is permafrost in Canada? in the world?
   d) Where does permafrost occur in the United States?
   e) How deep is permafrost in Canada's Arctic Islands? in Siberia?
2. a) What is the "active layer"?
   b) How deep is the active layer in the far north?
   c) What is its average depth?
3. a) What is muskeg?
   b) What causes muskeg to form?
4. Describe the vegetation mat on the active layer.
5. What is thermokarst?
6. Describe two examples of natural thermokarst.
7. Describe how each of the following can cause thermokarst:
   a) an oil pipeline   d) water and sewage pipes
   b) a building   e) pedestrian and vehicle tracks
   c) a road or parking area
8. Describe the steps taken in Inuvik to prevent thermokarst.
9. Make a summary of the effects of human activities on wildlife in the Arctic.

8.5   *ACTIVITY* **Arctic Development**

The Arctic has resources, particularly oil, natural gas, and minerals, which we need. The Arctic must be opened up, or "developed", if we are to get these resources. This development, if done improperly, can cause serious damage to the tundra ecosystem. Yet proper development requires expensive research. This could delay projects by many years. Further, proper development will be more costly.

In this activity you are to imagine that oil has been discovered deep in the ground near Tuktoyaktuk, NWT (see Fig.8-14). Planners want to enlarge this town to a population of 10 000. And a pipeline could be built along the Mackenzie River valley to take the oil south. A similar discovery of oil has been found on the Alaskan north shore. A proposal has been submitted to run a pipeline from that oilfield to link up with the Mackenzie River pipeline near Fort McPherson.

A public hearing has been called to assess the project proposals. In this activity you will participate in that public hearing.

Problem

Should these proposed developments proceed? And, if so, how?

Materials

maps of Alaska and northern Canada
reference books on Arctic wildlife
reference books on northern communities

Procedure

a. Appoint five people from your class to be the Hearing Panel. This group will listen to the presentations. Then it will make a decision regarding the project proposals.

b. If you are not on the Hearing Panel, select one of the following roles or any other role approved by your teacher:
   • president of the Far Arctic Oil Company of Canada
   • a self-employed wildlife biologist
   • a wildlife biologist working for the Canadian Wildlife Service
   • a wildlife biologist working for the U.S. Fish and Wildlife Service
   • a construction worker living in Tuktoyaktuk
   • an Inuit who makes his or her living largely by trapping and hunting near Tuktoyaktuk
   • Canada's Minister of Energy, Mines, and Resources
   • Canada's Minister of the Environment
   • Canada's Minister of Tourism
   • Canada's Minister of Indian and Northern Affairs
   • president of the North Alaska Oil Company
   • a stockholder in either of the oil companies
   • the mayor of Tuktoyaktuk
   • a representative of Greenpeace or any other environmental protection organization
   • a representative of the government of the Northwest Territories
   • a representative of the government of the Yukon
   • a representative of the government of Alaska
   • a tourist outfitter working in Tuktoyaktuk
   • president of a steel company which makes pipelines
   • the owner of a store in Tuktoyaktuk
   • a Canadian or American citizen living in the south who will receive the benefits of the oil and who pays the taxes which will subsidize some of the development

   Note: More than one person can choose the same role. Suppose, for example, two people choose to be the president of an oil company. They can work together on their submission. One can be the president and the other the vice-president.

c. Prepare a paper to present to the Hearing Panel. You may work on a joint submission with others who have similar points of view. You will be given 5 min to present your paper orally. Then you must leave a copy with the Hearing Panel. In your paper you should try to convince the Hearing Panel that your position is sound. You may wish to do a "Cost-

Benefit Analysis". To do this, make a list of the beneficial aspects (benefits) of your proposal. Then make a list of the negative aspects (costs) of your proposal. Now try to convince the Hearing Panel that the benefits outweigh the costs.

d. The Hearing Panel must listen to the presentations. Ask questions for clarification, if necessary. Then, after the hearing, the Panel must study the submissions and make a recommendation. Should the developments proceed? And, if so, how?

Discussion

1. Are you satisfied with the Hearing Panel's decision? Why or why not?
2. What is your opinion of the use of Hearing Panels for issues such as this?
3. In what ways could this procedure be made more effective?

Main Ideas

1. The average annual temperature in the tundra is below $0°C$; the annual precipitation is low (less than 25 cm).
2. Arctic summers have long hours of daylight but low light intensity.
3. Permafrost underlies the tundra.
4. Vast areas of muskeg dot the Arctic landscape during the summer.
5. Arctic plants and animals show striking adaptations to their environments.
6. Tundra vegetation consists mainly of lichens, mosses, grasses, sedges, and dwarf shrubs and trees.
7. Human activities tend to disrupt the tundra vegetation. This disruption can cause thermokarst.

Key Terms

active layer   muskeg   permafrost   thermokarst

Chapter Review

A. True or False

Decide whether each of the following statements is true or false. If the sentence is false, rewrite it to make it true. (Do not write in this book.)

1. The Arctic tundra is circumpolar.
2. Lichens and mosses are the dominant tundra vegetation.
3. Most Arctic plants are annuals.
4. Most Arctic plants reproduce vegetatively.
5. Most Arctic plants are short-day plants.

6. A spherical body shape helps an animal conserve heat.
7. Permafrost thaws in mid-summer.
8. The active layer of tundra soil has an average depth of 0.5 m.

B. Completion

Complete each of the following sentences with a word or phrase that will make the sentence correct. (Do not write in this book.)
1. Soil which never thaws is called ▨▨▨▨▨▨ .
2. The two main trees (dwarfs) of the tundra are ▨▨▨▨▨ and ▨▨▨▨▨ .
3. ▨▨▨▨▨▨ are mammals which migrate south to the tree line to escape the Arctic winter.
4. Arctic birds generally lay ▨▨▨▨▨▨ eggs than their southern relatives.
5. The most common tundra animals are ▨▨▨▨▨▨ , ▨▨▨▨▨▨ , and ▨▨▨▨▨▨▨ .
6. The most critical animal in the tundra food web is the ▨▨▨▨ .
7. Arctic homes can be built on ▨▨▨▨▨ to prevent thermokarst.

C. Multiple Choice

Each of the following statements or questions is followed by four responses. Choose the correct response in each case. (Do not write in this book.)
1. Which one of the following best describes the tundra climate?
   a) cold, windy and dry   **c)** cold, calm and dry
   b) cold, windy and wet   **d)** cold, calm and wet
2. The soggy soil which covers low areas of the tundra is best called a
   a) marsh   **c)** muskeg
   b) swamp   **d)** thermokarst
3. Which statement below is the best description of permafrost?
   a) a solid chunk of ice under the soil
   b) frozen, heaving soil containing chunks of ice
   c) a solid chunk of frozen soil
   d) a large solid mass of frozen soil containing chunks of ice
4. A fire in the tundra can seriously affect caribou numbers because
   a) it blocks migration routes
   b) it burns vegetation among which the caribou hide for protection from wolves
   c) many die as they attempt to outrun the fire
   d) the fire destroys lichens, the main food of caribou
5. A vehicle path in the tundra gradually changed into a deep gully. The main cause was likely
   a) destruction of the vegetation cover
   b) compaction of the soil
   c) a decrease in the depth of the active layer
   d) excessive ice in the permafrost

Using Your Knowledge

1. What major problems would a gardener face trying to grow vegetables in the Arctic during the summer?
2. Why is muskeg important to Arctic vegetation?
3. Why is tundra soil nutrient-deficient?
4. Why are reptiles and amphibians rare in the Arctic?
5. As the world's population grows, more and more food is needed. Is farming the tundra feasible? Could grains, developed for a short growing season, be successfully grown in the Arctic? What problems do you foresee? Discuss them.
6. Design an "ideal" Arctic mammal. Describe its shape, size, body covering, and other special adaptations.
7. a) Make a list of the ecological problems which can result from careless exploration for and extraction of Arctic resources.
   b) Propose ways of avoiding these problems and defend your ideas.
8. Suppose you found it necessary to travel over the tundra using a vehicle.
   a) Describe the vehicle you would use to lessen the chances of thermokarst occurring.
   b) When would you do your travelling? Why?
9. a) What benefits will increased tourism bring to Arctic communities?
   b) What harm could increased tourism do to Arctic communities and their surrounding environments?

Investigations

1. a) Find out what oil and gas pipelines now exist in Alaska and northern Canada.
   b) What pipelines are proposed for the future?
   c) Give your opinion of these proposals.
2. Find out all you can about the James Bay power project. It is guided by the James Bay Energy Corporation, a division of Hydro Québec. How extensive a land area does it cover? How were Native people affected? Just exactly what did the project do? Why was the project undertaken? What ecological damage, if any, did it do? What benefits does it bring to the residents of Québec, Canadians as a whole, and Americans?
3. Snow geese are important to tundra vegetation. Nutrients leach from the land into ponds and lakes. The snow geese return these nutrients to the land. Find out how they do this.
4. Research travel arrangements for a trip to Inuvik from your home. What is the cost? How long is the trip? What is the route? What will food and accommodation cost per day?

9 The Boreal Coniferous Forest Biome

South of the Arctic tundra is an **ecotone**, or transition zone. Physical factors gradually change as one moves from north to south in this ecotone. For example, it becomes warmer and wetter. These changes are accompanied by a gradual change in vegetation and animal life. Clumps of dwarf trees, scattered in sheltered nooks, gradually increase in size and number. Finally one reaches a fairly distinct **tree line**. It marks the northern edge of the **boreal coniferous forest**. (**Boreal** means "northern" and **coniferous** means "cone-bearing".)

This vast forest stretches across North America, Europe, and Asia (see Figure 7-14, page 140). We will take a look at the features of the North American part. It stretches coast to coast, from Alaska to Newfoundland, in a belt that is 650-1300 km wide (see Figure 7-16, page 144). It is largely south of latitude 57° N. Most of it is in Canada. However Alaska is mainly boreal forest. And it extends south into northern areas of New York State and the New England states. A strip of boreal coniferous forest follows the high Appalachians south to North Carolina.

9.1 Abiotic Factors

Climate

This biome is closer to the equator than the tundra is. Therefore it receives more of the sun's radiant energy. As a result, average monthly temperatures are higher. They range from a winter low of –30°C to a summer high of

20°C. In other words, some winter days can be bitterly cold. And some summer days can be surprisingly hot. The growing season is longer than in the tundra. It varies from 60 d in the north to 150 d in parts of the south.

Winters are not as long or as severe as those in the tundra. But snowfall is heavier. The total annual precipitation is greater than that of the tundra but is fairly low in some places. It varies from about 50 to 125 cm. Summer rains provide most of this moisture.

Light

Summer days are shorter but warmer and brighter than further north. Unlike the tundra, most of this biome does not have 24 h of daylight in the summer and 24 h of darkness in the winter. On the average, then, the light intensity is higher and the photoperiod shorter than in the tundra.

Soil

Permafrost extends south into the northern parts of the boreal forest. But, in general, the soil thaws completely during the spring and summer. Even where permafrost exists, the active layer is much deeper than in the tundra. Trees cannot grow where the active layer is less than 45 cm deep. But stunted black spruce trees grow where the active layer is from 45-120 cm deep. Mature black spruce are joined by white spruce and poplars where the active layer is deeper than 120 cm.

Centuries ago a massive glacier, thousands of metres thick, covered the boreal coniferous region. This ice sheet scraped away topsoil and gouged out countless depressions in the land. It then deposited loose rock and earth as it melted. The depressions filled with water. This activity formed the endless pattern of lakes, swamps, and bogs which runs among the trees (Fig. 9-1). The Soviets call the boreal forest the taiga, meaning "swamp forest".

The shifting ice cover altered the surface features. In doing so, it hampered the formation of an effective river drainage system. Thus water does not drain off readily. As well, the cold air reduces evaporation. Therefore most of the water stays in the soil. As a result, boreal forest soil in lower areas is usually waterlogged. Furthermore, this trapped water tends to turn acidic as organic matter in it decays.

In this cold, wet, acidic soil, earthworms are rare. The action of bacteria is slowed down. The most effective decomposers of organic matter are fungi. But they too operate slowly in this environment. As a result, conifer needles and other organic matter decompose slowly. Partly decayed organic matter called peat accumulates. Water, percolating through the peat, becomes acidic. This acidic water leaches plant nutrients from the soil. Among them are important nutrients such as nitrogen, potassium, calcium, and iron. This leaves a grey, acidic, nutrient-deficient topsoil called a podsol, from a Russian word meaning "ashes".

Fig. 9-1 The boreal forest is dotted with lakes, swamps, and bogs.

Section Review

1. Describe the ecotone between the Arctic tundra and the boreal coniferous forest.
2. **a)** What is meant by "tree line"?
   b) What does "boreal coniferous forest" mean?
3. **a)** Describe the location of the boreal forest over the earth.
   b) Describe the location of the boreal forest in North America.
4. Describe how the boreal forest differs from the Arctic tundra with respect to each of the following:
   a) average monthly temperatures
   b) length of growing season
   c) duration of sunlight throughout the seasons
   d) intensity of sunlight
   e) depth of snowfall
   f) total annual precipitation
5. **a)** Why did the boreal forest form where it did in North America?
   b) Why does the boreal forest contain numerous lakes, swamps, and bogs?
   c) Why do the Soviets call the boreal forest "taiga"?
6. Why do the lakes of the boreal forest tend to be acidic?
7. **a)** What is peat?
   b) Why does peat form in the boreal forest?
8. **a)** Describe the soil of the boreal forest.
   b) Explain how the soil got these characteristics.

9.2

Biotic Factors: Vegetation

Conifers: The Dominant Vegetation

Coniferous trees, or conifers, dominate the boreal forest. All but one of these cone-bearing species are evergreen. That is, they keep their needles (leaves) during the winter. The tamarack, or larch, is deciduous. It drops its needles just before winter (Fig.9-2). It may interest you to know that evergreens *do* drop their needles. But they do so a few at a time throughout the year. They also grow new needles each spring. Therefore the trees have needles all the time.

Figure 9-3 shows a closer view of the boreal forest than you saw in Figure 9-1. Almost all the trees in this photograph are conifers called spruce trees. The ones with the knobby tops are black spruce. The others are white spruce. These two species dominate much of the boreal forest. If you try to walk through this forest, you will have some problems. Except around lakes and in harvested or recently burned areas, the trees are very close together (Fig. 9-4). Also, deadfalls (fallen trees) will block your path. And you will have to walk on a deep carpet of spongy moss (Fig. 9-5).

Fig. 9-2 The same tamarack (American larch) was photographed in the early spring and in the summer.

Fig. 9-3 A closer look at the boreal coniferous forest. In this area, spruce trees dominate. Note the bog at the near end of the lake. The acidic water in the lake helped form it.

Fig. 9-4   Inside the boreal coniferous forest. Note the close spacing of the trees, the deadfalls, and the carpet of sphagnum moss.

Fig. 9-5   Much of the forest floor is covered with sphagnum moss. It forms a deep mat in low wet areas. It thrives in acidic conditions.

At first glance, the boreal forest looks monotonous—wall-to-wall conifers on a carpet of sphagnum moss. But a closer look reveals a wider variety of both vegetation and animals than exists in the tundra. Yet the somewhat harsh climate restricts the variety to fewer species than one finds in warmer areas. However, like Arctic species, the species living in the boreal forest have striking adaptations.

Tree Species in the Boreal Forest

The tree species present vary from place to place in this biome (Fig. 9-6). In much of the vast northern section from Alaska to Newfoundland, the dominant species are black spruce, white spruce, and balsam fir. The tamarack, or American larch, is found in moist areas. The same species dominate the forests of the Adirondacks and White Mountains in the north-east United States. Red pine, white pine, eastern hemlock, and white cedar are characteristic of the Great Lakes region.

The peaks of the southern Appalachians are marked by Fraser fir and red spruce (Fig. 9-7). The highest peaks occur in the Smoky Mountains of Tennessee and North Carolina. Here the higher peaks reach elevations of about 2000 m. This is the only place Fraser fir lives in all of North America. Red spruce also occurs along the St. Lawrence River valley and in the Maritime provinces. But they grow much larger in the Smoky Mountains because of the heavier precipitation there (Fig. 9-8).

Jack pine is common in dry and burned areas. Its dominance in burned areas is largely due to the structure of its cone (Fig. 9-9). The cone will

Red pine

White pine

Hemlock

White cedar

Tamarack

White spruce

Black spruce

Balsam fir

Jack pine

Fig. 9-6   The most common trees of the boreal coniferous forest.

Fig. 9-7   This view from Clingman's Dome in Smoky Mountains National Park shows the blanket of Fraser fir and red spruce which covers the higher peaks.

Fig. 9-8   The Smoky Mountains receive abundant precipitation. As a result, all trees, like this red spruce, grow larger than in other regions.

Fig. 9-9 The jack pine cone usually remains tightly closed. Dry conditions or a forest fire can cause it to open.

generally not open to release seeds until after a forest fire. A forest fire may burn all the trees and seedlings in an area. But after the fire has passed, jack pine cones release seeds. These seeds germinate and colonize the area with jack pine. Because of this behaviour, jack pine is called a fire successional species.

Certain hardwoods (deciduous trees) also invade burned and harvested areas of this biome. The common ones are white birch, poplars (trembling aspen and balsam poplar), and alders. Hardwoods are also common on the moist soil of riverbanks and wet valleys.

The low winter temperature slows down tree growth throughout most of this biome. Despite this the boreal forest of North America is very productive. In fact, it ranks high among the great wood-producing regions of the world.

Adaptations of Conifers

Plants of the boreal forest must cope with poor soil, low temperatures, and limited precipitation. The soil contains enough water to support tree growth. But it is frozen during much of the year. Humidity is often low, both summer and winter. Therefore, boreal vegetation must be able to tolerate long dormant periods when water is not available. And it must be able to use any available moisture to full advantage.

Conifers thrive in this environment because they are well adapted to dry conditions. Their leaves are modified into needles or scales. The reduced surface area lessens water loss by evaporation. Also, these leaves are covered with a thick cuticle. This waxy skin greatly reduces water loss through evaporation. And the stomata, or breathing pores, of many conifers are located in a groove on the underside of the needle. The needles can also withstand freezing. This, too, helps reduce water loss by evaporation.

The slope and structure of conifers are ideally suited for northern winters (Fig. 9-10). Snow can often crush a tree. But large masses of snow cannot collect easily on the small surface area provided by needles. Further, conifer branches are quite flexible. They tend to bend when snow builds up. And clumps of snow slide down the sloping boughs. Freezing rain and wet snow can, however, cling to the needles and branches. And this can do considerable damage to the trees.

The northern summer provides the warmth, sunlight, and moisture needed for tree growth. This summer is too brief for most deciduous trees, however. They would lose more stored energy when their large leaves were shed in the fall than they could replace in the short growing season. Moreover, deciduous leaves decay quickly. Therefore plant nutrients released during decay would be leached from the soil before the trees could absorb them in the spring.

The summer is not too brief for conifers, however. All conifers but the larch (tamarack) are evergreens. They keep their needles during the winter.

Fig. 9-10 This spruce tree has flexible branches. Therefore snow slides off before it gets heavy enough to break the branches.

Dead needles are gradually shed throughout the year. They are replaced during spring growth. The needles have a high resin content and thick cuticle (outer covering). These resist the action of decomposers (bacteria and fungi). Therefore fallen needles decay slowly. By not losing too many leaves at once, conifers conserve energy and nutrients. Also, they are ready to photosynthesize whenever conditions permit. Measurable photosynthesis occurs in conifers at temperatures as low as $-6°$C. Even at that low temperature enough photosynthesis occurs to replace food reserves used in respiration.

Conifers have a further defence against the rigours of the north. If the bark is damaged, a sticky resin quickly covers the wound. It helps prevent attack by bacteria and fungi.

Other Vegetation in the Boreal Forest

The conifers form a dense canopy all year round. Thus little light reaches the forest floor. Most ferns and mosses thrive in low light conditions. Therefore they are abundant in the boreal forest (Fig. 9-11). One particular moss, sphagnum moss, grows in great abundance in the acidic soil of the boreal forest (see Figure 9-5). Lichens also do well in the boreal forest environment. In fact, in many places dense masses of lichens hang from the conifers (Fig.9-12). They also cover rocks and live among the mosses on the ground (Fig.9-13).

Fig. 9-11 Ferns and mosses thrive in the boreal forest.

Fig. 9-12 This lichen, Old man's beard, hangs from spruce trees and other conifers in much of the boreal forest.

Fig. 9-13 *Cladonia* is called reindeer moss. But it is a lichen, not a moss. It is common in the boreal forest where it is a favourite food of caribou. They paw down through the snow to reach it.

Fig. 9-14 Three common flowering plants of the boreal forest.

Bunchberry   Blueberry

Fig. 9-15 Mushrooms are important decomposers in the boreal forest. This one is *Amanita virosa*, the "destroying angel". Members of the genus *Amanita* are common in the boreal forest. And they are very poisonous.

Figure 9-14 shows three common flowering plants of the boreal forest. These plants prefer shade and acidic soil. All three produce berries. The berries are important food for many birds and mammals.

Fungi are vital decomposers of the boreal forest. Over 100 000 km of hyphae (the thread-like "roots" of fungi) may weave through just one cubic metre of soil! They break down the dead needles and absorb them for food. Many of these hyphae belong to mushrooms. The caps, or fruiting bodies, of the mushrooms are a common sight on the forest floor (Fig. 9-15).

Section Review

1. **a)** What is a conifer?
   b) What is the difference between an evergreen and a deciduous conifer?
   c) Name the only deciduous conifer in the boreal forest.
2. Name the conifers which dominate each of the following regions of the boreal forest:
   a) the vast northern part from Alaska to Newfoundland
   b) the Adirondacks and White Mountains
   c) the Great Lakes region
   d) the high peaks of the southern Appalachians

3. Why is jack pine called a fire successional species?
4. Name three hardwoods which invade open areas of the boreal forest.
5. a) State three problems faced by boreal plants.
   b) Describe six features of conifers that enable them to live in the boreal forest.
   c) Give two reasons why deciduous trees are not suited to this region.
6. a) Describe two factors which limit the types of vegetation that can grow on the boreal forest floor.
   b) Why do mosses and ferns thrive in the boreal forest?
   c) Why is sphagnum moss the most common boreal moss?
7. a) Name five flowering plants of the boreal forest.
   b) Of what ecological importance are these plants?

Identifying Conifers of the Boreal Forest

9.3   *ACTIVITY*

Some conifers, like white pine and white spruce, are used for lumber. Others, like black spruce and balsam fir, are used to make wood pulp. Still others are used to landscape homes and parks, and for erosion control. And most conifers provide excellent habitats and food for birds, squirrels, and other wildlife. In short, conifers are very important, both ecologically and economically. Can you identify these important trees?

For this activity your teacher has brought in twigs from several conifers. Where possible, these twigs bear cones. You are to use the following key to identify these conifers. The key contains most of the common boreal forest species. It also contains a few commonly planted non-native species.

If you don't live in an area with boreal forest trees, your teacher will provide a key for the conifers of your area. Then you can still practise identifying conifers.

Fig. 9-16   Some conifers have needle-like leaves.

Fig. 9-17   Some conifers have scale-like leaves that hide the twigs.

Key to the Conifers of the Boreal Forest

A   Leaves needle-like, not hiding twig (see Fig. 9-16)
- Leaves in bundles → B
- Leaves single → BB

AA   Leaves scale-like, hiding twig (see Fig. 9-17)
- Twigs leaf-covered and flat → White cedar
- Twigs leaf-covered and rounded → Eastern red cedar

B   Leaves (needles) in bundles
- Deciduous; 10-50 needles per bundle → C
- Evergreen; 2-5 needles per bundle → D (pine)

C   Deciduous
- Cones 1 cm long → Tamarack (American larch)
- Cones 2-5 cm long → European larch

D   Pine
- 5 leaves per bundle → White pine
- 2-3 leaves per bundle → E

E   2-3 leaves per bundle
- 3 leaves per bundle → Pitch pine
- 2 leaves per bundle → F

F   2 leaves per bundle
- Leaves usually under 5 cm long → G
- Leaves usually over 5 cm long → Red pine

G   Leaves usually under 5 cm long
- Leaves 2-5 cm; cones curved; mature cones often closed → Jack pine
- Leaves 4-5 cm; bluish green and twisted; young bark orangish-red; mature cones usually open → Scots pine

BB   Leaves single
- Leaves 2-sided (flat) → H
- Leaves 4-sided → CC (spruce)

H   Leaves 2-sided (flat)
- Leaves with stalk → I
- Leaves stalkless → Balsam fir

I   Leaves with stalk
- A shrub; leaves pointed at top, yellow-green above & pale green below → Canada yew
- A tree; leaves rounded at tip; many lengths of leaves on same twig → Hemlock

CC   Leaves 4-sided (spruce)
- Leaves green → J
- Leaves silvery-blue, sharp & very stiff → Blue spruce

```
                              Leaves roll easily          ──→ K
                              between fingers; cones
                              2-5 cm long
      J    Leaves green   <
                              Leaves slightly flattened;   ──→ Norway spruce
                              do not roll easily;
                              cones 10-15 cm long

                              Cones 2-4 cm long;          ──→ Black spruce
                              twigs with dense short
                              hairs; not common in
                              Southern Ontario
      K    Leaves roll easily; <  Cones 4-5 cm long;      ──→ White spruce
           cones 2-5 cm long     twigs usually hairless

                              Cones 2-5 cm long; twigs    ──→ Red spruce
                              orangeish-brown, with
                              dense short hairs; scales
                              on terminal buds
                              sometimes longer than
                              buds
```

9.4 *ACTIVITY* Adaptations of Conifers

Conifers of the boreal forest must be able to cope with several environmental factors. Among these are poor soil, low temperatures, and limited precipitation. You read in Section 9.2 how conifers, in general, are adapted to cope with such factors. In this activity you will find out how one particular conifer has adapted.

Problem

How has a conifer adapted to cope with environmental factors in your area?

Materials

notebook	conifer (growing)
pen	hand lens
probe	dissecting microscope (optional)

Procedure

Note: Read Sections 9.1 and 9.2 carefully before you begin this procedure. They contain information which will help you decide what to look for in this activity.

a. Select a conifer growing in your area. Identify it using the key in Section 9.3 or a key provided by your teacher.

b. Make a list of the main environmental stresses which could affect the tree. Consider soil, temperature, wind, moisture, and light factors.

c. Copy Table 9-1 into your notebook. List in the first column structural features of the tree *as a whole* which help it cope with environmental stresses. This could include factors such as shape, size, and flexibility of branches.

d. Describe in the second column how each of the features helps the tree survive.

e. Remove a few needles from the tree. Examine these closely with a hand lens and, if possible, a dissecting microscope. Look for adaptations which help the tree cope with the environmental stresses. Add these to your table. Then complete the second column for each adaptation.

Table 9-1 Adaptations of Conifers

Adaptation	Benefit of adaptation
Branches slope down and out	Snow slides off easily

Discussion

1. Could the tree you selected cope with conditions at the northern edge of the boreal forest? Give your reasons.

2. Which of the adaptations you noted would you probably *not* see on a conifer growing in the tropical rain forest? Why?

3. Which of the adaptations you noted would probably be more noticeable on a conifer growing in a semi-arid climate? Why?

9.5   Biotic Factors: Animals

Hare, Lynx, and Wolverine

Animals of the boreal forest have adapted in structure and behaviour to several environmental factors. Among these are the long cold winter, a thick blanket of snow, and frozen ground. Foxes, wolves, and moose are common in the boreal forest. They remain active even when the temperature dips to –45°C. They can do this because they develop a thick winter fur. The snowshoe hare is also well adapted (Fig. 9-18). It turns white for camouflage. And it travels about on built-in "snowshoes"—large tufts of fur that cover its feet.

Fig. 9-18 The snowshoe hare is a key link in the boreal forest food web.

Fig. 9-19 The lynx, a cat of the boreal forest.

Like the lemming of the tundra, the snowshoe hare plays a major role in the boreal forest food web. It eats grasses, mosses, and herbs, as do most of the other herbivores. A single doe can produce five yearly litters of three to four young. Not all of these survive, of course. But a ten-year period can still result in as many as 1500 hares for every square kilometre of forest. Predators such as weasels, hawks, and owls raise large families during this time of plenty. Suddenly, however, the hare population crashes. Factors such as competition for food, increased predation, and the stress of overcrowding are possible causes. Now predator numbers also decrease. Of all the predators, the **lynx** is most heavily hit (Fig. 9-19). In some parts of North America, the hare provides 70% of its diet. The lynx will travel long distances to seek other prey such as squirrels and grouse. But it is still largely dependent on the hare. As a result, its cycle trails closely behind the ten-year cycle of the hare (Fig. 9-20).

Fig. 9-20 Snowshoe hare populations peak every 10-11 years. Then they fall sharply. Records kept by the Hudson Bay Company many years ago show that lynx populations have corresponding fluctuations.

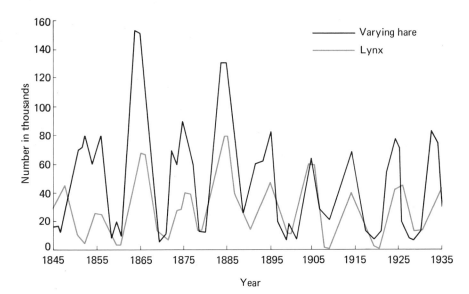

The **wolverine** is another predator of the snowshoe hare (Fig. 9-21). It is the swiftest mammal in the forest during the winter. Spreading toes let this stealthy hunter chase prey over deep snow without sinking. The photograph shows the powerful legs which give the wolverine its speed. The wolverine is a true wilderness animal and generally avoids people.

Fig. 9-21 The wolverine has an enormous appetite. As a result, it has the common name "glutton".

Moose

Like spruce trees, **moose** are a symbol of the boreal forest (Fig. 9-22). In fact, this biome is often called the "moose-spruce biome". Moose wade through wetlands and snow as deep as one metre on stilt-like legs. Moose are normally solitary. But in the winter they gather. Then, as a group, they trample the snow into "yards". Now they can more easily reach tree shoots, twigs, and brushwood below. They even pack snow into mounds so they can reach twigs on branches above. A grown moose must eat 3600-4500 kg of vegetation to live through a boreal winter. Starving moose will even chew conifer bark. By spring, the hungry survivors are thin from their winter ordeal. But they soon gain weight by browsing on aquatic plants in lakes and marshes.

Fig. 9-22 The moose, symbol of the boreal forest, is the largest of all deer species.

Timber Wolf

Wherever there are moose, there are usually wolves. A wolf's unmistakable howl can send chills up your spine on a quiet dark evening. Yet to those who love the northern woods, this call is a symbol of true wilderness. The **timber**

Fig. 9-23 The timber wolf, an important carnivore of the boreal forest.

or gray wolf is the largest of our wild dogs (Fig. 9-23). This predator ranges over a territory which can be over 100 km in diameter. It feeds on almost anything it can catch. Birds and small mammals make up much of its prey at times. But it also preys on large mammals like moose and caribou.

No animal has been more persecuted by humans than the wolf. There are three reasons for this. First, childhood stories and myths (the "big bad wolf") have created a fear of and hatred for this animal. Second, when human settlements invade wolf territory, wolves do kill some livestock. Third, and most important today, wolves prey on large game mammals such as deer, moose, caribou, and bighorn sheep. And so do humans. Humans hunt these animals for food, trophies, and the challenge of the kill. Wolves hunt them for food. Between them, humans and wolves have seriously lowered the numbers of large game mammals in some areas. In fact, the numbers are too low to meet the needs and wants of both wolves and humans. When another animal competes with humans for the same resource, it seldom wins! Indeed, wolves have, in the past, been deliberately exterminated in some areas. Even today, wolves are "managed" in some parts of North America. They are being killed to help species like bighorn sheep and moose increase in numbers. Yet, at the same time, humans continue to kill these species. Those who manage game populations have made a decision: It is more important for humans to have big game to kill than it is for some wolves to live and kill the same game. What do you think of this decision?

Some Small Herbivores

Air spaces trapped in plant undergrowth between the snow and soil create a microclimate. Here the temperature seldom drops more than one or two degrees below freezing. Here lemmings, voles, and other rodents are active all winter long (Fig. 9-24). They feed on grasses, mosses, herbs, and the bark of shrubs and tree saplings. Shrews also live in this habitat during the winter. Due to its high metabolic rate, a shrew must eat constantly to survive. A person with a matching appetite would have to eat 230 kg of food daily!

Chattering red squirrels often shatter the silence of the winter forest (Fig. 9-25). Their main food is conifer seeds. They obtain these by stripping off the scales of the cones. This activity is very time-consuming. A squirrel may work away at over 200 cones but end up with less than 15 g of seeds. When the cone harvest is poor, these animals eat conifer buds instead. This, of course, can seriously affect the growth of the trees.

Porcupines also inhabit the boreal forest (Fig.9-26). These heavy-bodied clumsy animals may be seen lumbering along the forest floor. More likely, though, they will be seen rolled up into a large black ball in the upper branches of a tree. They climb awkwardly. But they are more at home in the branches of a tree than on the ground. They are nocturnal (most active at night). Strong, curved claws help porcupines climb to the upper branches. There they feed on small twigs, buds, and the inner bark of trees. When you

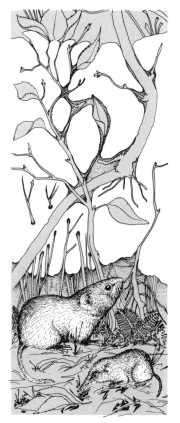

Fig. 9-24 The tiny shrew collects dormant insects from the soil litter. The larger rodent is a vole. It feeds on vegetation. Both live in an airspace beneath a blanket of snow.

Fig. 9-25 The red squirrel is a common mammal of the boreal forest.

Fig. 9-26 The porcupine is common throughout the boreal forest.

see trees with the upper branches debarked, you know porcupines are around. Porcupines fear few predators, since they are protected by a layer of quills. However, some predators, such as the wolverine, have learned how to carefully roll the porcupine over and attack its unprotected belly. Porcupines love salt. They can often be seen at night licking salt from roadsides in areas where salt is used to melt ice on roads. Experienced woodcutters know that you never leave your axe outside in porcupine territory. The porcupine will gnaw on the handle just to get the salt your hands left on it!

Some Small Carnivores

The smaller carnivores of the boreal forest—minks, martens, weasels, and wolverines—all belong to the weasel family. They prey on rabbits, rodents, birds, and insects. They will also eat most other types of food when the need arises. Prey in the boreal forest is widely scattered. Therefore these carnivores claim unusually large hunting territories. One short-tailed weasel may range over an area of 35 ha (350 000 m²). The larger wolverine is chiefly a scavenger. It feeds on animals which other carnivores kill. But it does not wait until its host has completed its meal. Instead, this aggressive and vicious animal will challenge even a bear or wolf for a fresh kill—and win!

Members of the weasel family do not hibernate. Instead, they grow thick protective coats. Their coats have lured trappers since the earliest settlements. Weasels are the only carnivores in the boreal forest which turn white in the winter. The short-tailed weasel keeps the black tip on its tail. In its winter robe it is better known as an ermine (Fig. 9-27).

Hibernating Mammals

The woodchuck is one of the few hibernating animals (Fig. 9-28). This herbivore is also called a groundhog or marmot. It feeds mainly during the

Fig. 9-27 The short-tailed weasel is called an ermine when its red-brown summer coat turns to winter white.

Fig. 9-28 The woodchuck or groundhog. Though it is a herbivore, it aggressively defends its territory when predators invade it.

Fig. 9-29 The eastern chipmunk is a common mammal of eastern parts of the boreal forest. The least chipmunk is widely spread through central and western regions.

day on succulent vegetation. In farming areas it selects crops such as alfalfa and clover for food. Therefore, farmers consider it a costly pest. It dens in a burrow which may be up to 2 m deep and 10 m long. The openings to these burrows are common sights on hillsides in the boreal forest. They are also seen in fields cleared for farming. There they can cause broken legs among livestock. In agricultural areas, then, they are a pest. But in wilderness areas they play an important ecological role. They are food for a wide variety of predators. And, when they are killed, their burrows become refuges and homes for other animals.

A woodchuck may "sleep" for as long as eight months in its burrow. During this period, its metabolism is reduced to the minimum needed to keep body cells alive. The heartbeat rate, normally 200 beats/min, drops to a mere 4-5 beats/min. The woodchuck may breathe only twice a minute. And stored body fat is consumed very slowly. As a result, body temperature falls. However, if the outside temperature drops too much, the animal awakens. And activity is resumed for a few hours to restore normal circulation.

Chipmunks also hibernate. But they wake up at intervals to feed on stored nuts and other seeds. The "chuck-chuck-chuck" call of the eastern chipmunk is often heard before the animal is seen (Fig. 9-29). This tiny member of the squirrel family is a real attraction around campgrounds. It feeds on fruits, nuts, seeds, insects, and bulbs. It, in turn, is preyed upon by hawks, owls, and some mammalian predators.

Bears

Two species of bear inhabit the boreal forest. Grizzly bears are found only in western regions, including Alaska, the Yukon, and the Northwest Territories. The black bear, however, is much more common (Fig. 9-30). It lives in all parts of the boreal forest. With a mass of 90-225 kg it is a large mammal. But it is also the smallest bear in North America. Though classified as a car-

Fig. 9-30 The black bear is in the order Carnivora, which means "flesh-eater". But it is better called an omnivore.

nivore, it is best called an omnivore. It dines much of the year on berries, nuts, roots, and honey. It does eat animals, however. It digs up insects and their larva. It eats small mammals like chipmunks when it can catch them. It also eats the remains of dead animals. And, of course, it loves human garbage! It is important to keep campsites free of garbage. Bears and humans cannot mix for long without one or the other being harmed.

Bears den under fallen trees, in hollow logs and trees, and under overhanging boulders. They semi-hibernate in the winter in northern parts of their range. Their body temperatures drop only slightly during this period. And their breathing rates also decrease just a little. Therefore they are not true hibernators.

Insects

As in the tundra, the most common animals are insects. Hordes of black flies, mosquitoes, and deer flies attack anything with blood! They rule the boreal forest in the summer. Large mammals are driven to distraction by these insects. Moose escape from time to time by submerging in lakes and marshes.

Few insect species can feed on conifers. But every part of a conifer can be attacked by some type of insect. Forest areas dominated by just one or two tree species can be wiped out by insect attacks. Outbreaks of spruce budworm and larch sawfly have destroyed vast tracts of boreal forest. For example, large parts of Cape Breton in Nova Scotia have been completely denuded by spruce budworm. These insect herbivores graze on conifer needles. But other insects—bark beetles, wood borers, and long-horned beetles—damage the bark of trees.

Insects have two main seasons. The summer season is a short but active period of feeding and reproduction. The winter season is a long dormant period. During it the insects live as larvas or pupas in bark crevices and in the soil.

Birds

Small birds called warblers are common in the boreal forest in the summer. They feed largely on the abundant insects. Then they migrate south for the winter. But woodpeckers, chickadees, and a few other species continue to feed on insects during the winter. They seek out the larvas and pupas hidden in bark crevices. And, as well, woodpeckers dig deep into dead wood for further insect larvas and pupas.

The choice of food in the coniferous forest is greatly limited, regardless of the season. After insects, the only other major source of food for birds is the conifers themselves. And both the seeds and needles of the conifers are eaten by birds. Only about 50 species of birds can feed on the tough resinous conifers. Most of these, such as the evening grosbeak, are seed-eaters. These birds have strong jaw muscles. These muscles control short, sturdy beaks

Fig. 9-31 Note the strong beak of the grosbeak.

Fig. 9-32 The crossbill has a strong curved beak for cutting through the tough cone scales. The upper and lower parts of the beak cross over one another. This helps the bird flick the scales apart. Then its long tongue reaches inside to get the seeds.

Fig. 9-33 The spruce grouse eats only the needles of mature spruce trees.

with sharp cutting edges (Fig. 9-31). These beaks easily crack open seeds found in the forest.

The beak of the red crossbill is especially adapted for extracting seeds from cones (Fig. 9-32). These birds hang from any angle on the twigs while their beaks and tongues rapidly gather seeds. The red crossbill has adapted to the problems of the boreal forest in other ways as well. When the parent is away from the nest gathering food, the baby crossbills get very cold. (Spring in the boreal forest is cold.) To survive this cold, the baby crossbills lapse into a coma. They revive as soon as the parent returns and warms the nest.

The winter diet of the blue grouse consists chiefly of conifer needles. These have a low nutrient content. Therefore, to survive on this food, the blue grouse must eat from morning till night. The spruce grouse feeds only on the needles of mature spruce trees (Fig. 9-33). One bird may spend days robbing a single tree of its needles. Grouse chicks feed on insect pupas. They cannot live more than a few hours without this food. They seek food on their own. These fragile balls of fluff often starve on cold wet days. In such conditions they cannot leave the protective warmth of the hen to find food. If they do, they die from exposure.

The birds of prey which patrol the forest sky include owls, hawks, falcons, ospreys, and eagles. These birds have many special adaptations. The most important of these are keen vision, sharp curved claws, and a strong hooked beak (Fig. 9-34). Owls are silent night hunters. They use sensitive hearing to detect the activity of small birds and rodents. Owls have the widest field of binocular vision of all the birds of prey. Some can spot objects in light 100 times less intense than humans require. Hawks, falcons, ospreys and eagles hunt by day. They usually hunt in clearings and along the forest edge. Their large wingspan makes flying difficult in dense forest. Some of the hawks are best adapted to hunt near trees. Their rounded wings enable them to hover and then turn sharply to catch birds flushed from treetops.

Fig. 9-34 This keen-eyed hunter has sharp claws for grasping prey and a strong hooked beak for tearing meat.

Forest Sounds

You have seen how forest animals have many adaptations to their habitats. One adaptation, however, has not yet been mentioned. But you would certainly notice it if you visited the forest in the spring or summer. It is a well-developed vocal system. In a habitat where trees limit visibility, vision is often a secondary sense. Animals rely more on sounds. Therefore they tend to have well-developed vocal and hearing systems. During nesting season, the air is vibrant with bird songs. The sounds of squirrels, chipmunks, and wolves echo through the trees. And the evening throbs with the calls of frogs and insects. Most of this "music" is made to attract mates and to proclaim territorial limits. But to most human listeners, it conveys the magic and mystery of the northern woods.

Section Review

1. Name three major environmental factors with which boreal forest animals must cope.
2. a) Describe how the snowshoe hare and wolverine have adapted to winter in the boreal forest.
   b) Describe how the snowshoe hare population affects the numbers of predators.
   c) Which predator is affected most? Why?
3. Describe how moose have adapted to winter in the boreal forest.
4. a) What are the main prey of the timber wolf?
   b) Why are wolves persecuted by humans?
5. a) What is the main food of red squirrels in the boreal forest?
   b) Describe how porcupines have adapted to life in the boreal forest.
6. a) Name four of the smaller carnivores of the boreal forest.
   b) How is the short-tailed weasel adapted to winter in the boreal forest?
7. a) Describe the niche of the woodchuck.
   b) Describe a hibernating woodchuck.
8. a) Describe the niche of the chipmunk.
   b) How does its hibernation differ from that of a woodchuck?
9. a) What does a black bear eat?
   b) Why do we say that a black bear "semi-hibernates"?
10. a) Which insects dominate the boreal forest in summer?
    b) Name two insect species which destroy boreal trees.
11. a) What are the two major sources of food for birds in the boreal forest?
    b) How are the evening grosbeak and red crossbill adapted for feeding on conifer seeds?
    c) Why do blue grouse have to eat almost continuously during the day?
    d) Name three adaptations of birds of prey.
    e) Why are well-developed hearing and vocal systems an advantage to forest animals?

9.6 Human Impact on the Boreal Forest

Fig. 9-35 Trees like this white pine provide high quality lumber for home and furniture building.

Fig. 9-36 Accessible parts of the boreal forest are being used more and more by campers.

Overall Importance of Forests

Forests have long been a major resource in many countries on earth. They provide firewood for heating and cooking. They produce lumber for building homes and furniture (Fig. 9-35). They are a source of pulpwood for making paper. They yield foods such as fruits, nuts, and sugars. And, recently, they have become popular places for recreation—camping, hiking, and nature walks (Fig.9-36).

Forests also help prevent rapid runoff of water. This, in turn, lessens soil erosion, helps prevent flooding, and helps keep water quality high in streams. And forests are the habitat for a wide variety of plants and animals. Forests also play a role in forming the microclimate of an area. In fact, large forested areas can greatly affect the climate of a whole continent and, perhaps, the entire earth.

Economic Importance of Forests

Forests are very important to the economy of both Canada and the United States. In 1985, for example, the forest industry contributed over $23 000 000 000 to the Canadian economy and $49 000 000 000 to the American economy. Canada has only one-tenth the population of the United States. Therefore forests play a greater role in the Canadian economy than in the American economy. Canada now produces about 14% of the world's timber and other forest products. This is the third largest share in the world. And Canada is the world's leading exporter of forest products. Much of this export goes to the United States. This provides Canada with $15 000 000 000 annual trade surplus. Over 250 000 000 trees are cut each year to keep Canada's forest industry going.

About 300 000 people are employed directly in the Canadian forest industry including loggers, sawmill workers, pulp and paper employees. Another 700 000 people have jobs that depend directly on the forest industry: newspaper employees, home builders, and furniture builders. Canada's population is near 25 000 000. Of this number, about 10 000 000 are employed (the rest are children and young adults still in school). Therefore, about one working Canadian in every 10 depends on forestry. In British Columbia this ratio jumps to one in every 4. As you can see, if the forest industry is in trouble, the national economy will suffer as well.

Present Condition of the World's Forests

Clearly, the earth's forests are important. But what condition are they in? As Table 9-2 shows, about one-third of the land area of the earth is forest. This is a generous figure, since it includes savanna and scrubland, where trees are few and scattered. Before humans began to exploit the forest, this figure probably stood at two-thirds.

These numerals are approximate, of course. No one knows exactly how fast forests are being cut on any particular continent. In fact, they are disappearing so fast in South America that some experts have put the USSR on the top of the list in Table 9-2.

Table 9-2 Forested Areas of the World

Location	Forested area (km²)	Total land area (%)
World	42 300 000	32
South America	9 600 000	47
USSR	9 200 000	41
Africa	8 300 000	27
North America	6 500 000	34
Asia (minus USSR)	5 100 000	29
Oceania & Australia	1 900 000	22
Europe (minus USSR)	1 800 000	36

Present Condition of Boreal Forests

The numerals in Table 9-2 include *all* forest types:
- boreal coniferous forest
- tropical rain forest
- savanna
- temperate deciduous forest
- warm temperate evergreen forest
- temperate rain forest
- mountain forest

As far as boreal forest is concerned, the USSR is the most important region on earth. About 78%, or 7 200 000 km², of that country's forest is boreal coniferous growth. This figure exceeds the total forested area of North America.

Some of North America's most productive boreal forest is in Maine and the northern parts of a few other states. And, of course, Alaska's forest is largely boreal. But the bulk of North America's boreal forest is in Canada. Of Canada's 3 417 000 km² of forest, about three-quarters is boreal.

The Canadian Situation   The seemingly endless supply of trees in Canada has encouraged over-exploitation and improper management. In fact, a Science Council of Canada report says that the forests have degenerated to a dangerous point. Wastage is great. One estimate suggests that to get the 250 000 000 trees marketed each year, over 3 000 000 000 are cut. In other

Fig. 9-37 Countless thousands of hectares of forest are destroyed each year by fires. What harm is done by fires? What benefits do they bring?

Fig. 9-38 This tree farm grows red pine trees. They can be thinned soon for pulpwood. Then, in another decade or two, they can be thinned for lumber.

words, only 1 of every 12 trees cut is used. The others are cut and left to rot. Perhaps they are too small, hard to get at, damaged, or not quite perfect. Regardless of the reason, the waste is great.

Fires destroy about six times more forest than loggers cut each year (Fig. 9-37). Careless users of the forest cause much of this loss through discarded cigarette butts and improperly set and extinguished campfires. Insect pests also cause great damage. In the 1970s the spruce budworm alone defoliated 75 000 000 ha (750 000 km²) of forest in Ontario, Québec, and the Maritimes. This area is almost equal to the land area of Ontario. And recent studies suggest that acid rain is affecting growth and regeneration of forests.

What Can Be Done? There are currently from 20 000 000-25 000 000 ha (200 000-250 000 km²) of logged but unreforested land in Canada. And Canada's forests are reduced a further 1 000 000 ha (10 000 km²) each year by poor management. This is an area about equal to the size of Prince Edward Island. A first step, then, is to replant more actively and effectively.

A second step is to reduce losses by fires. Prevention is much more effective than trying to put out fires once they start. You should know the fire regulations before beginning a camping trip in the forest. You should also know how to make a safe campfire. (Generally, the safest campfire is a small portable stove.) And people who must smoke should be *absolutely certain* that butts are extinguished.

A third step involves better pest control. Some pesticides seem to be effective against major insect pests. But they can also pollute streams, kill wildlife, and affect human health. The trend today is toward Integrated Pest Management. This method uses lower amounts of pesticide along with other control measures. Among these other methods are

- Thinning of the forests through controlled burning and cutting. Pests seem to thrive in the thick forests which have developed since forest fires have been better controlled.
- Development of resistant tree species. Cut areas of forests can be replanted using species which are resistant to major diseases.
- Biological controls. Forests are sprayed with bacteria, fungi, and other organisms which control the pests.

A fourth step is to recycle wood products such as newspapers. If we recycle, fewer trees will have to be cut from our forests. Finally, tree farms could be used to supply more of our pulpwood (Fig. 9-38). Species have been developed which are large enough to cut for pulpwood in about 5 years. These should be more actively planted as crops on marginal farmland.

Canada must move toward sustained yield forestry. In such forestry, the government and industry ensure that cut trees are replaced. Further, cutting is done in such a way that there will always be a supply of marketable trees. Overall, Canadian forest management techniques lag behind those of the United States, Sweden, and Norway. Sweden, for example, has only one-quarter of the forest land Canada has. But it produces two-thirds as much wood product. In recent years, Canada's share of the world pulp market has dropped from 70% to 30%. Clearly a strong effort is needed to revitalize the forest industry. This effort will have to be guided by well-trained foresters. Canada now has only one forester for every 500 000 ha of forest. This ratio is one for every 14 000 ha in countries like Sweden and Norway.

The American Situation   The overall forest situation is not quite so bleak in the United States. The forests of the United States were exploited long before Canada's. Therefore the need for conservation was recognized sooner. Also, outside Alaska, most American forests are not boreal. Because of a more favourable climate, these forests grow faster than boreal forest. Among them are the hardwood forests of the northeast, the pine-oak forests of the southeast, and the coniferous forests of the west coast.

Table 9-3 summarizes the history of American forests. Note that, after an all-time low in 1920, the area of forest has stayed constant. Yet the average American uses 272 kg of paper a year. This is four times more than was used in 1920. Note, too, that the population has doubled in that time. Today, about 25% of the continental United States is forested. When Alaska is included, the figure rises to about 35%.

Both the population and the per capita use of paper have increased. But the area of American forests has stayed constant. This is partly due to good forest management. But a major factor is that much of America's paper comes from Canada's boreal forest. Therefore, recycling paper in the United States could help conserve Canadian boreal forest. The average European uses only 61 kg a year. And the average Asian uses still less—10 kg a year. Why do North Americans use so much more?

Section Review

1. List eight reasons why forests are valuable.
2. **a)** Explain why forestry is so important to the Canadian economy.
    b) In what ways does Canada's forest industry affect the economy of the United States?
    c) How important is forestry to the American economy?
3. Describe the location of the boreal forest in North America.
4. Make a summary of the state of Canada's forests.
5. **a)** What is Integrated Pest Management?
    b) Why is it better than the use of pesticides alone?
    c) What is sustained yield forestry?
6. **a)** Make a summary of the state of the United States' forests.
    b) Give two reasons why American forests are overall in better shape than Canadian forests.

Table 9-3 History of American Forests

Approximate date	Forested area (km²)	Population	Effects on the forest
before 1600	4 200 000	about 1 000 000 Aboriginal Peoples	used for firewood and homes; in some cases large areas burned to drive out game
1700	4 150 000	1 250 000	European settlers began to arrive in 1607; forests cleared for agriculture, lumber, fuel; export of lumber began
1800	4 000 000	5 230 000	vast areas cleared for agriculture; wood shortages developed near cities; timber industry began to move west
1850	3 640 000	23 250 000	vast areas still lost to agriculture and harvesting; heavy losses during Civil War of the 1860s; conservation began; first National Park (Yellowstone) established in 1872; in 1898 Pinchot heads Forestry Division of Agriculture Department (became U.S. Forest Service); National Forests began
1900	3 240 000	76 000 000	virgin pine of east gone; timber industry moved south and then to far west
1920	2 460 000	107 000 000	forest reduced to lowest level by demands of World War I; fire control began; 120 000-160 000 km² burned each year
1940	3 120 000	132 000 000	total area began to increase; Civilian Conservation Corps planted 2 356 000 000 trees; depression encouraged farmers to move to cities; farms reverted to forest
1945	3 100 000	140 000 000	World War II placed extra demands on forests; western forests now supplied 55% of American lumber, south 35%, north 10%
1960	3 130 000	183 000 000	government and industry increased conservation efforts; amount cut now equalled amount grown; forest industry began to expand
1985	3 050 000	230 000 000	conservation efforts continue

Main Ideas

1. The boreal forest has more moderate temperatures and greater precipitation than the tundra.
2. The boreal forest soil contains a great deal of peat.
3. All conifers but the larch are evergreen.
4. The vast northern part of the boreal forest is dominated by black and white spruce, balsam fir, and tamarack.
5. Conifers have many adaptations to the boreal climate.
6. Sphagnum moss, lichens, and fungi live on the forest floor.
7. Animals of the boreal forest are well-adapted to their habitats.
8. The boreal forest is important to humans and to the ecology of the region.
9. The boreal forest is of great economic worth to Canada and the United States.
10. Conservation measures are necessary if the boreal forest is to continue to play a major role in the economy.

Key Terms

boreal	integrated pest management
coniferous	peat
deciduous	sustained yield forestry
ecotone	tree line
evergreen	

Chapter Review

A. True or False

Decide whether each of the following statements is true or false. If the sentence is false, rewrite it to make it true. (Do not write in this book.)

1. The tundra and boreal forest are ecotones.
2. The boreal forest receives less precipitation than the tundra.
3. Boreal forest soil is often waterlogged and nutrient deficient.
4. All conifers are evergreens.
5. Black spruce is a common tree in the northernmost parts of the boreal forest.
6. Fungi are vital decomposers in the boreal forest.
7. Small herbivores like voles and shrews hibernate.
8. The boreal forest contains only coniferous trees.
9. Canada has the most boreal forest of any country on earth.

B. Completion

Complete each of the following sentences with a word or phrase that will make the sentence correct. (Do not write in this book.)

1. Most of North America's boreal forest is in ▓▓▓▓▓ .
2. Soviets call the boreal forest the ▓▓▓▓▓ which means "swamp forest".
3. Partly decayed organic matter is called ▓▓▓▓▓ .
4. The needles of conifers are adapted to decrease ▓▓▓▓▓ loss.
5. The most common moss of the boreal forest is ▓▓▓▓▓ moss.
6. The ▓▓▓▓▓ plays a role in the boreal forest similar to the one the lemming plays in the tundra.
7. Large areas of boreal forest have been denuded by two insects: and ▓▓▓▓▓ .

C. Multiple Choice

Each of the following statements or questions is followed by four responses. Choose the correct response in each case. (Do not write in this book.)

1. The tree line occurs
    a) at the northern edge of the tundra
    b) at the southern edge of the tundra
    c) at the northern edge of the boreal forest
    d) at the southern edge of the boreal forest
2. The country with the most boreal forest is
    a) the USSR   c) Canada
    b) the United States d) Sweden
3. Which one of the following is mainly responsible for the formation of peat in the boreal forest?
    a) a lack of sufficient fungi
    b) a lack of nutrients in the soil
    c) the presence of a gray ash in the soil
    d) the cold, wet, acidic soil conditions
4. A large area is dominated by black spruce, white spruce, and balsam fir. It has tamarack in wetter places. This area is most likely in
    a) the Great Lakes region
    b) the peaks of the southern Appalachians
    c) northern Canada
    d) the southeast United States
5. Conifers are able to survive in the boreal climate because
    a) they have adapted to high humidities
    b) they have adapted to dry conditions
    c) they are able to live for many months without photosynthesizing
    d) they are fire successional species

6. Which one of the following statements is true?
    a) Wolves prey just on deer, moose, and other large herbivores.
    b) Wolves never kill livestock such as cattle.
    c) Wolves often compete with humans for the same prey.
    d) Wolves stay within a very small territory (10 km or less in diameter).
7. The black bear is best called a
    a) omnivore   c) carnivore
    b) herbivore   d) scavenger

Using Your Knowledge

1. a) Describe the soil of the boreal forest.
   b) What major problems would a farmer face in this region?
2. Hardwoods (deciduous trees) often invade burned or cut areas of the boreal forest. The trees which normally do this are white birch, poplars, and alders. Why are these particular hardwoods found instead of others such as oaks and maples?
3. Conifers have many adaptations for life in the boreal forest environment. Which of these adaptations are likely to be found on conifers growing in sandy hot areas of low precipitation? Why?
4. In many areas of North America, wolves are shot to prevent them from killing moose, bighorn sheep, and other large herbivores. The main reason for this killing is to provide more big game for sport hunters to shoot. What do you think of this "wolf management" program? Defend your position.
5. Why are road kills of porcupines quite common?
6. If you have ever camped in bear country, you have probably seen this sign: Do Not Feed The Bears. Pretend that you are a park ranger. A camper has come up to you and asked you what's wrong with feeding a hungry bear. Make a list of the things you would tell the camper.
7. Why is a forest with just two or three tree species in it very vulnerable to insect damage?
8. Warblers are beautiful birds to observe. However, most species live in the boreal forest in the summer. And, if you go there in the summer to see these birds, the blackflies and mosquitoes will "eat you alive". What do you think of a plan to spray a large section of forest to kill the insects so birdwatching will be more comfortable? Defend your position.
9. What relationship would you expect to find between spruce grouse numbers and spruce budworm numbers? Why?
10. Calculate the percentage of the world's forests that is in North America.
11. Imagine that you are the government official in charge of forest policy for your province or state. What major policies would you try to implement?

Investigations

1. For this investigation you will need a map that shows the major cities of Canada and the United States. Refer to it and Figure 7-16, page 144, to answer the following question. If you lived in each of the cities in Table 9-4 where would you go to visit boreal forest? Assume you want to make the shortest possible trip.

Table 9-4   Visiting Boreal Forest

City	Location of nearest boreal forest
Montreal, Québec	
Chicago, Illinois	
Calgary, Alberta	
Washington, D.C.	
Ottawa, Ontario	
Seattle, Washington	
Regina, Saskatchewan	
Atlanta, Georgia	
St. John's, Newfoundland	
Billings, Montana	
Winnipeg, Manitoba	
Galveston, Texas	

2. Use the key in Section 9.3 on page 182 or one provided by your teacher to identify the conifers in an area selected by your teacher.
3. All conifers are not evergreens. For example, the larch is a conifer but it is not an evergreen. Similarly, all evergreens are not conifers. Find the name of one evergreen plant in your area which is not a conifer.
4. Jack pine is a fire successional species in much of the boreal forest. Most parts of North America have a fire successional pine. Find the name of the one where you live.
5. Write a paper of about 200 words on the nature of hibernation.
6. Investigate the paper recycling program in your community. How successful is it? What happens to the collected paper? How much is it worth? Who runs the program?
7. The spraying of boreal forest to kill spruce budworm has become a very controversial issue. Some people say the spraying is necessary to protect the forest. Others say that the spraying harms humans, wildlife, and the ecology of the forest. Research both sides of this issue. Then write a paper of about 300 words which states and explains your position.

10 The Temperate Deciduous Forest Biome

In North America, the temperate deciduous forest occurs on the southeast edge of the boreal forest (see Figure 7-16, page 144). This biome is recognized by its temperate (moderate) climate and deciduous trees (Fig. 10-1). Deciduous trees drop their leaves in the winter. In Canada, only the most southern parts of Ontario, Québec, and the Maritimes are in this biome. However, as Figure 7-16 shows, most of the eastern half of the United States is in it.

Fig. 10-1 This deciduous forest appears bleak in the winter. The occasional evergreen adds some green to the landscape (A). In the summer, however, the forest has an understory of green shrubs and saplings, shaded by a dense canopy of leaves (B).

A large ecotone (transition zone) occurs between the boreal forest and the deciduous forest. This zone dominates the Great Lakes region. A mixture of coniferous and deciduous trees occurs in it. Temperate deciduous forest biomes also occur in large areas of Europe and China. However, we will examine the North American forest.

10.1   Abiotic Factors

Climate

The temperate deciduous forest is found largely in the eastern half of our continent. There, the climate is moderate. The average annual precipitation varies from 75 to 125 cm. That is, moisture is abundant, but not excessive. (The Gulf states generally receive more precipitation—up to 150 cm a year.) Further, precipitation is fairly evenly distributed throughout the year. The winter snow is not as deep as that of the boreal forest. Nor does it stay as long.

The four seasons are well-developed. And the temperature gradually changes with the seasons. Temperatures are more moderate than those of the boreal forest. Average January temperatures range from $-12°C$ in the north to $15°C$ in the south. And average July temperatures range from $21°C$ in the north to $27°C$ in the south. The growing season ranges from 4 to 6 months. During that time, the relative humidity is usually high.

Light

This biome is closer to the equator than the boreal forest is. As a result, the average light intensity is higher. But the average photoperiod (length of daylight) is shorter.

Winters are shorter than in the boreal forest. But they are still long enough to greatly reduce photosynthesis and, as a result, growth rates. Deciduous trees enter a dormant period in the winter. During this period they shed their leaves. One hectare of forest floor may be carpeted with more than 25 000 000 leaves each fall! (A hectare is about the area of two football fields.)

Soil

Fallen leaves and other organic matter decay quickly during the warm moist summer. This produces a nutrient-rich layer of soil called humus. Typical deciduous woodland soil is called "brown earth". It is formed where the downward drainage of rain water (percolation) is balanced by the upward movement of water (capillarity). Capillarity brings water to the surface to replace water which evaporates. As it does so, it brings nutrients to the surface. In other words, it brings up those nutrients that percolation tends to leach out of the soil. As a result, nutrients are circulated through the soil. They are not leached from it as they are in boreal soils.

Rocky areas and areas with porous soils tend to be much drier. Precipitation drains off quickly. Such areas do not usually have enough moisture to support deciduous trees. They will, however, grow conifers and shrubs. In some pockets of land, water movement is slow. Bogs may form in these areas.

Section Review

1. Compare the temperate deciduous forest and the northern boreal forest with respect to each of the following factors:
   a) average monthly temperatures
   b) length of growing season
   c) intensity of sunlight
   d) photoperiod
   e) depth of snowfall
   f) annual precipitation
   g) appearance of the soil
   h) soil nutrients

10.2   Biotic Factors: Vegetation

At one time the eastern shore of this continent was a vast forest. It was so dense, legend says, that a squirrel could travel through the treetops from the Atlantic coast to the Mississippi River without ever having to set foot on the ground. But today only patches of that forest remain (Fig. 10-2). Because the soil is rich, much of this biome has been cleared for farming. And urbanization covers a fair portion of the cleared area. Small animals have adapted to live in small scattered woodlots. And some large herbivores like the whitetail deer thrive in this more open environment. But, generally, large carnivores do not. They have been wiped out or forced to retreat to a few remaining pockets of wilderness. Some, like the timber wolf, have retreated to the boreal forest.

Clearing this biome has greatly affected the nature of the life in it. But a wide and interesting variety of plants and animals still exists. Foremost among these are the trees. Let us first take a look at them.

There are three main types of deciduous forest in the temperate deciduous forest biome:

- northern hardwood forest
- central hardwood forest
- southeast pine-oak forest

The species present in each forest depend on the local climate.

Fig. 10-3 Sugar maple and beech dominate the northern hardwood forest in many areas. The beech tree is the one with the smooth gray bark.

The Northern Hardwood Forest

A **northern hardwood forest** occurs in the moister and cooler northern regions. It begins in southern Canada (specifically southern parts of Ontario, Québec, and the Maritimes). It extends south into the United States, covering the mountainous regions of New England and following the Appalachian Mountains south to North Carolina and Tennessee. It also spreads west in a belt under the Great Lakes from New York to Minnesota.

In the eastern part of the northern hardwood forest, the dominant species are sugar maple, beech, and yellow birch (Fig. 10-3). Black cherry, white ash, and red oak are also common. Hemlock, a conifer, is co-dominant in wet cool areas. And majestic white pines tower above the hardwoods in drier areas (Fig.10-4). White pines used to be the most striking feature of this forest. But heavy logging has removed most of the large trees. And you know from your study of succession in Chapter 4 that pine cannot regenerate in the dense shade of trees like maple and beech. Moving west from western New York to southern Indiana, the northern hardwood forest is mainly a maple-beech forest. Maple-beech extends to parts of Illinois and central Minnesota. But from central Wisconsin and Minnesota south to Missouri, it is mainly a maple-basswood forest.

Fig. 10-4 White pine can often be seen towering above the deciduous trees.

Fig. 10-5 Yellow poplar (A) and buckeye (B) dominate the cove hardwood forest.

The Central Hardwood Forest

South of the northern hardwood forest is the vast central hardwood forest. It occupies the central part of the temperate deciduous forest biome. This forest consists of three main types:
* cove hardwood forest
* pine-oak forest
* oak-hickory forest

Cove Hardwood Forest This forest occurs throughout the central region. But it is best developed in the deep mountain coves of the southern Appalachians. In Smoky Mountains National Park (in North Carolina and Tennessee) this forest ranks in majesty and beauty with the best on earth. It contains a wide variety of species, including most of those of the northern hardwood forest. But the dominant trees are towering yellow poplars and yellow buckeyes (Fig. 10-5).

Pine-Oak Forest This forest is found in drier upland regions of the central hardwood forest. It is dominated by a wide variety of oaks and pines. Among the oaks are red, white, chestnut, and scarlet oak. And among the pines are Virginia, pitch, shortleaf, and white pine. Several species of hickory also live here.

One of the most devastating ecological disasters of all time happened in the pine-oak forest. When the European settlers first moved into this area, one of the dominant trees was the American chestnut. It was one of the finest, most common, and most valuable of the native trees. Humans and many animals shared its nuts. And its timber was of top quality. But it was struck by a disease, the chestnut blight. This disease is caused by a parasitic fungus. It entered the United States before plant quarantine laws were enacted. It came from Asia about 1925 on plants closely related to the chestnut. As is often the case with disease organisms, the blight was much more virulent in its new home than in its native land. In a matter of a decade or so, almost all the American chestnuts were dead. The last good crops of chestnuts were collected in the early 1930s. Today a few living trees still occur in isolated areas such as Ontario's Niagara Peninsula. But throughout the pine-oak forest, dead trunks still stand as reminders of this disaster (Fig. 10-6). No remedy has been found for chestnut blight. But resistant varieties of chestnut are being developed and planted.

Along streams and in wet valleys throughout both the pine-oak and cove hardwood forests, one finds cottonwoods, sycamore, elm, and willow. Elms are not as common as they used to be. Like the American chestnut, elms have been almost eliminated by a fungus which causes the Dutch elm disease. It, too, is an imported fungus. It has spread to elms throughout most of their range. It is carried from tree to tree by a beetle called the Japanese bark

Fig. 10-6   This chestnut has been dead for over 60 years. The high quality wood of this hardwood resists rotting.

Fig. 10-7   Pines surround this campsite in the Pine Barrens of New Jersey.

Fig. 10-8   Longleaf pine is easily identified. Its needles are up to 45 cm long! And its cones can reach 25 cm in length.

beetle. Specimen trees have been preserved in city parks by expensive treatments. But most trees die two or three years after they are attacked.

Oak-Hickory Forest   This forest occurs along the western edge of the central hardwood forest. It dominates the Ozark Mountains of Missouri. And it follows the river valleys through the prairies.

The Southeast Pine-Oak Forest

This forest occupies the coastal plain from New Jersey south through the Atlantic states to the Gulf states. It occurs on sandy, well-drained soils. Such soils are nutrient-poor and low in water-holding capacity. Pines thrive in such an environment. As a result, they dominate this forest.

It may seem strange to you that we call this forest a deciduous forest when it is dominated by evergreens. Ecologists agree that the pines are just a successional stage. If cutting and fires are halted, the pines are usually replaced by deciduous trees. Oaks dominate, but hickories and magnolias are found in many areas.

Pitch, Virginia, and shortleaf pine dominate northern areas. Figure 10-7, photographed in the Pine Barrens of New Jersey, includes these species. Further south, shortleaf, longleaf, slash, and loblolly pine dominate (Fig. 10-8). These pines invade as far south as most of Florida and the Mississippi delta. But oaks and magnolias dominate the climax forest in most of the southern region.

Fig. 10-9 How many strata (levels of vegetation) can you see in this deciduous forest?

Other Vegetation in the Deciduous Forest

The temperate deciduous forest has a long, warm growing season. It also has abundant moisture and rich soil. As a result, it supports a wide variety of other plant species in addition to trees. These species usually live in levels, or strata, in the forest (Fig. 10-9). The taller trees form the first stratum, or upper canopy. This canopy receives full exposure to the sun. The broad leaves permit maximum absorption of light energy. A small oak tree with a trunk diameter of 60 cm has more than 100 000 leaves. Their total surface area is about the size of two tennis courts!

Some sunlight filters through to the second stratum. This layer contains smaller "understory trees". Beneath these is the third stratum, a shrub layer. This layer includes shrubs and saplings. Saplings are young trees up to 3 or 4 m tall. And, finally, at ground level, the fourth stratum occurs. This ground layer consists of mosses, ferns, tree seedlings, and a wide variety of flowering plants (Fig. 10-10).

Trillium

Wild ginger

White Adder tongue

Blood root

Fig. 10-10 A few of the flowering plants of the deciduous forest.

Fig. 10-11 Flowers cover this forest floor "wall to wall". The trees, however, are still dormant.

When the sun is overhead, the ground layer in an oak forest receives only about 6% of the sunlight that strikes the upper canopy. At other times of day, it receives even less. As a result, the plants of the ground layer show many adaptations to low light intensity. Their leaves are generally quite broad. This allows them to capture extra energy. And the leaves are densely packed with chloroplasts. (You may have noticed that plants of the forest floor are dark green.) These extra chloroplasts promote additional photosynthesis.

If you have ever walked through the woods in the spring, you have seen another adaptation to low light intensity (Fig. 10-11). While the trees are still dormant and leafless, the ground layer plants resume activity. They leaf out and begin to photosynthesize. While abundant light still reaches them, they store food in roots or underground stems. Much of their photosynthesis and flowering occurs in the short days of early spring. Once they have formed seeds, these plants become dormant until the following spring.

Why Deciduous Trees Drop Their Leaves

The Reason for Loss of Leaves Deciduous leaves are usually thin and delicate. They are easily injured by frost. Furthermore, they are easily dried out by winter winds. Therefore, even if they could remain on the trees undamaged during the winter, the frozen soil could not replace lost water. As a result, the leaves are shed in the fall. Photosynthesis ceases. And the trees live on food stored in roots, trunks, and branches.

How Loss of Leaves Occurs The falling temperatures and shorter days of autumn cause chemical changes in the leaves. These changes cause certain cells at the bases of the leaf petioles to separate from each other. (The separation takes place where the leaf petiole joins the leaf to the twig.) The leaves are now attached to the twigs only by their veins. They are easily knocked off by wind or rain. Where the petiole falls off, a layer of cork forms over the exposed stem. The cork prevents water loss. These corky areas form leaf scars. You have likely seen these on twigs in the winter (Fig. 10-12).

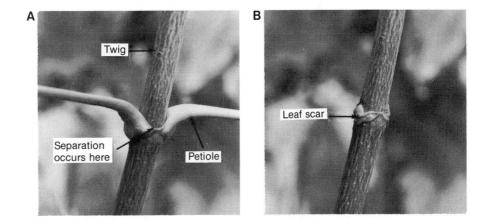

Fig. 10-12 When the petiole separates from a twig (A), a leaf scar forms (B).

Spring Returns When the air gets warm enough, the trees resume activity. All deciduous trees are flowering plants. Some, like the maple, beech, and oak, form inconspicuous flowers. These trees depend on the wind to carry pollen from one tree to another. As a result, they usually flower before the trees completely leaf out. Then the wind can spread the pollen around more effectively. Other trees such as the yellow poplar and black cherry have brightly coloured fragrant flowers (Fig. 10-13). These trees depend largely on insects for pollination.

The flowering of deciduous trees usually produces a bounty of seeds and fruits. As a result, a deciduous forest can support a wide variety of mammals and birds.

Fig. 10-13 These bright, fragrant cherry blossoms attract insects.

Why Leaves Change Colour

Deciduous trees in temperate climates often become brightly coloured before they drop their leaves. Why does this occur?

A leaf usually has many pigments, or colours, in it. Table 10-1 lists the names and colours of the main ones. Fall colours are caused partly by a loss of chlorophyll. This loss is triggered by falling temperatures. The cold nights of early autumn break down the chlorophyll. Now you can see the yellow and orange pigments which were masked by the green of the chlorophyll. They are responsible for the beauty of poplar (cottonwood), beech, and white birch

Table 10-1 Leaf Pigments

Pigment	Colour
Chlorophyll	green
Xanthophylls	yellow
Carotenes	orange
Anthocyanin	red

leaves. The production of anthocyanin, a red pigment, is triggered by low temperatures. And it is greater when there are many cool sunny days. The leaves of maples, sumac, and poison ivy often turn brilliant red. This colour is due to an abundance of anthocyanin in the vacuoles of their leaf cells.

Section Review

1. **a)** Why has the temperate deciduous forest been largely cleared?
   b) State the overall effects of this clearing on wildlife.
2. Name the three main types of forest in the temperate deciduous forest biome.
3. **a)** Describe the location of the northern hardwood forest.
   b) What tree species dominate the eastern part of the northern hardwood forest?
   c) In what ways does this dominance change as you move west?
4. **a)** Describe the location of the central hardwood forest.
   b) What three forest types occur in it?
5. **a)** Where is the cove hardwood forest best developed?
   b) What species dominate it?
6. **a)** Where is the pine-oak forest best developed?
   b) Which species of pine dominate it?
   c) Which species of oak dominate it?
   d) Why did the chestnut blight develop into such a disaster?
7. Where is the oak-hickory forest?
8. **a)** Describe the location of the southeast pine-oak forest.
   b) Which pine species dominate the northern areas of this forest?
   c) Which pine species dominate the southern areas?
9. Name the four main strata in a deciduous forest.
10. Name and describe three adaptations of ground layer plants to low light intensity.
11. **a)** Why do deciduous trees drop their leaves?
    b) What causes the dropping to begin?
    c) What causes the leaf to break away from the twig?
12. Describe two different ways in which trees have adapted to ensure pollination.
13. Explain why deciduous trees usually change from green to many other colours in the autumn.

Making and Using a Classification Key for Deciduous Leaves

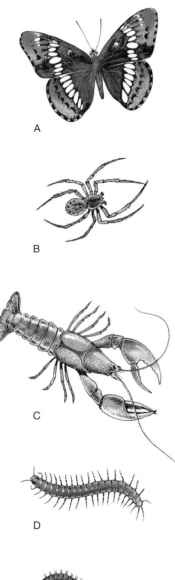

A

B

C

D

E

Fig. 10-14 Can you identify these animals?

You may have already used a classification key in Chapter 9 to identify conifers. In this activity you will learn how such keys are made by making one. Then you will learn more about how these keys work. As a result, you should feel confident using them to identify trees, in this case, deciduous trees.

Classification puts similar organisms in groups. Grouping makes it easier to keep track of organisms. It also makes it easier to "find", or identify, a certain organism. For example, suppose you come across an unfamiliar animal and you want to know whether or not it is an insect. There are close to one million species of insect. To look through books for a picture of this animal to see whether or not it is an insect would be a hopeless task. Fortunately, biologists have classified, or grouped, all animals with three pairs of legs into the class Insecta of the phylum Arthropoda. Therefore, you only need to count the animal's legs to know if it is an insect.

In this activity, you will prepare a classification system for the leaves from several species of trees. If you set up your classification system properly, it can be used as a classification key which someone else could use to identify an unknown leaf. To set up a classification key, you write down pairs of opposing characteristics in couplets. Study the following example to see how your key should look. Then proceed to make a classification system for the leaves provided. Your system could be used as a classification key.

Example

The following is a classification key for the five animals in Figure 10-14.

1a. Has wings....................................... butterfly
1b. Has no wings.................................... go to 2
2a. Has 8 or fewer legs............................... spider
2b. Has more than 8 legs.............................. go to 3
3a. Has 10 or fewer legs............................. crayfish
3b. Has more than 10 legs............................ go to 4
4a. Body flattened; 1 pair of legs per body segment.......... centipede
4b. Body rounded; 2 pairs of legs per body segment......... millipede

Materials

2 sets of leaves arranged as follows:

SET A: 10 leaves, each from a different species of tree, mounted on cards, numbered from 1 to 10, with the names of the leaves attached.

SET B: Identical to Set A, but without the names.

Procedure

a. Spread the leaves of Set A on the top of your desk.

b. Examine them closely and decide on the main characteristics that distinguish one leaf from another. In what ways is one leaf the same as the others? In what ways is it different? Use the terms shown in Figure 10-15.

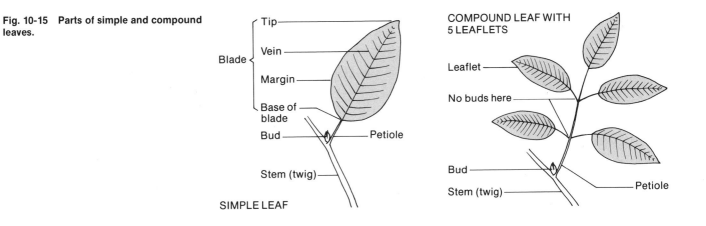

Fig. 10-15   Parts of simple and compound leaves.

COMPOUND LEAF WITH 5 LEAFLETS

Leaflet

No buds here

Bud

Petiole

Stem (twig)

Tip

Vein

Blade

Margin

Base of blade

Bud

Petiole

Stem (twig)

SIMPLE LEAF

Ask yourself questions such as the following:

1. Is the leaf **simple** (all one piece) or **compound** (divided into many separate leaflets)?

2. Is the leaf margin smooth, finely notched, coarsely notched, or wavy?

3. What shape is the blade—long and narrow, oval, heart-shaped, spearshaped, circular?

4. Does the leaf have both a petiole and a blade?

5. Are the leaves smooth or hairy? On which side?

6. What is the length of the blade?

7. Do the veins fan out from the base of the blade or are they parallel to one another from the mid-rib?

8. Is the petiole flattened or rounded?

9. What colour is the upper surface of the leaf? the lower surface?

c. Now pick 2 contrasting characteristics, one which about half of the leaves have and the other which the rest of the leaves have. Separate the leaves into 2 groups based on these characteristics.

d. Repeat step (c) for each of the 2 groups. Continue to do this until you have only 1 leaf in each group.

e. Prepare a "tree diagram" for your classification system. Figure 10-16 will give you a start. Of course, you may choose a different starting characteristic than we did.

f. Now take the information from your "tree diagram" and make a true classification key out of it. Use the number-letter format that we used in

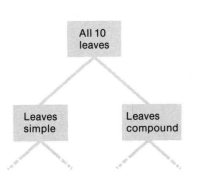

All 10 leaves

Leaves simple

Leaves compound

Fig. 10-16   A possible beginning for a "tree diagram".

the example. Your key might have the following as its first couplet:

1a. Leaf simple.................................go to 2
1b. Leaf compound............................go to 3

g. Put Set A to one side. Without looking at Set A, try to identify each of the leaves in Set B by using your classification key.
h. Check your results by looking at Set A. If you made any mistakes, something is wrong with your key. Correct any errors in your key.
i. Here is the final test of your key: Give your key and Set B to another student. Ask that student to identify the leaves using your key. If the student has any problems, find out what they are. Then, if necessary, change your key to eliminate the problems.

Discussion

1. Take your key home. Collect two or three leaves that can be identified using your key. Have someone in your family use your key to try to identify the leaves. Write a brief report on the success (or failure) of your key when used by another person.
2. Obtain a "real" classification key for deciduous trees from your teacher. Use it to identify the specimens your teacher gives to you.

10.4   Biotic Factors: Animals

Fig. 10-17   The woodpecker has four toes per foot. Two toes point backwards. Why? Note, too, the use of the tail as a prop.

The deciduous forest provides a wide variety of habitats for animals. The animals, in turn, show unique adaptations to these habitats. Many, for example, have adapted in structure, function, and behaviour to live in trees. Here they find shelter, protection, and nesting sites. From the branches they can spot predators. And they can also proclaim and protect territorial boundaries. Many other animals dwell in the shrubs and ground layer. Still others live under fallen trees or in the rich litter and humus of the soil. And others simply take advantage of the shade, moderate temperatures, higher humidity, and protection from wind which the forest offers.

Tree Dwellers

Tree dwellers are well equipped for moving among branches. Woodpeckers have sharp claws on opposing toes for balance (Fig.10-17). They also have a tail which is just the right length and structure to serve as a prop.

Squirrels and chipmunks also have sharp claws with opposing toes. As well, they have powerful hind legs for jumping from branch to branch. And most have a bushy tail for balance. The eastern gray squirrel is an example. It lives in all parts of the deciduous forest (Fig. 10-18). It rarely ventures far from trees. It feeds on a wide variety of nuts, fruits, and seeds. It will even eat

Fig. 10-18 The eastern gray squirrel. In most of the deciduous forest, this squirrel is gray. But in some places, like southern Ontario, a black phase occurs. Both the gray and black squirrel are the same species.

Fig. 10-19 After the leaves have fallen from the trees, squirrel nests are often visible.

Fig. 10-20 The tree frog clings to bark with suction discs on its toes.

fungi and the cambium (growing layer) beneath the bark of trees. In the fall, it stores nuts in the ground. But because its memory isn't always good, many of these nuts germinate in the spring. In this way, squirrels play an important role in forest regeneration. Gray squirrels nest in hollow trees or in nests made of leaves (Fig. 10-19).

The southern flying squirrel is also found throughout most of the deciduous forest. But it is seldom seen because it is nocturnal. It only appears in the open at deep dusk. This squirrel is adapted for gliding from tree to tree and from tree to ground. It has a folded layer of loose skin along each side of the body. This skin extends from front to hind legs. When the squirrel spreads its legs, the skin extends and forms "wings".

Also among the tree dwellers are tree frogs (Fig. 10-20). They use suction discs on their toes to cling to bark. Snails and slugs use a slimy "foot". And white-tailed mice and opossums use their tails for climbing and grasping, much as monkeys do.

Whitetail Deer

Unlike conifers, deciduous trees are a major source of food for a wide variety of herbivores. The most concentrated food (protein, fat, and carbohydrate) is stored in buds and seeds. These provide a year-round source of food for birds and mammals. Buds are most valuable during the late winter and early spring. Little other nourishment is available then. However, autumn produces a rich harvest of seeds. These seeds persist far into the winter in the form of berries and nuts. Acorns, for example, feed jays, deer, squirrels, chipmunks, and many other animals.

The dominant herbivore throughout most of the deciduous forest is the whitetail deer (Fig. 10-21). Deer prefer to feed in brushy areas along the edge of woods rather than in deep forest. But they seldom move far from the protective cover of the forest. In fact, the view of a whitetail deer you will most likely see is a white "flag" waving back and forth as the animal bounds for the cover of the forest.

Fig. 10-21 The whitetail deer lives in almost all parts of the deciduous forest. It can often be seen browsing in the early morning or evening. A loud "snort" means that it has scented you.

This browser feeds on twigs of trees, shrubs, nuts such as acorns, fungi, grasses, and other plants. It is the most important big game animal of the east. And, because of hunter demand, its habitat is managed in many areas to produce more deer. Unfortunately, management can produce a surplus of deer. This surplus does considerable damage to farmers' crops and fruit orchards. It can also lead to mass starvation of the deer. Most of the deer's natural predators, such as the wolf, have been driven out of the east. Therefore, control of this animal's numbers rests largely with humans.

Deer are herd animals. They commonly live in groups of 25 or more in the winter. In the summer and fall, however, they usually live alone or in family groups (the doe with her one or two fawns).

In the northern part of the deciduous forest, snow and cold are problems for these narrow-hoofed animals. As a result they often migrate to swamps for protection from the cold. There they work together to break trails and trample the snow to form a "deer yard". They feed on twigs and buds they can reach. They will even stand on hind legs and use the front legs to bend upper boughs down so they can reach the tender twigs.

Rabbits and Small Rodents

Rabbits and small rodents form important links in forest food chains. Cottontail rabbits nibble at herbs, tree bark, and small plant growth (Fig. 10-22). They prefer the forest edge and clearings for a habitat. But in winter they stay close to the protective cover of forest shrubs. Deer mice are agile climbers. They forage in small trees and surface litter for buds and seeds. They store these and nuts, in particular, in their nests. They use their sharp incisor (gnawing) teeth to crack open even the toughest shells.

Rabbits and small rodents are food for a wide variety of predators: owls, hawks, foxes, and, in the north, coyotes.

Beavers

Beavers, the largest North American rodents, are found throughout much of the deciduous forest. They are nocturnal but occasionally appear during the day. It is best to look for them at sunset. They prefer to feed on poplar (aspen), birch, willow, and older trees. They eat small twigs and the inner bark. They store branches and small logs underwater near their lodges (Fig. 10-23). They eat this underwater food in the winter. Two adult beavers can chisel through a trunk 10 cm in diameter in less than 15 min (Fig. 10-24)!

From the days of the first fur-traders, the beaver's pelt has been widely sought. In fact, years ago, trappers, along with settlements that destroyed their habitats, exterminated the beaver from much of its range. Today, however, the beaver has returned in numbers exceeding those of the past.

Beavers feed near ponds, lakes, and rivers. They cannot move too far from water because they must haul branches back to their homes. To keep water deep near their homes, beavers work as a colony to build dams. These dams slow the runoff of water. Because of them, beavers are important agents in

Fig. 10-22 The cottontail is a common sight in the open parts of the deciduous forest.

Fig. 10-23 Note the size of this beaver lodge. It is made largely of branches cemented together with mud.

Fig. 10-24 Have you ever heard the phrase "work like a beaver"? Their reputation for being industrious is well-earned.

Fig. 10-25 Hundreds of tent caterpillars come from this nest. They can strip the tree of its leaves. At night, the gorged feeders return to the nest.

water conservation in many areas. Unfortunately (for the beavers), they often build their dams near roads, lanes, cottages, and fields. The resulting flooding causes some annoyance. As a result many people see beavers as pests. They are also blamed for destroying valuable timber. However, the trees they eat are mostly low-grade timber species.

Beavers, like all rodents, have just 2 incisors (gnawing teeth) on each of the upper and lower jaw. They use their incisors regularly to chew through tough material such as tree trunks. As a result, the incisors wear down rapidly. But, like a blade of grass, they grow from the bottom to replace the lost parts.

Insects

Large herbivores do little damage to the leaves of trees. But two major groups of insects are highly destructive. The leaf-chewers, such as caterpillars and beatle and fly larvas, use biting jaws to eat all of the leaf tissue (Fig. 10-25). Some will attack any tree. But most are specialists and will feed on just one or two species. Oak trees are the host for many such invaders. Over 50 000 caterpillars may share the same tree! Large trees are generally not killed. An oak tree, for example, simply produces new leaves in midsummer after the insects have passed.

Sapsuckers, such as aphids, have piercing and sucking mouthparts. These operate like a hypodermic syringe to suck sap from leaves and other tissues. This sap contains little protein. To get enough protein to grow, aphids must gorge themselves on sap. Therefore they ingest (take in) excess sugars. The excess must be egested (gotten rid of). It is egested in drops of "honey dew". Ants and flying insects feed on these liquid feces. Ants also store aphid eggs for their winter diet.

In return for proteins and sugar, bees and other insects act as pollinating agents for blossoms. And the army of caterpillars provides a meal for birds, tree frogs, and even squirrels. Insect parasites also feed upon the caterpillars. And shrews, mice, and toads feast upon those caterpillars which drop to the soil to pupate. Spiders weave their webs everywhere to trap insects and other arthropods. The spiders, in turn, are preyed upon by birds.

As you can see, the food web of a forest is complex. It is not possible to spray a forest to kill an insect pest without disrupting the entire web. Ecological considerations must be a part of every decision to spray.

Carnivores

The large carnivores of the deciduous forest have suffered greatly because of human intrusion. Most of them have retreated to mountain or boreal forests. Hunting, trapping, and habitat destruction have largely eliminated wolves, gray foxes, cougars, and bobcats from the deciduous forest. Large carnivores used to play an important role in controlling small mammal numbers. Now, however, that role is played largely by birds of prey such as hawks and owls. Weasels and the red fox are still abundant. They, too, prey on small mammals.

Fig. 10-26 The red fox is a resourceful feeder. It will eat just about any small animal it can catch. It often feeds on plant materials.

Fig. 10-27 The raccoon is well-known to many city dwellers. It thrives on garbage.

Fig. 10-28 The opossum, an expert climber, is a marsupial, or pouched animal.

Omnivores

The red fox is best described as an omnivore (Fig. 10-26). This nocturnal hunter prefers mice. But it will settle for birds, large insects, fish, and even berries and grass. When birds' eggs are abundant, foxes often bury them. Then they dig them up and eat them months later when food is scarce.

The raccoon is another well-known omnivore (Fig.10-27). Its menu includes eggs, fruit, seeds, nuts, insects and aquatic organisms such as crayfish. And, as many city dwellers will tell you, it also feeds on their garbage and gardens!

Another omnivore, the skunk, dines, in part, on grubs and insects. City dwellers often awaken to find their lawns full of holes. These were dug by skunks foraging for food. Skunks also eat mice, eggs, and the occasional carcass of a dead animal. The opossum—the only marsupial in North America—eats almost anything from vegetables and fruits to insects and carrion (Fig. 10-28). But the most resourceful feeders of all omnivores may be crows. These intelligent sociable birds are equipped with hardy digestive systems. And, furthermore, they quickly adapt their feeding behaviour to almost any kind of food at hand.

Life in the Soil

The yearly blanket of fallen leaves combines with other organic matter to form a rich soil. The greatest feeding activity of the forest occurs in this soil. One square kilometre of soil litter may be home to more than 120 different species of invertebrates. Each one is a specialized eater. Earthworms, roundworms, and millipedes feed on organic matter. And centipedes feed on them. Bacteria and fungi break down dead organic matter. This process releases nutrients which support the growth of plants. The surface of the soil and the litter layer are alive with animals. Among these are hungry spiders, beetles, snakes, toads, and small mammals like shrews. All of these organisms are links in complex food chains.

The Low and High of Forest Activity

The bounty of food disappears with the coming of winter. Some birds, such as chickadees and nuthatches, remain in the forest. They eat insect pupas, insect eggs, and, in some cases, seeds. Specialized food preferences allow several wintering species to share the same area without competition.

Most birds, however, migrate to regions of insect activity. Amphibians and reptiles lapse into a hibernating coma. The tiny shrew, however, cannot afford to sleep through a single winter day. It must constantly find dormant insects in the soil litter to survive (Fig. 10-29).

Forest activity reaches a peak during the spring and early summer. Most of the animals breed then. However, some, such as deer and bats, mate in the fall. Owls and some squirrels wait until winter. But at any time of year life is diverse and abundant in the deciduous forest. The interrelationships are complex. But the same principles which govern a simple biome like the tundra also govern this biome. We can use our knowledge of those principles to understand and protect the deciduous forest.

Fig. 10-29 To match the shrew's appetite, you would have to eat over 200 kg of food daily! How does that compare to your mass?

Section Review

1. Copy Table 10-2 into your notebook. Complete it as a summary of adaptations to tree life.

Table 10-2 Adaptations to Tree Life

Animal	Adaptations to Tree Life
woodpeckers	
eastern gray squirrels	
southern flying squirrels	
tree frogs	
snails and slugs	
white-tailed mice	
opossums	

2. a) What does the eastern gray squirrel eat?
   b) How does this squirrel help in forest regeneration?

3. Why are buds and seeds the favourite food of many forest animals?
4. a) Describe the habitat of the whitetail deer.
   b) What are the chief foods of these deer?
   c) Describe the positive and negative effects of deer management programs which are designed to create more deer.
   d) Describe the behaviour of deer in cold regions with deep snow.
5. Describe how rabbits and mice fit into forest food chains.
6. a) What are the preferred foods of beavers?
   b) Why are beavers often viewed as a nuisance?
   c) Why don't the teeth of beavers and other rodents wear out?
7. a) Describe the damage done by leaf-chewing insects.
   b) How do sap-sucking insects feed?
   c) Why do aphids give off "honey dew"?
   d) What beneficial role do caterpillars play in a forest?
8. a) Name four large carnivores of the deciduous forest.
   b) What three factors have eliminated these large predators from much of the region?
   c) What predators now serve as a check on small mammal numbers?
9. What are the common foods of each of the following omnivores: red foxes, raccoons, skunks.
10. Make a summary of the feeding activity in deciduous forest soil.
11. List three ways in which forest animals respond to the coming of winter.

Comparing the Deciduous and Boreal Forests

10.5   *ACTIVITY*

Between them, the deciduous and boreal forests occupy much of Canada and the United States. In Chapter 9 you explored the boreal forest in detail. In this chapter you did the same for the deciduous forest. These biomes are governed by the same ecological principles. Yet as you discovered they differ in many respects (Fig. 10-30). In this activity you will investigate those differences. Comparing them will help you gain a better understanding of the ecology of both biomes.

Problem

How do the deciduous and boreal forests differ?

Materials

Fig. 10-30   How do the deciduous and boreal forest differ? These photographs show just the obvious difference. What is it?

Deciduous forest

Boreal forest

Procedure

a. Locate London, Ontario and Chicoutimi, Québec on the map in Figure 10-31.

b. Study the climatograms given in Figure 10-32 for London and Chicoutimi.

c. Answer the discussion questions. Refer back to Chapter 9 and earlier sections of this chapter for the information you need.

Fig. 10-31   London, Ontario is at the northern edge of the deciduous forest. Chicoutimi, Québec is in the coniferous forest.

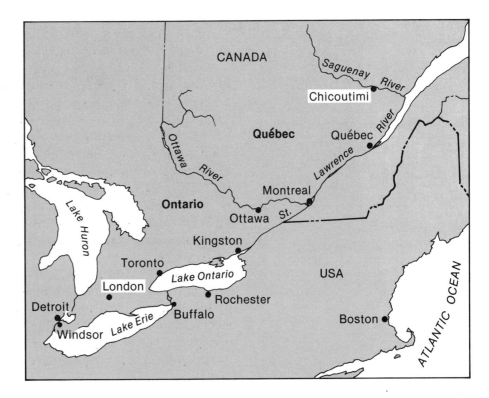

Fig. 10-32 Climatograms for London, Ontario and Chicoutimi, Québec.

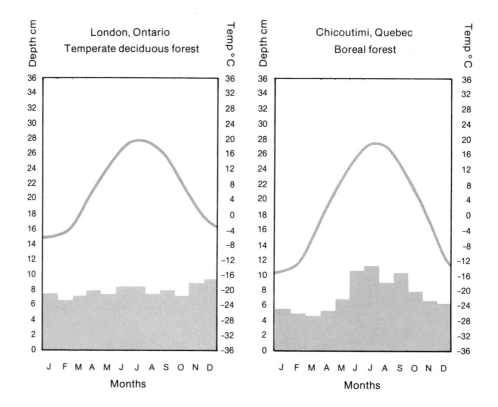

Discussion

1. **a)** There are three main types of forest in the temperate deciduous forest biome. In which of these is London?
   b) What tree species likely dominate the mature forest near London?
2. Different areas of the boreal forest are dominated by different conifers. What species likely dominate the forest near Chicoutimi?
3. Compare the two areas by answering the following questions. Refer to the climatograms to support your answers.
   a) Which area has the longer growing season?
   b) Which area has greater annual precipitation?
   c) Which area has greater annual snowfall?
   d) Which area has the wetter July?
   e) Which area receives heavier snowfall throughout December and January?
   f) Which area is warmer in July?
   g) Which area has more uniform precipitation throughout the year?
   h) In which area are temperatures more extreme?
4. Continue your comparison of the two areas by answering the following questions. The climatograms may help you deduce some answers. But to answer most of the questions, you will have to look back through the text.

a) Which area has greater light intensity?

b) Which area has the longer photoperiod during the growing season?

c) Which area has greater diversity of organisms? Why?

d) Which area has the greater number of migrating species? Why?

e) Which area has the faster rate of decomposition of organic matter?

f) Which area has the higher percentage of animals that change colour seasonally? Why?

g) Which area will likely have drier summer soil? How do you know?

5. Compare the soil of the London area with that of the Chicoutimi area.

6. Which area would you expect to be most like it was 300 years ago? Why?

7. Compare the two areas as a summer animal habitat with respect to each of the factors below:

a) availability of food

b) shelter from extremes of weather

c) protection from predators

8. Repeat question 7 for winter.

9. Which area is more suitable for agriculture? How do you know?

10. White spruce trees grow best in abundant light and abundant (but not excessive) moisture.

a) In which area will they likely grow faster?

b) In which area are they actually more abundant?

c) Why are they not as abundant in the other area?

10.6 Human Impact on the Deciduous Forest

Present State of the Deciduous Forest

In the United States and Canada, large tracts of deciduous forest still exist. It is more common, however, to see this forest in countless small woodlots. Almost every farm has a woodlot. Logging removed most of the virgin forest long ago. Fires and clearing for agriculture and settlements destroyed still more forest. In fact, much of this biome looks more like a grasslands (Fig. 10-33). In many prime agricultural areas, less than 5% of the land remains forested.

The rich soil formed by generations of trees makes this biome a prime agricultural area. However, large-scale agriculture has moved west. And agriculture in the east has gone into a slight decline. The best land in the east remains under cultivation. But the poorer land is being taken out of agriculture. Gradually this land is reverting back to forest. Close to urban areas, urbanites are buying up this land. Many plant trees on the land. Often, however, these trees are not native species. Therefore the forests may be a

Fig. 10-33 A dense forest of deciduous trees once covered this land. Today, the rich soil formed by generations of trees grows food.

long time returning to their former state, if they ever do. But at least trees are being planted.

You learned in Chapter 9 that the demands for timber and other wood products will soon exceed the supply. This trend is encouraging the development of tree farms on abandoned farmland. These tree farms are under intensive management. In most cases, the objective of the owner is to make money. As a result, tree farms are often planted to a monoculture (one species). And they often specialize in fast-growing hybrid species. Again, this type of reforestation may not bring the deciduous forest back. But it is better than leaving marginal agricultural land bare.

Because of planting programs, forest is returning in parts of the deciduous forest biome. But urban sprawl and highways still destroy countless hectares each year. Clearing for agriculture still occurs. And strip mining threatens vast tracts of some of the most beautiful and diverse forest on earth—the southern Appalachians.

Importance of Woodlots

Numerous woodlots dot the deciduous forest biome. They are of great importance ecologically, economically, and socially. They provide wildlife habitat and soil protection. They act as ground water recharge areas. They help moderate climatic extremes. They are sources of wood and wood products. They are prime sites for recreation. And they add greatly to the beauty of the countryside. For these and other reasons, these woodlots must be protected and improved.

Because of poor management (often no management), these woodlots are not making the contribution they could make. Proper thinning could greatly increase timber production from these woodlots. In many areas, the woodlots need to be expanded to make a noticeable contribution. Extensive replanting needs to take place. For example, trees need to be planted along fencelines to protect crops and soil from the winds. And trees should be planted along all creeks and rivers to reduce erosion and increase water quality.

Modern forestry practices can create forests which benefit an area ecologically, economically, and socially. We simply need enough vision as a society to plan a few decades into the future.

Section Review

1. List three reasons for the disappearance of most of the deciduous forest.
2. **a)** Why is this biome a prime agricultural area?
   b) What factors are helping to bring deciduous forests back?
   c) What factors are still removing deciduous forests?
3. **a)** What is a tree farm?
   b) What is a monoculture?

4. **a)** Describe the importance of woodlots.
    b) List three things we should do to increase the contribution of these woodlots.

Main Ideas

1. The temperate deciduous forest biome occurs in parts of southern Canada and most of the eastern United States.
2. The moderate climate, long growing season, and rich soil encourage a wide diversity of trees and other organisms.
3. This biome contains three forest types: northern hardwood, central hardwood, and southeast pine-oak.
4. Vegetation in the deciduous forest occurs in strata (usually four).
5. The dropping of leaves is the most striking adaptation of the trees to their environment.
6. Deciduous forest animals have adapted to life in trees, shrubs, ground layer, or soil.
7. Most of the original deciduous forest is gone.
8. Woodlots could be managed to play a much greater role ecologically, economically, and socially.

Key Terms

canopy
classification key
deciduous
monoculture

Chapter Review

A. True or False

Decide whether each of the following statements is true or false. If the sentence is false, rewrite it to make it true. (Do not write in this book).

1. The temperate deciduous forest biome contains only deciduous trees.
2. Canada has less deciduous forest than the United States.
3. Summer days are longer in the deciduous forest than in the coniferous forest.
4. The central hardwood forest occurs only in the United States.
5. Most deciduous trees have no flowers.
6. Squirrels eat only nuts.
7. Deer are herd animals in the winter.
8. Beavers often destroy valuable hardwoods.

B. Completion

Complete each of the following sentences with a word or phrase that will make the sentence correct. (Do not write in this book.)

1. The Great Lakes region is in an ▨▨▨▨▨ between the deciduous and boreal forests.
2. Precipitation in the deciduous forest is ▨▨▨▨▨ distributed throughout the year.
3. Deciduous woodland soil contains a rich layer of ▨▨▨▨▨ .
4. The northern hardwood forest is dominated by ▨▨▨▨▨ , ▨▨▨▨▨ , and ▨▨▨▨▨ .
5. The deciduous forest has been seriously affected by two diseases caused by imported fungi: ▨▨▨▨▨ and ▨▨▨▨▨ .
6. The dominant herbivore in much of this forest is the ▨▨▨▨▨ .
7. In many prime agricultural areas, less than ▨▨▨▨▨ % of the forest remains.

C. Multiple Choice

Each of the following statements or questions is followed by four responses. Choose the correct response in each case. (Do not write in this book).

1. The climate of the deciduous forest biome is *best* described as
   a) moderate
   b) warm and dry
   c) cool and wet
   d) warm and wet
2. In almost all parts of the deciduous forest, one is likely to find a species of
   a) beech
   b) pine
   c) hemlock
   d) buckeye
3. Which one of the following *best* describes the leaves of *many* ground layer plants?
   a) narrow and light green
   b) broad and light green
   c) narrow and dark green
   d) broad and dark green
4. The most concentrated foods of the forest are
   a) leaves and grasses
   b) bark
   c) buds and seeds
   d) twigs
5. The largest North American rodent is the
   a) beaver
   b) cottontail rabbit
   c) whitetail deer
   d) opossum
6. A common nocturnal omnivore is the
   a) beaver
   b) red fox
   c) cottontail rabbit
   d) whitetail deer
7. In which cleared area that follows are you *least* likely to see a forest or woodlot develop over the next few decades?
   a) rural land owned by a city dweller
   b) marginal farmland
   c) an abandoned farm
   d) an area with rich well-drained soil

Using Your Knowledge

1. **a)** If you live in the deciduous forest biome, name and describe the forest type near your home.
   b) Name any parts of the biome you have visited.

2. **a)** Explain why the rich "brown earth" of the deciduous forest does not lose its nutrients through leaching.
   b) Why are drier areas of this biome often dominated by conifers?

3. **a)** Which species of deciduous trees appear to prefer moister and cooler conditions?
   b) Where might you expect to find these species on a mountain in North Carolina? (Consider the height and the direction.)

4. Pines are often planted as pioneers to reestablish forest in a region.
   a) Why are pines used for this purpose?
   b) Which species of pine would you plant in each of the following regions: southern Ontario, northern Ohio, New Jersey, Georgia?

5. Deciduous trees under city street lights often hold their leaves longer than similar trees nearby. Why?

6. Some years, the fall colours are poor. What conditions likely cause poor colour?

7. Deer are managed in some areas to increase their numbers. Winter feeding programs and shrub planting are part of such management. In the same areas, the "surplus" deer cause considerable damage to crops. Therefore hunting is essential to control deer numbers. As a result, hunting is called an important part of deer management. What is your opinion of this total management program? Defend your opinion.

8. Within 100 km or so of many urban areas, dogs are major predators of deer. They are very effective predators when the snow has a crust on it.
   a) How do you think the dogs arrived in deer country?
   b) Why are they so effective when the snow is crusty?
   c) If you were in a position to take action, what would you do to lessen this slaughter?

9. Beavers generally do not cut down valuable trees. But they often wipe out large tracts of such trees.
   a) How do they do this?
   b) How would you protect these trees?

10. Imagine that a person has a forest dominated by large oak trees. A species of caterpillar has attacked the trees. The owner has decided to spray the trees to kill the caterpillars. Trace the ecological consequences of this spraying.

11. What problems can one expect to have if he or she operates a monoculture tree farm?

Investigations

1. The trees of the cove hardwood forests in the southern Appalachians grow faster and larger than the same species in other areas. Find out why.

2. Visit a nearby woodlot, with the permission of the owner. Prepare a management plan for the woodlot. Your plan should permit sustained yield harvesting without upsetting ecological balance. You should look back to Section 4.9, page 79, for ideas. You may want to team up with 3 or 4 classmates to conduct this activity.

3. Get the official policy on the management of privately owned woodlots from your provincial or state government. Evaluate it.

11 The Grassland Biome

A

B

Fig. 11-1   Two views of the grassland biome. In places this biome is quite flat. In other places it is rolling (A). The best of the flat land is farmed (B).

The interior of North America was once covered by a vast expanse of grassland. It stretched a distance of about 4000 km from north to south. Edmonton, Alberta sits at its most northerly point. And Mexico City occupies its most southerly point. This grassland reached from the Rocky Mountains in the west to the central hardwood forests of the United States and the boreal forest of Canada in the east (see Figure 7-16).

The early explorers called this flat to rolling sea of grasses "prairie", from a French word meaning grasslands. Ecologists call it the grassland biome. In many places, one can still see the original grasses of this biome (Fig. 11-1). But most of it has been converted to agriculture. It still grows mainly grasses, however. Some of these are grasses on which livestock graze. Others are grasses such as corn and wheat which are food crops for livestock and humans.

Our grassland biome is just one of many large grassland biomes on earth. The other great grassland regions include the *veldt* in South Africa, the *steppes* of Asia and eastern Europe, and the *pampas* of South America. At one time, grasslands covered about 42% of the earth's land. Today, however, most of this biome is farmed.

All these grasslands have six things in common:

- rolling to flat terrain
- a climax vegetation of grasses
- low and irregular precipitation
- a high rate of evaporation of soil moisture
- occasional severe droughts
- an animal community dominated by burrowers and grazers

This chapter examines the unique features of grasslands listed above.

Abiotic Factors

The grassland biome lies between the same latitudes as the deciduous forest. As a result, seasonal changes are similar. Light intensity and duration are about the same. But great differences exist in climate. These, in turn, produce great differences in soil conditions. And, of course, these abiotic factors support a far different plant and animal community than one finds in the deciduous forest. Let us look at these two abiotic factors, climate and soil.

Climate

Precipitation The main factor responsible for a climax vegetation of grasses is the low rainfall. The continental pattern of air circulation from west to east produces low and irregular precipitation. Also, because the winds are usually dry, evaporation of water from the soil is high.

The annual precipitation is just 25-75 cm. Precipitation is lowest in the west and gradually increases across the continent toward the east. The low precipitation is enough to support grasses. But it is too low for extensive tree growth. And it is too high to encourage the formation of a desert.

Ecologists believe that the climax vegetation of grasses is not due entirely to climate. It is true that most tree species cannot tolerate the low precipitation. And most cannot live through the severe and prolonged droughts. But some species like trembling aspen (a poplar) can. However, periodic fires used to rage across the grasslands. They killed the trees and kept them from covering the land. Grasses, however, quickly recover from fires. Today, agriculture, not fires, keeps the trees in check. In some areas, though, the aspen parklands of the north are gradually creeping south.

Temperature Look ahead to the climatograms in Figure 11-13. You can see that the *average monthly* temperatures are similar to those of the deciduous forest. But the *daily* temperatures are not. The grassland biome is an area of violent temperature extremes. At Medicine Hat, Alberta, for example, the temperature can drop to -45°C on a January day. Yet the famous Chinook winds can send the temperature soaring to well above freezing a day or so later. July highs in the same area reach 42°C on occasion.

Soil

The brown to black soils of the prairies are among the most fertile on earth. There are two reasons for their fertility. First, if the grasslands are natural (ungrazed, unmowed, and unburned), a deep layer of mulch builds up. It consists of slowly decaying vegetation, mainly grasses. Up to four years is necessary for natural grasslands vegetation to decompose completely. But once the mulch comes into contact with the mineral soil, decomposition is rapid. And a deep layer of dark humus forms. The humus adds nutrients to the soil. The mulch cover helps the soil retain water and nutrients.

Second, surface evaporation of water causes capillarity (upward movement of water) to exceed percolation (downward movement of water). This leaves the topsoil rich in nutrients, especially calcium and potassium.

Grazing, mowing, and fire tend to reduce mulch. If these are extensive, the grassland can no longer maintain itself. Instead it is replaced by weeds, cacti, and xerophytic shrubs.

The semi-arid climate of the far west helps form the characteristic brown soils of that region. The greater precipitation further east helps form the dark brown and black soils of that region.

Section Review

1. a) Describe the extent of the grassland biome of North America.
    b) Name and give the location of three other grassland biomes in the world.
    c) List the six things all grasslands have in common.
2. a) Describe the characteristic features of the precipitation in the grasslands.
    b) How is the temperature of the grasslands like that of the deciduous forest?
    c) How is the temperature of the grasslands different from that of the deciduous forest?
3. a) Describe the role of mulch in the formation of prairie soils.
    b) How does surface evaporation help keep the soil nutrient-rich?
4. Name three factors that discourage tree growth in the grasslands.

11.2   Biotic Factors: Vegetation

Differences in precipitation produce three distinct regions in the grasslands (Fig. 11-2). They are:
- tall grass prairie
- mixed grass prairie
- short grass plains

Tall Grass Prairie

This region is a narrow strip next to the deciduous forest in the east. It receives moderate rainfall, around 75 cm a year. This rainfall is sufficient to support trees. In fact, oak-hickory forest can still be found along some rivers. But fires, often set by humans, kept these trees from colonizing the area. Today, agriculture serves much the same role. Corn and wheat now cover much of this area.

Rich soil and the moderate rainfall make the eastern prairies a tall grass zone. Where natural vegetation exists, it is dominated by a grass called tall bluestem. This grass soars as high as 2.4 m. And the plants are supported by

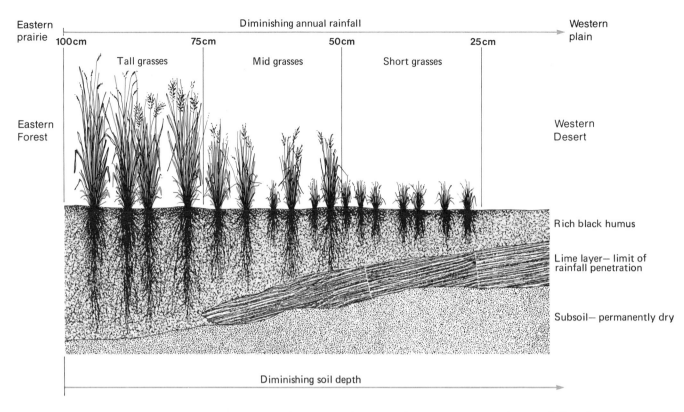

Eastern prairie

Eastern Forest

Western plain

Western Desert

Diminishing annual rainfall

100cm   75cm   50cm   25cm

Tall grasses   Mid grasses   Short grasses

Rich black humus

Lime layer— limit of rainfall penetration

Subsoil— permanently dry

Diminishing soil depth

Fig. 11-2 From prairie to plain. Soil characteristics and precipitation combine to produce three distinct types of grassland. They occur between the deciduous forest in the east and the desert in the southwest.

roots buried 1.8 m in the soil. Tall bluestem is a sod-forming grass. Such plants develop into a solid mat over the ground.

Mixed Grass Prairie

Further west, the drier central prairie supports two main kinds of grasses (hence the name "mixed"). Mid grasses occupy lower areas. And short grasses occupy the drier higher areas. Mid grasses grow from 60-120 cm tall. These grasses are "middle" in height between tall grasses and short grasses. Short grasses are less than 40 cm tall.

Most mid grasses are bunch grasses. They grow, as the name suggests, in bunches or clumps. The clumps are well-spaced. And other species of plants grow between them. Some of the short grasses are also bunch grasses; others are sod-forming.

Most of the mixed grass prairie has been converted to agriculture. Wheat and other grains are the main crops. And cattle ranches are common.

Short Grass Plains

This region occurs in the arid western plains. Here the winds are strong, humidity is low, and precipitation is sparse. Most regions receive only 25 cm of precipitation a year. The wettest regions receive only 50 cm. Much of North America's short grass plains occurs in the southwest United States.

There, it gradually blends into the desert. Large tracts of short grass plains are also in southeast Alberta and southern Saskatchewan in Canada.

The short grass plains are dominated by short grasses (less than 40 cm tall). Most species are sod-forming. These grasses are shallow-rooted. They absorb moisture from the upper soil zone. But they do not grow down into the permanent dry zone beneath.

Much of the short grass plains has been ruined by overgrazing and cultivation. Farmers tried to grow wheat on this land. But, in general, the land is too dry to grow this crop. With the grass cover gone, drought and strong winds caused extensive soil erosion. You may have heard of the "Dust Bowl" of the 1930s. Recovery from that catastrophe is still occurring.

Other Regions

A strip called desert grassland runs from southeastern Texas, through southern New Mexico and Arizona, south into Mexico. This grassland is similar to but drier than the short grass plains. Like the tall grass prairies of the east, the desert grassland exists largely because of fires. If there were no fires, this region would be dominated by cacti and mesquite (a tree in the legume family). Grasses, growing under cacti and mesquite, recover from the fires more rapidly than the other plants.

Trees, largely cottonwoods (poplars) dominate many river valleys. They also occur in low mountain ranges such as the Cypress Hills of Saskatchewan and Alberta and the Black Hills of South Dakota.

Strata in Grasslands

Grasslands have three strata (layers) which can be easily seen:
- the root layer
- the herb layer
- the ground layer

Root Layer Prairie soils are generally quite dry. Therefore plants have large root systems so they can absorb the water they need. At least half the mass of most plants is in the soil. Often this is in the form of roots. But sometimes it also includes underground stems called rhizomes. Rhizomes serve two functions. First, they help propagate (spread) the species. They run horizontally under the ground. Then they send up shoots to start new plants. Second, rhizomes store water and food. This stored material supports the plant during adverse conditions.

Ground Layer The ground layer consists mainly of the mulch described under "Soil" in Section 11.1. This layer is shaded by the grasses. Therefore it has a low light intensity. It also has a low wind speed. Because of these two factors, it remains cooler during the hot growing season. The sun's heat and the warm winds are intercepted by the grasses above.

The mulch helps increase the soil moisture content. (It slows down evaporation and decreases runoff.) It helps moderate soil temperatures by insulat-

Fig. 11-3 This plant, the cinquefoil, is one of a wide variety of species beneath the grasses.

Fig. 11-4 Coneflower is a member of the composite family which includes daisies, dandelions, and sunflowers. It is one of many flowering species in the grasslands.

ing the soil from heat input in the summer and heat loss in the winter. It also adds nutrients to the soil and helps the germination of seeds. Clearly it is vital to the existence of a natural grassland. Its loss, as you read earlier, can lead to a complete change of species in the community.

Herb Layer The herb (plant) layer can change from year to year. The species that dominate it in a given year depend largely on the precipitation that falls. Usually, though, three layers can be seen. The lower layer consists of plants which are flat on the ground or nearly so. Among these are mosses, lichens, dandelions, wild strawberries, and cinquefoil (Fig. 11-3).

If sufficient moisture is present, these plants are partly hidden by a middle layer of short grasses and other plants. Among these are members of the composite family such as fleabane and coneflower (Fig. 11-4). The middle layer, in turn, may be partly hidden by the upper layer. This layer consists mainly of tall grasses.

The grasslands, then, are more than a sea of grasses. Among the grasses is a wide assortment of other plants. This diversity of plants helps ensure a wide diversity of animals. It also increases the stability of the ecosystem. If an environmental stress such as a drought strikes the area, some species may die. But other more tolerant species will live. And the ecosystem continues to function.

Section Review

1. Name the three regions in the grasslands.
2. Copy Table 11-1 into your notebook. Then complete it as a summary of the nature of the grasslands.

Table 11-1   Regions of the Grasslands

Name of region	Location	Precipitation	Grasses and their nature
Tall grass prairie			
Mixed grass prairie			
Short grass plains			

3. What caused the "Dust Bowl" of the 1930s?
4. Name and describe each of the three main strata in the grasslands.

11.3   Biotic Factors: Animals

A History of Survival and Extinction

American Bison   When you drive through the prairies today, it is hard to imagine what they used to be like before non-Native people arrived. However, historians think that at least 45 000 000 American bison roamed the grasslands at one time (Fig. 11-5)! These animals, commonly called buffalo, seldom overgrazed an area. Instead, they stayed constantly on the move. Ecologists believe they are, in large part, responsible for the nature of the prairies. They helped mould the prairies into what they are by killing invading trees. The bison rubbed against the trees to remove loose fur. They stripped off bark with their horns. And they browsed on seedlings. (Cattle perform the role of the bison now.)

Fig. 11-5   Enormous herds of bison once roamed the grasslands. They were slaughtered by the millions when European settlers invaded this area. This largest of North American animals almost became extinct. But the governments of both Canada and the United States have introduced small herds into a number of places.

Then the population of the prairies began to increase. As early as 1859 people, particularly the Métis and the Plains Indians, became aware of the declining numbers of buffalo. Many factors contributed to this. Ranchers and farmers shot bison that wandered onto their lands. The Métis and Plains Indians bought repeating rifles. This allowed them to hunt far more efficiently than before. In addition to this, sport hunters slaughtered bison in great numbers just for fun. "Buffalo robes" became popular. And for 25 years, over 100 000 bison hides went down the Missouri River alone each year! Bison tongues were eaten as a delicacy. But the rest of the meat was left to rot. By 1879, the Blackfoot in Canada could find no more bison. In the United States, the remaining bison were trapped in one herd between two rivers. About 150 000 were killed in 1883. The next year, only 300 could be found and killed. And by 1888 the government reported that only 6 bison remained!

But just before this animal became extinct, governments took conservation measures. Now, small herds exist in a number of places in North America. A large herd (about 12 000) is established in Wood Buffalo National Park in northern Alberta. There, American bison mingle with wood bison. A smaller herd is maintained in Elk Island Park near Edmonton, Alberta. In the United States, herds can be seen in the Black Hills of South Dakota, Yellowstone National Park, and several other state and national parks.

Pronghorns   In the early 1800s, the grasslands were also home to millions of pronghorns (Fig. 11-6). These animals are among the most graceful and swift on earth. And, at that time, their numbers rivalled the bison's. They and the bison competed very little. Bison feed mainly on grasses. Pronghorns eat plants such as sagebrush, roses, cacti, and juniper.

Pronghorns, commonly called antelope, also narrowly escaped extinction. Their troubles began when the bison had vanished. The Plains Indians turned to antelope as a source of food. Ranching reduced their feeding grounds. And their speed and agility made them a special challenge for sport hunters. By 1890 the herds were becoming dangerously small. Then a severe winter in 1906-07 reduced their total number to about 2000. (Pronghorns are not well-adapted to deep crusty snow which lasts several days. They feed mainly by sight. If they cannot see the food, they will not paw through snow to get it.)

By 1915 pronghorns faced extinction. But again, conservation measures were taken just in time. The Canadian government started a herd with just 42 animals. Under protection, they multiplied by the hundreds. Now up to 20 000 pronghorns roam freely through southern Alberta alone. They compete little with cattle because they feed mainly on plants cattle will not eat. Therefore they are tolerated on rangeland. As a result, you can see these animals all over the western plains. They live mainly in this short grass region because it is where their preferred food is. Controlled hunts ensure that their numbers will not drop again to the near-extinction level.

Fig. 11-6 Speed means survival for the pronghorn. When alarmèd, the white rump hairs bristle, flashing a danger signal to the herd.

Speed means survival for many grassland animals. With few places to hide, the only defence may be to run. In this sense, pronghorns are well-adapted to live in the grasslands. They have sturdy legs, large lungs and windpipe, and a heart double the expected size. With such adaptations, they can race with bursts of speed reaching 100 km/h!

The Fates of Other Animals In the early 1800s, several other hoofed animals shared the grasslands with the bison and pronghorns. Among these were mule deer, whitetail deer, and elk. They roamed the prairies in incredible numbers. All these herbivores were followed by a host of carnivores: great plains grizzly, great plains wolf, coyote, lynx, bobcat, and cougar. And scavenging foxes—kit fox and swift fox—joined the parade.

Small mammals, however, far exceeded the large mammals in number. Hordes of ground squirrels, gophers, prairie dogs, mice, voles, shrews, cottontails, jackrabbits, weasels, badgers, skunks, and raccoons lived on and in the land. And bird life was no less rich.

What is the status of these animals today? The great plains grizzly and great plains wolf were hunted to extinction. A combination of hunting and ranching eliminated elk from the plains and almost drove mule and whitetail deer to extinction before 1900. Moose and black bears vanished from the prairies before 1900. The kit and swift fox disappeared from Canada (see Figure 12-7). **Prairie dogs** now live only in a handful of scattered colonies or "towns". One prairie dog town in Texas used to cover 65 000 km² and was home to over 400 000 000 of these rodents! Today a small population resides

Fig. 11-7 This position helps the ground squirrel see predators. Unfortunately (for the ground squirrel) it also helps predators see the ground squirrel!

there. Prairie dogs compete with cattle for food. As a result, they were killed by the millions with poison bait. Conservation efforts have restored small colonies in southern Saskatchewan, Texas, and a few other places. Among birds, the beautiful trumpeter swan and whooping crane no longer nest on the prairies.

Hunting in the early days and then ranching brought a few species to extinction and several to the brink of extinction. Others were forced to migrate from the grasslands. But many species still remain. These have adapted to the presence of humans. And they still show the unique adaptations of grassland animals.

Adaptations of Grassland Animals

Mammals Grassland mammals have many fascinating adaptations to open country. Long distance vision is very important to both predator and prey. The eyes of grazing mammals are usually located well above the snout. Then they can see above the grass while feeding. Smaller mammals like the ground squirrel stand up on their haunches to see over the vegetation (Fig. 11-7). Others, like the kangaroo rat, hop up and down on well-developed hind legs (Fig. 11-8).

Fig. 11-8 Note the long "foot" of this tiny kangaroo rat. This foot, powered by a muscular upper leg, propels this rat well above the vegetation.

The prairies have few trees to provide hiding places. Therefore many animals rely on camouflaging colours for protection. If they sense danger, they remain motionless in the deep grass to escape notice. If the enemy approaches too closely, these animals suddenly flee by running, hopping, or in the case of birds, flying. Such sudden motion often startles the predator for a moment. This gives the intended prey a head start in its escape. Pronghorns, at 100 km/h, hold the escape speed record. But jackrabbits are close behind. They bound across the prairie at 70 km/h, using 8 m leaps and easily clearing obstacles 2 m high! Many other mammals escape predators by diving into underground burrows. These shelters also offer protection from the summer's heat and the winter's cold.

Fig. 11-9 The northern harrier hovers a few metres above the ground. When it spots a small rodent, it dives quickly to catch it.

Fig. 11-10 Over 30 species of birds were in this pothole when this photograph was taken.

Birds The grasslands abound in insect life, notably grasshoppers and their relatives. The large number of insects and seeds attracts a wide variety of birds. Grassland birds must be strong fliers to combat the high winds. In the absence of trees, many birds attract mates with songs delivered in flight. Nests are concealed in the tall grass. Among the insect and seed-eating birds are meadowlarks, bobolinks, longspurs, lark buntings, a variety of sparrows, prairie chickens, sage grouse, and sharp-tailed grouse.

Hovering, gliding, and diving in the sky above the smaller birds are hawks, eagles, falcons, and other birds of prey (Fig. 11-9). And vultures soar high in the sky looking for dead animals to feed upon.

The prairies are dotted with nutrient-rich potholes and sloughs. These small bodies of water, along with lakes and marshes, are home to a host of bird species—ducks, geese, shorebirds, swans, herons, cranes, and pelicans, to name a few (Fig. 11-10). The nutrient-rich water supports plant and algal growth. They, in turn, feed invertebrates and other small animals. And, together, the plants and animals are food for the birds.

In the fall, the skies are filled with migrating birds. The sloughs, potholes, marshes, and lakes provide food and resting places. And, to the regret of farmers, grain fields also feed many migrating species.

Section Review

1. **a)** Describe how American bison were brought almost to extinction.
   b) What is their present status?
2. **a)** List the four factors responsible for the decline of pronghorn numbers to the near-extinction level.
   b) What is their present status?
3. **a)** Name two grassland species that humans caused to become extinct.
   b) Why were prairie dogs poisoned?
   c) What is the present status of prairie dogs?
4. List six adaptations of grassland mammals which help them avoid predators.
5. **a)** Why do the grasslands support a wide variety of birds?
   b) Describe the role of potholes and sloughs in the prairie ecology.

11.4   *ACTIVITY*   Comparing Grassland and Deciduous Forest Biomes

The grassland and deciduous forest biomes lie, roughly, between the same latitudes. As well, they are governed by the same ecological principles. Yet, as you discovered, they differ in many respects (Fig. 11-11). In this activity you will investigate the reasons for their differences. By doing this, you will gain a better understanding of the ecology of the two biomes.

Grasslands

Deciduous forest

Fig. 11-11 Comparing grasslands and deciduous forest. The difference in dominant vegetation is easily seen. What other differences are there? And why do they exist?

Problem

How do the grasslands and deciduous forest differ?

Materials

Procedure

Fig. 11-12 Locate Cheyenne, Wyoming (in the grasslands) and Pittsburgh, Pennsylvania (in the deciduous forest).

a. Locate Cheyenne, Wyoming and Pittsburgh, Pennsylvania on the map in Figure 11-12.

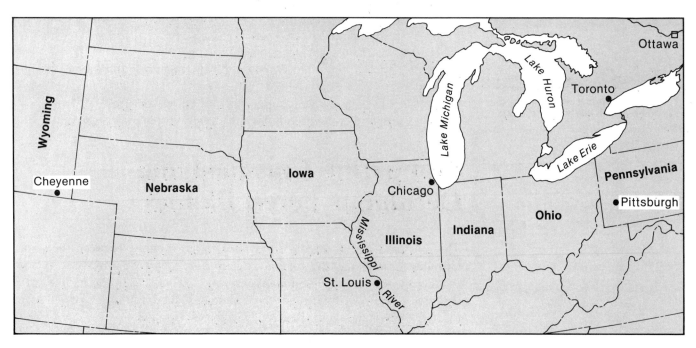

b. Study the climatograms given in Figure 11-13 for Cheyenne and Pittsburgh.

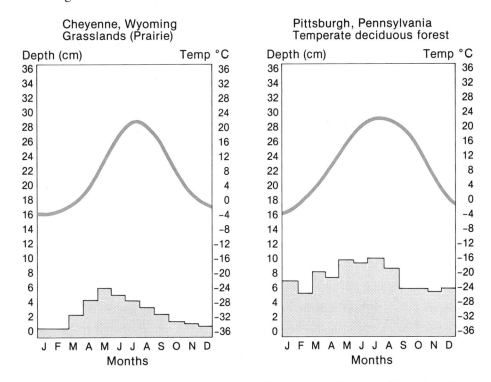

c. Answer the discussion questions. Refer back to Chapter 10 and earlier sections of this chapter for the information you need.

Discussion

1. **a)** What are the three distinct regions in the grasslands?
    b) In which one is Cheyenne located?
2. **a)** What are the three main types of forest in the temperate deciduous forest biome?
    b) In which one is Pittsburgh located?
3. Cheyenne and Pittsburgh are at about the same latitude. As a result, some of the abiotic factors of their ecology are similar. What are they?
4. **a)** What is the main difference in abiotic factors between the two areas?
    b) What role does this difference play in determining the dominant vegetation?
5. Compare the soil of the Cheyenne area with that of the Pittsburgh area.
6. Compare the two areas under the following headings:
    a) length of growing season
    b) annual precipitation
    c) annual snowfall
    d) month with the heaviest precipitation
    e) month with the lowest precipitation

f) distribution of precipitation over the year

g) annual temperature extremes

h) average monthly temperatures

i) daily temperature extremes

j) snowfall in December and January

7. Which area likely grows the most productive food crops? Why?

8. Cheyenne is at an altitude of 1870 m and Pittsburgh is at an altitude of 230 m. How might this affect the climatograms?

11.5   Human Impact on the Grasslands

We have completely changed the grasslands. They are no longer a sea of grasses. We have made them into the main food-producing region of the earth. This section summarizes the changes which occurred when the grasslands were changed into farms and ranches. Then it looks at the results of present-day agricultural methods.

A Summary of Changes

There is little doubt that humans have drastically changed the grasslands. In fact, probably no other biome has undergone such widespread and dramatic change. Many of these changes have been described in earlier sections. The following list is a summary of the changes:

- Most of the biome has been converted to agriculture.
- The tall grass prairie is intensively farmed to grow corn, wheat, and other crops.
- The mixed grass prairie is intensively farmed to grow grains and raise cattle.
- Much of the short grass plains has been overgrazed and improperly cultivated. But large natural areas still exist.
- Overgrazing, mowing, and fires have reduced the mulch layer in many places. This reduction completely changed the plant and animal community in those places.
- Bison and pronghorn have been reduced to a fraction of their original numbers. But they are now protected by conservation measures.
- The great plains grizzly and great plains wolf were hunted to extinction.
- Large predators such as the cougar, bobcat, and lynx have largely disappeared.
- Prairie dogs are a tiny fraction of their original numbers.
- Elk, moose, and black bears have been eliminated from the grasslands.
- The kit fox and swift fox disappeared from Canada.
- The trumpeter swan and whooping crane no longer nest on the prairies.
- Many species adapted to the presence of humans and the changed environment.

This list is just a small fraction of the changes since the mid-1800s. How serious are they? What impact have they had on the grasslands?

Fig. 11-14 This food pyramid existed in the grasslands up to about 1850. Some species shown here are now extinct. Can you spot them? Others are endangered. What might today's pyramid look like?

Fig. 11-15 The black-footed ferret, North America's rarest mammal.

Figure 11-14 shows a food pyramid that existed in the grasslands before human intervention. Study it carefully. Can you see species which no longer exist? Can you see species which are present in lower numbers than before? Now try to imagine a pyramid which might exist in the grasslands today. What are the major differences?

Here is just one example of how changes in one species affect an entire ecosystem. Prairie dog colonies used to support millions of these rodents. Such a community also supported bears, wolves, badgers, weasels, ferrets, burrowing owls, coyotes, foxes, hawks, snakes, and a host of other predators. Now prairie dog colonies are much fewer and much smaller. You can imagine how this change has affected predator types and numbers. One predator, the black-footed ferret, preys mainly on prairie dogs (Fig. 11-15). It also nests in prairie dog burrows. Poisoning campaigns almost eliminated the prairie dogs. The black-footed ferret, being further along the food chain, was hit even harder. Today, sightings are rare. It is probably the rarest mammal in North America. In fact, until recently, it was thought to be extinct.

Summary The most productive areas of the grasslands, the tall grass and mixed grass prairies, are intensively farmed. Most of the natural plants are gone. They have been ploughed under. And with them went many animals. In their place are domestic grasses: corn, wheat, barley, oats, rye. These cereal crops make the prairies the "bread basket of the world".

The short grass plains contain many natural areas. But much of this area was devastated by agriculture and has not yet recovered.

Impact of Agriculture

Tillage Practices   Abnormally wet years in the late 1880s fooled farmers and ranchers. The rains produced dense tall stands of grasses. But the bison were no longer around to eat these grasses. Therefore the land looked like it was more productive than it really was. As a result, land that should never have been cultivated was ploughed. And too many cattle were allowed to graze on the land. However, severe winters in the early 1900s and the drought of the 1930s changed farmers' thinking. Soils were devastated. And crop yields dropped drastically. Many marginal farms were abandoned. Some of these today are slowly changing back to grasslands.

Gradually, new tillage methods have been developed. Today, some farmers no longer use the deep-cutting moldboard plough which caused soil problems. Instead, conservation tillage implements are used which do not turn the soil over. They leave a residue of plant material on the surface. This residue helps prevent erosion. It also helps conserve soil moisture, just as the mulch of the original grasslands did. Many farmers now use other soil conservation measures—contour tillage, strip-farming, and crop rotation. Also, shelterbelts of trees have been planted to slow down prairie winds.

Unfortunately, far too many farmers are not practising soil conservation measures, as we will see later.

Irrigation   Irrigating lands has become popular in many areas. It greatly increases crop yields. It also allows new crops like sugar beets to be grown. But it can also drain too much water from wildlife habitats. It can increase the salt content of the soil. And it can lead to soil erosion.

Pesticides   The use of herbicides (weed killers) is widespread. Their use has greatly increased crop yields. It also reduces the amount of tillage needed. But often this method of weed control is used alone, without other methods such as crop rotation. If this is done, soil structure (the proper particle size) can be destroyed. Then soil losses through wind erosion increase.

The use of insecticides (insect killers) is also widespread. Their use, too, has greatly increased crop yields. But insecticides can have negative effects on the fish and wildlife that feed in food chains involving the target species.

Fertilizers   Commercial (inorganic) fertilizers are widely used to increase crop yields. They are needed to maintain the productivity of these foodlands. But often they are used as the *only* method of adding nutrients to the soil. If this is done, the soil structure gradually breaks down. And, once again, soil erosion increases. Organic matter is needed to maintain soil structure. Some farmers add it by putting animal wastes on the soil. Others plant legumes such as alfalfa. This plant adds both organic matter and nitrogen.

Summer fallowing   Many farmers still use this process to control weeds. Land is left fallow (without a crop) for a year (Fig. 11-16). During the year,

Fig. 11-16 Summer fallowing. The dark fields are those which were summer fallowed. The others grew crops.

the soil is tilled, when necessary, to kill the weeds. Summer fallowing does control weeds well. But it can destroy the soil. First, it speeds up the decay of organic matter. Loss of organic matter lowers the water-holding capacity of the soil. This allows water to run off more quickly, causing erosion.

Loss of organic matter, along with tillage, also affects soil structure. The soil aggregates are broken down into small particles. Now they can be easily blown away by wind. Sometimes the particles cake together, forming a hard crust on the soil.

Humus is a storehouse of nitrogen. Therefore, the loss of organic matter also lowers the amount of nitrogen in the soil. As a result, farmers practising summer fallowing must add more nitrogen fertilizer to keep yields up.

In arid regions, **salinization** is the major soil problem. During salinization, the soil becomes very salty. Its main cause is the wheat-summer fallow rotation many farmers use. Wheat does not require as much water as native grasses. Therefore extra water percolates into the soil. This raises the water table. The rising water brings salts up with it. Capillarity takes this salt-rich water to the surface. Tillage during summer fallow increases the rate of evaporation of this water. Then more water is drawn up by capillarity. After a time, more salts are carried up than are washed down. The soil becomes very salty. It even appears white. Canada's prairie provinces now have at least 2 200 000 ha of saline soil. And this area is increasing by 10% each year! Salinization has already reduced crop yields by 50% in many areas.

Soil Erosion

Why Is It Getting Worse? Many experts call soil erosion North America's most serious environmental problem. Many farmers and ranchers have changed their agricultural methods to conserve the soil. But most have not. And, strange as it may seem, city dwellers are an important cause of the problem. Those of us who live in cities simply will not pay a proper price for food. Therefore, the only way farmers can make a decent living is to grow more food on the land they have. One way to do this is to bring more land into production. Much of this land, however, should never be tilled. It includes hillsides, fence rows, windbreaks, natural water drainage systems, and arid land.

Other ways to grow more food (at least for a time) are to

- cut back on crop rotations and grow cash crops like corn every year (Fig. 11-17).
- use more chemical fertilizer.
- use more pesticides.
- irrigate more and more land.

You know the long term effects these measures can have.

How Serious Is It? Each year, Canada and the United States lose their best farming soil at the rate of 6 000 000 000 t a year! Losses are most serious in

Fig. 11-17 One form of water erosion. Corn was grown here, year after year. This broke down the soil aggregates into tiny particles. Then a heavy rain washed the soil downhill.

cash crop areas (wheat, corn, barley, beans, and soybeans). In the United States, these areas are mainly in Iowa, Illinois, and Missouri. These three states alone account for one-third of American soil losses. A single storm in Iowa recently washed away enough soil to cover over 900 000 ha to a depth of 5 cm!

The United States has a total of about 170 400 000 ha of farmland. Of this figure, about 39 300 000 ha are eroding twice as fast as natural processes can rebuild the soil. In all, 40% of farms are losing soil at alarming rates. In Iowa, the hardest hit state, topsoil which was 30 cm deep a few decades ago is now only 15 cm deep. About 25 t of soil leave each hectare every year. In parts of southern Missouri, half the topsoil is gone. The rest is eroding five times faster than it is being replaced. About 13 400 000 ha of American farmland is so prone to erosion that the soil can only be saved by turning the land back to grasslands.

The situation is similar in Canada. Prairie soils in many areas have lost 60% of their organic matter. Wind erosion has reduced crop yields up to 30% on higher ground. All told, erosion costs Canadian farmers over $1 000 000 000 a year in lost income. Not all erosion occurs, of course, on the prairies. Other major food-producing regions such as southern Ontario (corn and soybeans) and New Brunswick (potatoes) also have serious erosion problems. Losses in Ontario are about 12 t per hectare every year. In parts of New Brunswick, about 2-5 cm of topsoil disappear each year.

Solutions   What can be done to stem the tide of soil erosion? Many farmers say that if they try to use conservation methods, they will go bankrupt. They would have to buy new machinery and, at the same time, take land out of production.

But other farmers have already taken action. They say that conservation pays. Reduced tillage means a saving in fuel costs. Crop rotation eventually increases yields. It also lowers fertilizer and pesticide costs.

Fig. 11-18   The prairies still offer "wide open spaces".

The United States generally leads Canada in soil conservation measures. About one-third of American farms now practise some form of conservation tillage. Even in Iowa, 50% of the farmers do this. The United States Department of Agriculture thinks 90% of farmers will be using such tillage by 2010.

Conservation tillage is not so widespread in Canada. But a growing number of farmers are practising it.

Summary   The grasslands can be preserved as the "breadbasket of the world". As well, they can support more of the native plants and animals that used to live there. But these two things can happen only if some changes are made. We must
- reduce summer fallow dramatically
- change from a grain monoculture to crop rotation
- use conservation tillage methods
- incorporate other soil conservation methods
- pay farmers a fair price for their crops
- return all marginal farmland to native grasses.

The prairies have lost much of their former grandeur. Yet they still have a wide diversity of plants and animals. Even in agricultural areas, the big skies and rolling fields offer much of the appeal of unspoiled wilderness (Fig. 11-18). And, with proper management, the grasslands can both feed the world and be home to native plants and animals.

Section Review

1. Make a brief summary of the ways in which the grassland biome has been changed by humans.
2. Why is the black-footed ferret almost extinct?
3. Early farmers tilled land which should never have been tilled. And early ranchers put too many cattle on the land. What led them to do these things?
4. **a)** What important thing do conservation tillage implements do?
   b) How does this benefit the soil?
   c) What other soil conservation methods do farmers use?
5. Copy Table 11-2 into your notes. Then complete it.

Table 11-2   Agricultural Practices

Practice	Good Effects	Harmful Effects
Irrigation		
Use of herbicides		
Use of insecticides		
Use of fertilizers		

6. **a)** What is summer fallowing?
   b) Why is it done?
   c) Summer fallowing reduces the organic matter in soil. What harm can this cause?
7. **a)** What is salinization?
   b) What is its main cause?
   c) Explain how the soil becomes salty.
   d) What harm does salinization do?
8. **a)** Why is soil erosion getting worse?
   b) Describe the seriousness of soil erosion in North America.
   c) How widespread is conservation tillage in North America?
9. Make a list of 5 things we must do to preserve the grasslands as a food-producing region and as a habitat for native plants and animals.

Main Ideas

1. The grassland biome covers a vast expanse of the interior of the continent.
2. Low and irregular precipitation is the main factor responsible for a climax vegetation of grasses.
3. The grasslands have three distinct regions: tall grass prairie, mixed grass prairie, and short grass plains.
4. Grasslands have three strata: root, ground, and herb.
5. Hunting and agriculture drove some grassland animals to extinction, lowered numbers of others, and forced others to leave.
6. Grassland animals have adapted to open country, hot dry summers, and cold winters.
7. Improper farming and ranching have caused serious soil problems in the grasslands.
8. New agricultural methods are being implemented to reduce soil degradation.

Key Terms

mulch	rhizome	slough	tillage
pothole	salinization	summer fallowing	

Chapter Review

A. True or False

Decide whether each of the following statements is true or false. If the sentence is false, rewrite it to make it true. (Do not write in this book.)

1. Most grasslands have occasional severe droughts.
2. Climate alone is responsible for the vegetation which dominates the grasslands.
3. The tall grass prairie receives the least rainfall of the three regions in the grasslands.
4. The short grass plains are a good wheat-growing area.
5. The grasslands often have cottonwoods (poplars) in the moister regions.
6. Conservation tillage leaves plant material on the soil's surface.

B. Completion

Complete each of the following sentences with a word or phrase that will make the sentence correct. (Do not write in this book.)
1. The animal community of the grasslands is dominated by burrowers and ▨▨▨▨▨ .
2. Grasses often spread by underground stems called ▨▨▨▨▨ .
3. Two grassland animals driven to extinction by hunting are the and the ▨▨▨▨▨ .
4. The fastest grassland mammal is the ▨▨▨▨▨ .

C. Multiple Choice

Each of the following statements or questions is followed by four responses. Choose the correct response in each case. (Do not write in this book.)
1. The grasslands have a climax vegetation of grasses mainly because of
   a) low and irregular precipitation
   b) hot, short summers
   c) long, cold winters
   d) moderate rainfall and temperatures
2. Which one of the following is a true comparison of the grassland and deciduous forest biomes?
   a) They have almost equal amounts of precipitation.
   b) They have almost equal amounts of snowfall.
   c) They have similar average monthly temperatures.
   d) They have similar soils.
3. Which one of the following describes one role of the mulch in the grasslands?
   a) It speeds up water runoff from soil.
   b) It slows down evaporation of soil moisture.
   c) It keeps the soil warm in the summer.
   d) It absorbs nutrients from the soil.
4. In the early 1800s, the grasslands were molded into what they are by
   a) cattle
   b) pronghorn
   c) moose
   d) bison

Using Your Knowledge

1. **a)** Which provinces of Canada have some grasslands?
    b) About what percentage of each province is grassland?
2. **a)** Which states of the United States have some grasslands?
    b) About what percentage of each state is grassland?
3. **a)** Describe the role of the American bison in maintaining the grassland biome.
    b) Explain how modern agriculture has assumed that role.
4. **a)** Describe how humans drove the American bison to the verge of extinction.
    b) Could this type of thing happen today? Give your reasoning.
5. Explain why pronghorns compete little with cattle.
6. **a)** Describe the past status of the prairie dog.
    b) What is its status today?
    c) Do you feel that further efforts should be made to increase prairie dog numbers? Why?
    d) Suppose you are in a position to bring about changes. What steps would you take to ensure that prairie dogs will not become endangered?
7. Prairie mammals and birds collect around potholes, sloughs, and marshes. List at least four reasons for their behaviour.
8. **a)** Describe the damage which summer fallowing can do to soil.
    b) Describe how a wheat-summer fallow rotation causes salinization.
    c) Why do farmers continue to use such practices when they know they cause soil degradation?
9. What do you think we, as a nation, should do to protect agricultural soils from erosion?
10. Describe some of the long-term consequences of poor soil management. (Try to think beyond your own country.)

Investigations

1. **a)** Find out where the aspen parklands are in Canada.
    b) What climatic changes could make them creep south at a faster rate?
2. Design and conduct an experiment to show that mulch does for soil what is described in Section 11.2.
3. Select one of the following birds: prairie chicken, whooping crane, trumpeter swan, golden plover, Eskimo curlew, bobwhite quail. Find out how its numbers were drastically reduced. Then find out what, if any, conservation measures have been taken to protect it.
4. Select one of the following animals: swift fox, kit fox, tule elk, black-footed ferret, prairie falcon. Find out how it has been brought to the verge of extinction. Then find out what, if any, conservation measures have been taken to protect it.

12 The Desert Biome

In the southwest corner of the United States is one of the most arid regions on earth—the **desert biome** of North America (see Fig.7-16). Vast stretches of desert also extend through Africa, Asia, Australia, and the southern tip of South America (see Fig.7-14). This chapter describes the abiotic and biotic features of only the North American desert biome.

12.1 Abiotic Factors

Climate

Precipitation   Most people think of deserts as very hot places. And, of course, many of them are, particularly in the summer. Yet lack of water, rather than heat, produces deserts. They are generally found in regions receiving less than 25 cm of precipitation a year. They are sometimes found where precipitation is heavier but comes only occasionally during the year.

In North America, the deserts are located in the "rain shadow" of the west coast mountains. The mountains include the Coast Range and, further inland, the Cascade Range and Sierra Nevada Range. These mountains are barriers to the moist ocean winds.

Long droughts often occur in the rain shadow. Then the water supply for an entire year may fall in one great deluge! It usually arrives as a thunderstorm or cloudburst. The sun-baked surface cannot, in many places, absorb much moisture. So much of it drains away in surface runoff.

The relative humidity of desert air averages less than 30% at midday. This warm dry air often stops rain from reaching the ground. Rain, falling from a cloud, often evaporates before a single drop reaches the ground!

Temperature   The range of latitudes in the desert biome produces two quite different deserts on this continent. A "cool" desert is found in the Great Basin in the north. And there is a "hot" desert in the southwest (Death Valley region). The average annual temperature in the Great Basin is about 10°C. But it is over 20°C in the southwestern desert. The values may seem low to you. Remember, though, that winter brings snow and cold weather to the Great Basin and, occasionally, even to the southwestern desert.

Summer temperatures in Death Valley have soared to 57°C—in the shade! But the greatest impact of temperature on desert organisms comes from the wide range in temperature during each day. An extremely hot day is often followed by a very cold night. The desert sand receives about 90% of the incoming solar heat. (There are few clouds, little water vapour, and no canopy of vegetation to absorb the incoming heat energy.) As a result, the sand gets very hot. It, in turn, makes the air hot. At night, the heat leaves just about as easily. About 90% of the heat absorbed by the sand radiates quickly into space. And the soil and air temperatures drop rapidly.

Soil

Steady winds erode rock into tiny particles. They also stir up dust storms which scour the land surface. As a result, desert soil is dominated by rock particles, or sand. The scanty desert plant life does not provide the sand with much organic matter. And soil organisms such as earthworms cannot endure the dry sand. Many burrowing rodents have been exterminated through pest control programs. With such organisms absent, the soil does not get loosened much. Therefore water cannot soak in easily. In many places, the result is a hard, sun-baked surface. When moisture can soak into the sand, the heat quickly evaporates it.

Section Review

1. What is the annual precipitation of most deserts?
2. Describe the location of the North American deserts.
3. What precipitation factors, other than amount, are important to the North American deserts?
4. Compare the location and average annual temperature of "cool" and "hot" deserts.
5. Why are the average annual temperatures of deserts so low?
6. **a)** Describe desert soil.
   b) Why does this soil sometimes go hard on the surface?

12.2   Biotic Factors: Vegetation

The abiotic factors which dominate the desert biome are harsh indeed:
- wide-ranging temperature extremes
- low, irregular precipitation
- dry soil, low in organic matter and nutrients

Yet many plants and animals thrive in the desert. They have adapted to the conditions listed above. And, like tundra organisms, their adaptations are striking.

Water is the key to desert life. To survive in the desert, organisms must be able to develop and reproduce *rapidly* during any period of rain. For many organisms, dew is an important source of water. It forms during many evenings in even the hottest deserts.

There are three main types of desert plants: annuals, succulents, and shrubs. All are xerophytes (see Section 5.3, page 93). Let us see how each has adapted to cope with the moisture conditions in the desert.

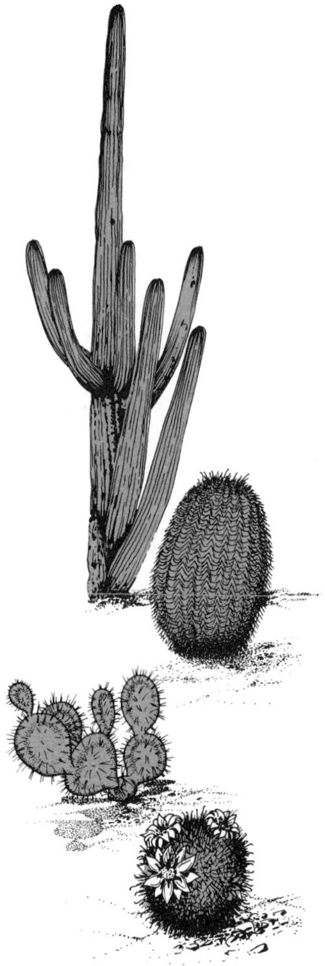

Annuals

Annuals are plants which live for only one year. Each generation must produce enough fertile seeds to continue the species. Annuals exist as dormant seeds during dry weather. The seeds will only germinate when enough water is available to enable rapid plant growth. The desert brightens with the flowers of these plants shortly after the winter and summer rains.

Succulents

Succulents, or "juicy" plants, such as cacti, survive long droughts by storing water (Fig. 12–1). Most cacti have a rounded shape. This shape minimizes the surface area exposed to the hot, dry air. Some fold like an accordian in dry periods. They can quickly expand by soaking up water during a rain. As they gradually use up their stored water, the plants shrivel back to their former shape.

Most plants lose water through stomata (breathing pores) in their leaves. Cacti do not. They are leafless evergreens. (The spines are thought to be the remnants of what were leaves in the early stages of the evolution of cacti.) Their green stems perform the role of leaves—photosynthesis. A thick, rubbery cuticle (skin) covers the stem. This cuticle further protects stored water.

The spines shade the cacti a little from the direct rays of the sun. They also reduce surface air currents that cause water evaporation. As well, the spines protect fleshy parts from browsing animals.

Shrubs

Desert shrubs have small, thick leaves. Many of the leaves have sunken stomata (as the needles of conifers do). They also have a waxy cuticle. It reflects heat and slows down water loss. During dry spells, the leaves are shed to help conserve water. But photosynthesis continues in the green stems. The creosote bush is the dominant shrub in the hot southwestern desert. Sagebrush is the dominant shrub of the cool northern deserts of the Great Basin.

Fig. 12-1 Most cacti have a rounded shape. This minimizes the surface area exposed to the sun. Sharp spines protect flesh parts from browsing animals.

Fig. 12-2 Competition for moisture is responsible for the long distances between desert plants.

Competition for Water

The competition for water keeps desert plants spaced well apart (Fig. 12-2). Most send out shallow, widely branching roots. The roots quickly soak up any traces of fallen water. Other plants such as the mesquite (a tree in the legume family), develop long tap roots. These may probe more than 30 m down to reach underground water sources!

The roots of the creosote bush produce toxins (poisons). These poisons are secreted into the ground. They kill other plants which try to invade the growth site of this plant. The creosote bush also has a pungent, distasteful juice. The taste discourages browsing animals.

Propagation by Animals

Some desert plants actually depend on animals for propagation. In June, birds eat and digest the sweet fruit of the saguaro cactus. The seeds pass through the digestive system unharmed. Often they drop to the shaded ground beneath the birds' nesting sites. The shade helps protect the seeds until the next rain causes them to germinate.

The seeds of the mesquite have a very hard seed coat. Its function is to protect the seeds from water loss. Unfortunately, it also prevents water from soaking in to stimulate germination. So before these seeds can germinate, they must be eaten. The hard seed coat is removed by animal digestive juices. Water can now penetrate the seed. Then after egestion, growth begins within the nutrient-rich animal manure.

Section Review

1. To survive, how must desert plants respond during periods of rain?
2. Name the three main types of desert plants.
3. **a)** What is an annual plant?
   b) When do desert annuals grow and bloom?
4. **a)** What is a succulent plant?
   b) Make a list of the ways cacti have adapted to desert conditions.
5. How have desert shrubs adapted to hot, dry conditions?
6. **a)** Why are desert plants spaced far apart?
   b) How does the creosote bush compete for space?
7. Describe how the saguaro cactus and mesquite tree depend on animals for propagation.

12.3   Biotic Factors: Animals

Fig. 12-3 Desert scorpions have enlarged claws for digging. They are also useful for capturing prey. These animals often eat their own mass in insects every day.

Desert animals must also cope with the problems of a limited water supply. The best way is to conserve body moisture. Body moisture can be lost in three ways:
- evaporation from the surface of the body
- exhalation from the lungs during breathing
- elimination through excretion of body wastes

Let's see how desert animals lessen their water loss.

One obvious precaution is to avoid the heat of the day. Therefore many desert animals are nocturnal—they are active only during the cool nights. Other animals have physically adapted to burrow. The desert scorpion has enlarged digging claws (Fig. 12-3). Certain snakes and lizards treat sand like water. They dive head-first into it. Their nostrils are upturned or fitted with valves to keep sand out.

A burrow has many advantages. The surface of the desert sand may be a scorching 65°C. But an animal burrow only 45 cm beneath the surface can remain a cool 16°C. At night, the surface temperature drops a great deal. But the burrow remains about the same temperature it was all day. Moisture from the animal's breath raises the relative humidity in the burrow. This greatly reduces water loss through evaporation from the body surface. Burrows, then, protect animals from temperature extremes. They also provide a cool storage site for food and a hiding place from many predators (Fig. 12-4).

Fig. 12-4 The air in a burrow is a good insulator. Therefore it maintains a fairly constant temperature, day and night.

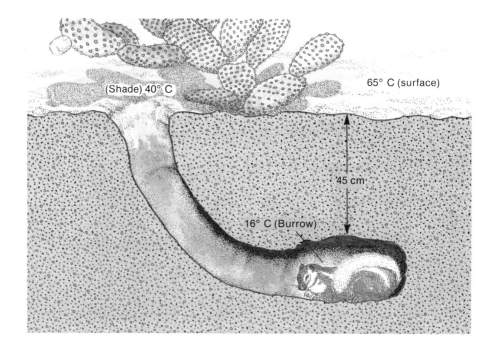

(Shade) 40° C

65° C (surface)

45 cm

16° C (Burrow)

Fig. 12-5 Some lizard species can run rapidly for short distances across the hot sand, using only their hind legs. The tail is raised to help maintain balance.

Animals which cannot burrow get protection from the hot sun by staying in the shade of cacti and other plants. Reptiles and scorpions have a hard body covering to reduce surface evaporation. Lizards and snakes have no sweat glands in their skins. Therefore they do not lose water through sweating, as many mammals do. Many desert spiders and insects are protected by a waxy exoskeleton. All desert animals try to minimize contact between their bodies and the hot sand. While hunting insects during the day, lizards use their legs to lift their bodies and tails off the sand. Some species can even stride for short distances with only their hind feet on the sand (Fig. 12-5).

Homeotherms ("warm-blooded" animals) sweat or pant in hot weather. They are simply using a built-in cooling system to keep body cells at or near the normal body temperature. The evaporation of water through sweating or panting uses up heat. Sometimes, though, mammals lose too much water. If they become severely dehydrated, they suffer "explosive heat death". Body water, lost by evaporation, is replaced by water from the blood. As a result, the blood thickens. Eventually it can no longer circulate fast enough to transfer heat from the interior to the surface. Then the body temperature soars, causing rapid death.

The body temperature of poikilotherms ("cold-blooded" animals) is regulated by their surroundings rather than by an internal system. "Cold-blooded" is a very misleading term for such animals. A lizard, basking on a desert rock measuring 38° C, has anything but "cold" blood! (Your blood temperature is about 37.5° C.) To maintain a functional body temperature, poikilotherms must move back and forth from sun to shade. Most lizards collapse if their body temperature rises above 40°C. And 10 min of direct exposure to the hot desert sun can kill a rattlesnake.

Birds are the most active animals during the day. They are not bothered by the heat as much as other animals for several reasons.

- They perch above the ground, away from the hot sand.
- During flight, the air stream cools their bodies.
- Feathers provide good insulation from the heat.
- They have no sweat glands in their skin.
- They have high body temperatures (between 40°C and 43°C). Therefore they can withstand heat more readily.

Fig. 12-6 This desert speedster, the roadrunner, preys on insects, lizards, and even rattle snakes. The prey is swallowed head first. Such prey provides needed water for the roadrunner.

However, birds lose more moisture through panting than small mammals do. Birds of prey and insect-eaters regain considerable moisture from their food (Fig. 12-6). But many desert birds, especially seed-eaters, must remain within flying distance of surface water. Certain birds, such as swifts and nighthawks, have an added defence against desert rigours. When wind or rain reduces their insect diet for several days, these birds face starvation. To conserve energy, they become torpid—sluggish and inactive—until conditions improve.

Many of the smaller mammals use a similar defence during the hottest season when water is desperately scarce. To conserve body moisture, the pocket mouse and ground squirrel enter a deep summer sleep called estivation. The animal's body temperature remains just slightly above that of the moist burrow. Larger animals must simply endure the days. They rest as motionless as possible in any spot of shade, until sunset brings relief from the burning heat. Many have very large ears (Fig. 12-7). Nocturnal hunters and their prey rely upon their hearing for survival. But heat can also be radiated from the body through the many blood vessels in the ears.

Fig. 12-7 Like the desert jackrabbit, the little kit fox has large ears. These ears are highly sensitive to sounds. And, just as important, they help radiate heat.

Most desert dwellers pass body wastes in a highly concentrated form to further minimize loss of body moisture. The waste product of protein digestion is poisonous. It must be eliminated in the form of urea or uric acid. Birds, insects, and most reptiles excrete crystallized uric acid using very small amounts of water. But mammals and some reptiles produce urea. Urea must be dissolved in water before excretion. Some desert mammals have far more concentrated urine than non-desert species. Mammals that eat meat and insects have a high protein diet. They lose more water through excretion than do vegetarian mammals that eat mainly sugars and starches. Thus, insect-eating bats must drink water daily. Seed-eating rodents need not do so.

The kangaroo rat is a perfect example of adaptation. On long hind legs, this agile little rodent can spring across the sand like a miniature kangaroo. It barely touches the hot surface. The short forelegs dig the burrow used to escape the heat. This remarkable character lives on a diet of dry plant food — and never takes a drink! Its digestive system breaks down the food to yield water. It has no sweat glands. And its urine is highly concentrated.

The rainy season brings water. And water brings life to the face of the desert. A throng of hatching insects clamours among the blossoming plants. Birds hasten to mate and rear their young while food and water are plentiful. It is a time of birth for many desert animals. Nursing mothers must obtain enough moisture to replace the fluid lost in milk production for their offspring. Even tadpoles and shrimp abound in scattered waterholes! All life struggles to perpetuate itself in this endless cycle of moisture and drought.

Section Review

1. State three ways in which animals lose water.
2. Why are many desert animals nocturnal?
3. Describe the adaptation of the desert scorpion for burrowing.
4. How are many snakes and lizards equipped for burrowing?
5. State four advantages provided by an underground burrow.
6. Describe five adaptations, other than burrowing, which help desert animals survive.
7. a) What built-in cooling device do homeotherms have?
   b) How does prolonged exposure to the sun kill homeotherms?
8. a) How do poikilotherms maintain a functional body temperature?
   b) Why will prolonged exposure to the sun kill poikilotherms?
9. State five reasons why birds are able to remain active during hot days.
10. a) What is estivation?
    b) Why is it an advantage to some small desert mammals?
11. Give two advantages of large ears to desert animals.
12. a) How do many desert animals lessen water loss during excretion?
    b) Why do kangaroo rats never need to drink water?
13. What is the normal season of birth in the desert? Why?

12.4

Comparing the Deserts of the North and the Southwest

All deserts are not alike. In this activity you will compare two deserts. One is a desert region, the Great Basin Desert, in the northern United States. The data for this desert comes from Boise, Idaho. Boise is at the top end of the Great Basin Desert. The other desert is the Sonoran Desert in the southwestern United States. The data for it comes from Yuma, Arizona.

Problem

How are the deserts of the north and southwest alike? And how are they different?

Materials

graph paper (2 sheets)
coloured pencils

Procedure

a. Locate Yuma, Arizona and Boise, Idaho on the map in Figure 12-8.
b. Obtain a physical map of the United States. Make a sketch map showing the extent of the desert which stretches from Boise down to Yuma.
c. Plot the climatogram for Yuma on one sheet of graph paper and the one for Boise on the other sheet. Use the data in Table 12-1.
d. Answer the discussion questions. The climatograms will help you answer many questions. You may have to look back through the chapter for information to help you answer other questions.

Table 12-1   Climate Data for Yuma, Arizona and Boise, Idaho

		J	F	M	A	M	J	J	A	S	O	N	D
Yuma, Arizona	Temp. (°C)	12.5	15.0	18.0	21.1	24.7	29.4	33.0	35.3	29.4	22.8	16.9	13.0
Altitude 43 m	Prec. (cm)	1.0	1.0	0.8	0.2	0.0	0.0	0.5	1.5	1.0	0.8	0.5	1.3
Boise, Idaho	Temp. (°C)	−1.9	1.1	5.1	10.0	14.3	18.2	23.7	22.3	17.3	11.4	3.9	0.1
Altitude 867 m	Prec. (cm)	3.4	3.4	3.4	3.0	3.2	2.2	0.5	0.3	1.0	2.2	3.0	3.3

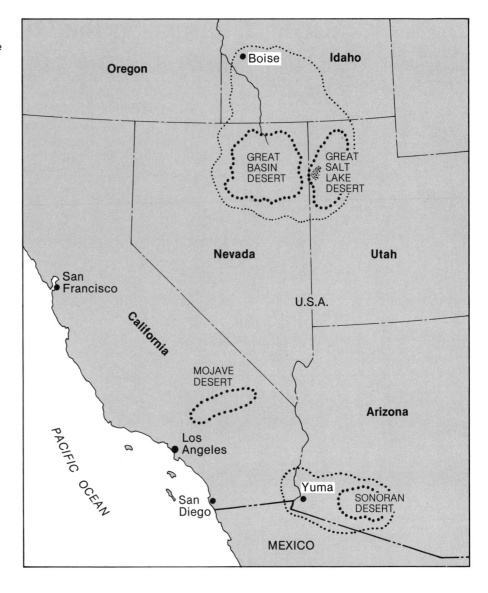

Fig. 12-8 Yuma, Arizona is in the Gran Desert (a "hot" desert) in the southwest. Boise, Idaho is at the northwest end of the Snake River Plain (a "cold" desert) in the north.

Discussion

1. a) Calculate the average annual temperature for Yuma and Boise.
    b) What two factors play a role in making these averages different?
2. a) Calculate the average annual precipitation for Yuma and Boise.
    b) What factors could be responsible for making these averages different?
3. When does a dry season occur in each area?
4. a) Which area has the greater range in average monthly temperature?
    b) What effects might this greater range have on the diversity of animals? Explain your answer.

5. What differences would you expect to find in biological activity during June in the two areas?
6. Which month would likely be the peak month for plant growth in each area? Why?
7. Which area probably has greater diversity of animals? Why?
8. Which area will have more grasses and shrubs? Why?
9. In which area are there likely to be more estivating species? Why?
10. Suppose unlimited irrigation water and fertilizer were available. Which area would likely be most productive for growing fruits and vegetables? Why?
11. April and May are favourite times for tourists in Arizona. Why?

12.5   Human Impact on the Desert

Like all the other biomes, the desert has been drastically changed by humans. The soil has been tilled. Crops have replaced native plants. Animals have been exterminated because they damage these crops. And other animals have been greatly reduced in numbers because their habitats have been destroyed.

Yet all is not bad. The deserts are rich in national and state parks. These parks offer habitats for native species and protection from "civilization". They also preserve some of the original beauty and grandeur that only deserts offer.

Water: A Scarce Resource

The face of the desert is being rapidly changed by three main factors:
- agriculture
- urbanization
- tourism

Unfortunately, all three factors demand a resource in short supply in the desert—*water*. Why are people developing the desert when we know that water is in short supply?

Agriculture   The deserts of the southwest produce bountiful crops of fruits and vegetables. Furthermore, they can produce crops in the winter. They put fresh fruits and vegetables on the tables of Canadians and Americans even in December. But there is a cost. The deserts can only yield food if they are heavily irrigated and fertilized.

Urbanization   The cities of the southwest deserts are growing rapidly. Industries are attracted to the area because of the climate. For the same reason, many Canadians and Americans from the north retire to homes in these cities. But industries need water. And homes need water. Further, people from the north expect green lawns, green golf courses, and swimming pools. All require water.

Tourism Because of the climate and scenery, the deserts of the southwest have become very popular with tourists. Tourists, too, expect green golf courses and swimming areas. They also require water for routine daily use.

Where Does the Water Come From? Clearly most of this water does not come from precipitation. An annual rainfall of 10 cm or so cannot meet all these demands. Where, then, does the water come from?

In some places it is brought in from dammed river systems. Demand has become so high, however, that once majestic rivers are reduced to tiny trickles by the time they reach the Pacific Ocean or the Gulf of Mexico. In other places, the water comes from underground deposits called aquifers. This water has been accumulating in underground caverns for thousands of years. But countless wells have been drilled to tap this water. And, in just a few decades, some aquifers are almost dry. In places, the desert is actually sinking into the empty space below.

The problem, incidentally, is not restricted to the deserts. A more serious problem exists on the High Plains east of the deserts. In just 40 years, farmers changed much of this area (mainly in Nebraska, Colorado, Kansas, New Mexico, Oklahoma, Texas, and Wyoming) from a barren dust bowl into one of the richest agricultural regions on earth. The change was made possible by the Ogallala Aquifer (Fig. 12-9). This aquifer, the largest on earth, underlies 570 000 km² of the High Plains. Water is disappearing from it at the rate of 27 000 000 000 m³/a. Because of irrigation, the High Plains produce 25% of the United States' cotton, 38% of its grain sorghum, 16% of its wheat, and 15% of its corn. About 40% of America's grain-fed cattle are raised here. Yet at the present rate of withdrawal the aquifer will be dry by 2025. Areas in the north, like Nebraska, still have a deep layer of water under them. But parts of the south are already having water shortages. Places in Texas have sunk because of water withdrawal. In parts of Oklahoma, the water may not last 20 years. As one expert said, "We are treating this water as we do any other mining operation. We use it up as fast as we can to make money. Then we will find something else to do." But this statement raises the question: Where else will we grow this needed food when the water is gone?

Solutions to the Water Shortage Problem

Solution 1: Find More Water Americans in the High Plains and Southwest have been "eyeing" Canadian water for years. Many rivers in Canada flow north to the Arctic Ocean and Hudson Bay. Countless schemes have been developed for diverting water south from these rivers. The cost is still prohibitive. But, more important, the effects of such diversions on Arctic ecology could be disastrous. With less warm water flowing north, the north-

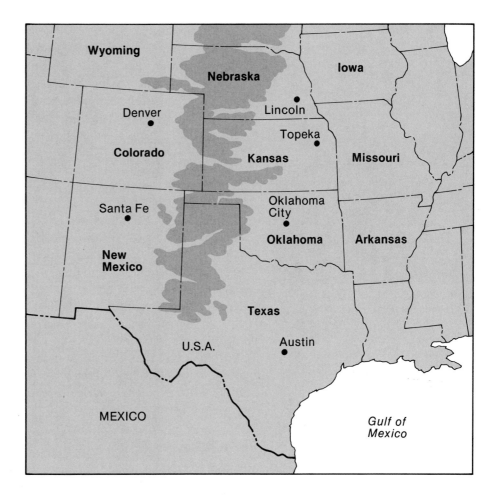

ern waters would freeze sooner and stay frozen longer. This change could seriously disrupt the ecological balance. It could even change the local climate and, perhaps, the global climate.

Plans have also been developed to divert water south from the Great Lakes. But Ontario and most of the eight Great Lakes states are opposed to such plans. There seems to be an endless supply of water in the Great Lakes. But a drop in lake levels of just a few centimetres could empty many marshes. These marshes support a wide variety of fish, birds, mammals, and other animals. Such a drop could also have a serious effect on power production and navigation. Further, northerners argue, the water is needed for local irrigation, industries, and cities.

It appears that finding more water will not be easy. What other solution is there?

Solution 2: Conservation Americans use about 1 137 000 000 000 L of water a day! Over half is for irrigation. And, says the United States General Accounting Office, half the water used for agriculture is wasted. Why does

Fig. 12-10 Spray irrigation wastes water, particular in hot dry climates. Much of the water evaporates before it reaches the ground.

this happen? Water is still cheap. The price charged for it does not reflect its true worth. Therefore it is handled wastefully. For example, spray irrigation is often used instead of drip irrigation (Fig. 12-10). When water is sprayed into hot dry air, much of it evaporates before it reaches the ground. Also, in places, poor irrigation methods allow water to wastefully run off the soil. Here are some things we can do to conserve water:

- Use less water on a given crop. Yields may be lower but the land will be productive longer.
- Change irrigation methods to reduce losses from evaporation and runoff.
- Grow only those crops which benefit the most from irrigation. Do not grow crops which can grow without irrigation on idle land in the north.
- Keep the organic content of the soil as high as possible. A higher organic content will increase the water-holding capacity of the soil. Then water will not drain away.
- Stop growing water-demanding crops in areas with mounting water deficits.
- Reduce non-agricultural irrigation such as watering lawns and golf courses. Do lawns and golf courses *really* have to be green?
- Introduce realistic water prices.

Arizona, more than any other state, has taken some of the above steps to conserve water. If others follow its lead, the Southwest and High Plains will continue to be productive agricultural regions for generations to come.

Section Review

1. What three factors are changing the face of the desert?
2. a) Why is agriculture popular in this region of poor soil?
   b) Why are cities growing rapidly in the southwest deserts?
   c) Why is tourism a big business in the southwest?
3. Make a summary of the demand for water made by agriculture, urbanization, and tourism in the southwest.
4. a) What are the two main sources of water for development in the southwest?
   b) What is the present status of these sources?
   c) What will happen to these sources if demand continues to increase?
5. a) What is the Ogallala Aquifer?
   b) How important is it to the High Plains?
   c) What is its present state?
   d) How long will it likely last at the present rate of withdrawal?
6. There are two possible solutions to the water shortage problems of the High Plains and southwest:
   a) find more water
   b) conservation
   Evaluate each of these solutions.

Main Ideas

1. Deserts usually lie in areas receiving less than 25 cm of precipitation a year.
2. The United States has "cold" deserts in the Great Basin and "warm" deserts in the southwest.
3. Desert plants are of three types: annuals, succulents, and shrubs. All have adapted to low precipitation and harsh temperature extremes.
4. Desert animals have adapted to reduce water loss by evaporation, exhalation, and excretion.
5. Humans have greatly changed the desert through agriculture, urbanization, and tourism.
6. The most crucial resource of the southwest is water. It must be conserved to keep the area functioning.

Key Terms

annual
aquifer
estivation
homeotherm
poikilotherm
succulent
xerophyte

Chapter Review

A. True or False

Decide whether each of the following statements is true or false. If the sentence is false, rewrite it to make it true. (Do not write in this book.)

1. Deserts are always hot and dry.
2. It sometimes snows in the desert biome of the United States.
3. An annual plant will blossom once a year, year after year.
4. The feathers of a bird insulate it from the desert's heat.
5. The kangaroo rat never drinks water.

B. Completion

Complete each of the following sentences with a word or phrase that will make the sentence correct. (Do not write in this book.)

1. A "cool" desert occurs in the ▓▓▓▓▓▓ of the north-central United States.

2. Cacti have ▨▨▨▨▨ stomata (breathing pores).
3. The ▨▨▨▨▨ is an example of a desert poikilotherm.
4. Ground squirrels enter a deep summer sleep called ▨▨▨▨▨ to conserve water.
5. The ▨▨▨▨▨ aquifer of the High Plains is the largest aquifer on earth.

C. Multiple Choice

Each of the following statements or questions is followed by four responses. Choose the correct response in each case. (Do not write in this book.)

1. Competition for water forces desert plants to be
   a) prickly   c) thick-leafed
   b) spaced far apart d) leafless
2. During the day, a burrow provides a desert animal with
   a) a hot humid home c) a hot dry home
   b) a cool humid home d) a cool dry home
3. Spring in the deserts of the southwest is best described as
   a) warm and dry c) warm and wet
   b) cool and dry d) cool and wet
4. The largest user of water in the deserts is
   a) industry c) tourism
   b) homes   d) agriculture

Using Your Knowledge

1. a) Small patches of desert exist in Canada. Where would you expect these to be? Why?
   b) With irrigation, the deserts in Canada are prime fruit-growing areas. What must their climate be like?
2. A brief rainstorm will not stimulate germination of desert annual flower seeds. Yet more than 50% of the seeds will sprout after a heavy rainfall. Also, the water must come from above, not beneath, the soil. Why is this adaptation so critical to desert annuals?
3. Some desert plants, such as the night-blooming cereus, have evolved flower petals that open only at night. The blossoms of such plants are usually white and highly fragrant. Of what advantage are these three characteristics to the plants?
4. Many desert plants have a special way of admitting carbon dioxide for photosynthesis. They absorb carbon dioxide through their stomata at night, rather than during the day. What advantage is this adaptation to the plants?
5. List A includes jurisdictions which may favour diverting Great Lakes water to the south. List B includes jurisdictions which may oppose such diversions.

List A	List B
Nebraska	Ontario
Kansas	Michigan
Oklahoma	New York
Texas	Wisconsin
New Mexico	Ohio
Arizona	Pennsylvania
Colorado	Minnesota
	Indiana
	Illinois

a) Imagine that you are the governor of a List A state. Prepare a statement of up to 200 words defending diversions. Give and defend your reasons.

b) Imagine you are the premier of Ontario or the governor of one of the List B states. Prepare a statement of up to 200 words opposing diversions. Give and defend your reasons.

6. a) Imagine that you are governor of one of the List A states in question 5. Make a list of water conservation measures you would implement immediately.

b) List the consequences of each of your conservation measures.

Investigations

1. Obtain a cactus. Examine its surface carefully with a hand lens. Strip some of the epidermis (skin) off the cactus. Make a wet mount of the epidermis. Then examine it with a microscope. Cut the cactus open. Examine the interior. Carefully dislodge the roots from the soil. Then examine them closely. Write a report of about 100 words on the adaptations of this cactus to xerophytic conditions.

2. Find out the official position of your provincial or state government on water diversions from the north to the High Plains and southwest.

3. Desert animals show many remarkable adaptations. Select *one* of the following and find answers to the questions asked:

a) The kangaroo rat. Why are these rodents vital to the life of the desert?

b) Desert birds. What are a few common species? Where do they nest? How does climate affect their breeding habits?

c) The antelope ground squirrel. How can this mammal remain active during the hot desert day?

d) The peccary. How does this wild pig survive in the desert?

e) Desert snakes. When are they most active? How do they find and capture prey?

13 Other Biomes

This chapter explores the five remaining biomes of Canada and the United States. It also looks at the tropical rain forest. Though not present in Canada or the United States, this biome is of great importance to the earth.

13.1   Mountain Biomes

Abiotic Factors

A change in altitude can affect the environment as much as a change in latitude. As altitude increases, the temperature falls as much as 1°C for every 150 m. Even in the Smoky Mountains of the southeastern United States, the temperature drops on the average 1.24°C for every 300 m increase in altitude. This decrease is equivalent to moving north about 640 km. Wind speed increases at higher altitudes. Mountain soil is eroded by rain, frost, and falling rock. Therefore it becomes thinner and more mineral deficient at higher altitudes.

Ecosystems resembling the circumpolar biomes of high latitudes are found on mountains (Fig. 13-1). A strip less than 6.5 km up a mountain at the equator provides as many different environments as a strip 10 500 km long from the equator to the north pole. A grassland has different organisms than the tundra. Similarly, the bottom of a mountain has different organisms than the top.

Northern species are found in mountain ridges where conditions match those of more northern latitudes. These mountain zones may resemble some of the biomes we have studied. But, as you will see later, many mountain species have unique adaptations.

The polar regions are cold because the sun's rays strike these latitudes at a very low angle (see Chapter 8). Much of the radiant energy is absorbed during its long path through the earth's atmosphere. In the mountains, the solar rays have a much shorter route through a thinner layer of atmosphere. The density of mountain air is very low. As a result, most of the heat is

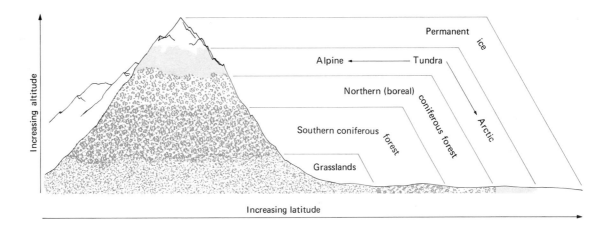

Fig. 13-1 If you climb a tall mountain, you will walk through several ecosystems. You would see similar ones if you walked from the southern grasslands to the Arctic icecap.

radiated back into space instead of being absorbed. Yet the mountain surface absorbs the remaining heat energy readily. This absorption results in a great difference between ground and air temperatures during the day. Since low-density air cannot retain much moisture, humidity is low. The clear, thin air permits more of the ultraviolet portion of the sun's rays to reach the ground. The high wind speeds increase evaporation, further reducing temperatures.

Alpine Tundra   Abiotic factors similar to those of the Arctic have established "islands" of tundra on mountains in high alpine regions. In **alpine tundra**, permafrost exists only at very high altitudes and on northern mountain ranges. As a result, the ground surface is drier than that of Arctic tundra. Yet the combination of frost and wind still produces thin, unstable soils except in small, protected pockets in the mountain sides. The temperature is usually low. But it can fluctuate as much as 32°C during a single summer day. Southern slopes are the warmest. The growing season is brief, as in the Arctic. But the alpine tundra is not subjected to the same extreme change in photoperiod. Although summer days are shorter in the mountains, the light intensity is much higher in the thin atmosphere.

The clouds and fog which often hide the mountain tops yield more precipitation to the alpine tundra. However, the steep land surface causes rapid water runoff before the water can soak in. Low atmospheric pressure and high wind speed increase the rate of evaporation. Yet humidity remains low because the thin air cannot retain much water vapour. The low density of air (and, hence, reduced concentration of oxygen) is a feature unique to the alpine tundra. How do you think this affects the plant and animal life of this region?

Biotic Factors

Zones   Five major zones can often be seen on the taller mountains in the Rocky Mountains (Fig. 13-2). Let's take an imaginary walk up a mountain through these zones.

Fig. 13-2 Zones in the Rocky Mountains. Each zone has a unique kind of vegetation. Differences in soil, temperature, moisture, and light form these zones.

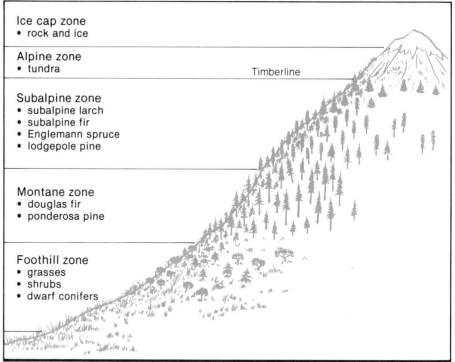

Ice cap zone
- rock and ice

Alpine zone
- tundra

Timberline

Subalpine zone
- subalpine larch
- subalpine fir
- Englemann spruce
- lodgepole pine

Montane zone
- douglas fir
- ponderosa pine

Foothill zone
- grasses
- shrubs
- dwarf conifers

Fig. 13-3 The large trees you see here are Englemann spruce. In drier areas, lodgepole pine dominate the subalpine zone.

Fig. 13-4 Subalpine larch, also called Lyall's larch, is usually the dominant tree at the top of the subalpine zone.

The first zone we walk through is the foothill zone. It is not surprising that this zone is often dominated by grasses. After all, the Rocky Mountains do rise from a vast sea of grasses. But this zone also contains a wide variety of deciduous shrubs. It also often has juniper, an evergreen shrub. And in most places, there are small coniferous trees.

Above the foothill zone is the montane zone. One of the characteristic trees of this zone is the ponderosa pine. If you consider only abundance and range, this tree is the dominant tree of western North America. Just above the ponderosa pine in the montane zone is the Douglas fir. It is one of the most abundant and valuable trees in western North America. The Douglas fir trees in the Rocky Mountains are a different variety from those in the temperate rain forest. They are hardier than their coastal relative.

A further hike up the mountain will take us into the subalpine zone. In the lower part of this zone, we walk among large conifers, usually Englemann spruce and lodgepole pine (Fig. 13-3). Toward the top of this zone, the trees become smaller. Subalpine fir join the forest. Subalpine larch, a deciduous conifer, tops the subalpine zone (Fig. 13-4). On drier ridges, we often find white-bark pine (in the north) and bristlecone pine (in the south).

The forest gradually fades away at the top of the montane zone. The uppermost limit at which trees can survive is called the timberline (Fig. 13-5). At the timberline, an interesting phenomenon occurs. The trees are stunted and unusual in shape. You saw in Figure 13-3 that Englemann spruce are tall

Fig. 13-6 A trail was cut through this dense stand of krummholz Englemann spruce. Otherwise, you could not walk here.

Fig. 13-7 This alpine meadow, at the timberline, closely resembles the Arctic tundra near the tree line.

trees in the subalpine zone. But here they are just one or two metres high. Their tops seem to be sheared off. And branches often remain only on the lee side. This condition is, of course, caused by the cold, strong, prevailing winds. It has a name—krummholz, or "crooked tree" in German. Krummholz trees often form a thick mat which you cannot walk through (Fig. 13-6). Often though, you can actually walk *on top* of this carpet of trees!

Above the timberline is the alpine tundra zone. In many ways, this zone resembles the arctic tundra (Fig. 13-7). The higher mountains have an icecap zone—an area of ice and rock—at the top.

Fig. 13-8 This willow is a mature tree. Yet it is less than 1 m tall!

Vegetation of the Alpine Tundra

As in the Arctic, alpine tundra plants are small and stunted (Fig. 13-8). However, mountain species are adapted to a shorter photoperiod with more intense sunlight. To survive the low temperatures and strong winds, alpine growth hugs the ground in a dense, compact mass. This tangle of foliage can absorb and trap heat energy. In fact, the temperature inside such growth can be twenty degrees higher than the surrounding air. This warm haven attracts pollinating insects. Some plants have a fuzzy coat of hairs. This coat resists wind chill, traps heat and moisture, and reduces the intensity of mountain sunlight. (Too much ultraviolet radiation can damage plant cells.) Many leaves are thick and waxy to resist both freezing and evaporation. Certain plants contain a red pigment. It converts light into heat energy. Others have a rich cell fluid containing dissolved nutrients which acts as an antifreeze. Alpine grasses have narrow leaves and stems. They bend easily instead of breaking in the wind.

Alpine plants use most of their energy just for survival. Hence growth and reproduction are very slow. Mountain soil is dry much of the year. Therefore, a large root system is needed to obtain sufficient moisture. Extensive roots also help secure plants against fierce winds and sliding rubble on the slopes. Most mountain species are perennials because the plants must be well established before flowering occurs. The first tiny blossom may appear after ten years of growth! Insects are not abundant at high altitudes. Therefore many plants are wind-pollinated or self-pollinated. Normal seed germination is difficult in the harsh mountain conditions. The seeds of some plants sprout while they are still attached to the parent. Many mountain plant species rely upon vegetative propagation.

Animals of the Alpine Tundra

Except for the caribou and pipet, the animals of the alpine tundra are very different from those of the Arctic tundra. Mammals include the collared pika, hoary marmot, singing vole, mountain goat, barren ground caribou, Dall's sheep, common pika, yellow-bellied marmot, and bighorn sheep. Bird life is represented by the white-tailed ptarmigan, water pipet, and finches. Reptiles and amphibians are rare. Blackflies and mosquitoes are less common than in Arctic tundra. Yet there is an abundance of other insects: grasshoppers, butterflies, spiders, bumblebees, ants, leaf-hoppers, springtails, mites, and ground beetles.

The warm spring sun melts the snow from the southern slopes first. Here, plant and animal activity has a head start over the northern slopes. Growth and reproduction also begin earlier on the lower portions of both slopes. Summer bird residents build their nests on the southern edges of thickets. There, their young can best benefit from the sun's warmth. These nests seem to be unusually compact. This structure likely provides better insulation against the cold mountain air.

Fig. 13-9 The pika, a tiny mountain rodent, lives in rock rubble. It roams far from its home to collect vegetation which it stores for winter.

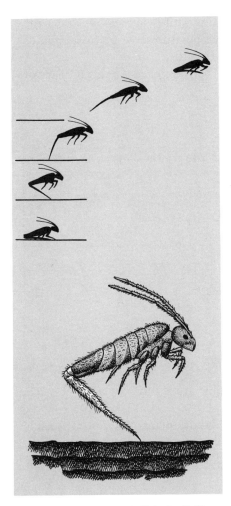

Fig. 13-10 The springtail flicks its "tail" downward to propel itself into the air. It can move many times its own body length by doing this.

Rather than combat the strong mountain winds, insects and even birds avoid flying, and remain close to the ground. In fact, 60% of alpine insects are wingless. Birds feed and rear their offspring in sheltered crevices or crawl into holes. When in the open, they always face toward the wind. Why?

Summer brings an invasion of bears, coyotes, weasels, badgers, mice, shrews, wapiti, and mule deer. Sandpipers and gulls frequent northern alpine ponds, seeking the scanty aquatic life. The little pikas which burrow among the rock rubble work through the summer, drying and storing up stacks of tundra vegetation. A single pika gathers as much as 23 kg of hay—150 times its own weight—to feed itself through the winter (Fig. 13-9).

The pocket gopher spends most of its life in underground burrows. It eventually kills the sedges and cushion plants above by chewing away at their roots. Any remaining growth is smothered by flying soil, scooped to the surface as the gopher tunnels. A different type of plant growth will invade the ruins. But the new vegetation is not acceptable to the gopher. It moves elsewhere in search of a more favourable residence. The original cushion plants gradually return and the sedges recover. Then back comes the gopher to try again!

Most of the active winter residents, such as the mountain goat and white-tailed ptarmigan, turn white. The marmots and ground squirrels hibernate. Wapiti, deer, and most of the birds depart to the slopes and valleys far below. Springtails can often be seen eating conifer pollen on the snow (Fig. 13-10). These insects freeze at night and then thaw out during the day.

The low oxygen concentration of the alpine tundra affects mammals the most. Birds are adapted to fly at high elevations. Invertebrates and plants have a much lower metabolic rate and, hence, a lower oxygen requirement. Increased heartbeat and breathing rates can temporarily help mammals, including humans, adjust to the thin atmosphere. But the animals permanently adapted to this high altitude have larger lungs and hearts. They also have an increased number of oxygen-carrying red blood cells.

Many alpine species have developed dark surface colours to absorb the increased ultraviolet radiation. This surface prevents damage to underlying tissues. Dark colouration also helps insects absorb and retain more body heat during the day. They cannot remain active without the warmth of the sun.

Snow meltwater is the main source of moisture in the mountains. At higher altitudes, where food supplies diminish, the population density of many alpine species is controlled by aggressive territorial behaviour and low reproductive rates.

Section Review

1. How much does altitude affect temperature?
2. Describe how a trip up a mountain can parallel a trip from the southern grasslands to the north pole.

3. Compare the upper regions of mountains with polar regions under the following headings: reason for low temperatures, permafrost, photoperiod, light intensity, soil moisture, oxygen.
4. Copy Table 13-1 into your notebook. Then complete it as a summary of the zones in the Rocky Mountains.

Table 13-1   Zones on a Mountain

Zone	Location	Dominant vegetation
foothill		
montane		
Subalpine		
alpine		
icecap		

5. What is the timberline?
6. **a)** What is the meaning of krummholz?
   b) What causes it?
7. **a)** How do alpine tundra plants resemble arctic tundra plants?
   b) How do they differ?
8. List six adaptations of different alpine tundra plants. Explain why each is an advantage.
9. **a)** Why are the rates of growth and reproduction of alpine tundra plants so slow?
   b) Give three benefits of a large root system to an alpine plant.
   c) Why are most alpine tundra plants perennials?
   d) How are many alpine tundra plants pollinated? Why?
10. **a)** Make a list of nine animals of the alpine tundra.
    b) Where does plant and animal activity first begin in the spring? Why?
    c) List four adaptations of alpine birds to their environment.
11. **a)** Why does the low oxygen concentration affect mammals more than birds or insects?
    b) How are alpine animals adapted to the oxygen-poor air?
12. List three ways in which alpine animals respond to the coming of winter.
13. Give two advantages to alpine animals of a dark body surface.

13.2

The Temperate Rain Forest Biome

Fig. 13-11 Giant conifers dominate the temperate rain forest.

Look back to Figures 7-14 and 7-16. Note the strip along the Pacific coast. It begins in Alaska and runs south through British Columbia, Washington, and Oregon. Then it ends in California. This unique forest of giant conifers lies between the Pacific Ocean and the coastal mountains. It is called the **temperate rain forest biome** (Fig. 13-11).

Abiotic Factors

This coniferous forest is quite different from the boreal coniferous forest you read about in Chapter 9. The trees are much larger and growth is more rapid. Also, the understory plants are more numerous and luxuriant in growth. These differences are mainly due to the unique climate of the coast—abundant moisture, high relative humidity, and moderate temperatures.

The winds along the coast are prevailing westerlies. They moderate the climate, resulting in average monthly temperatures from a low of 2°C to a high of 18°C. (Look ahead to the climatogram for Prince Rupert, B.C., Fig. 13-16.) The soil is frost-free for a period of 120 to 300 d.

In winter, the westerly winds pass over the warm Japanese Current. As a result, the winds become laden with water. When these winds move inland, they strike the coastal mountains. The mountains force the winds to rise. In the higher, colder atmosphere, the water in the air condenses. Then it falls as rain or snow. Some areas of this forest receive as much as 635 cm of precipitation a year!

In summer, the prevailing winds shift to the northwest. These winds are cooled by the northern seas. As a result, the colder air masses carry little water. But they do cause heavy fogs. The fogs soak the forest canopy. The water then drips from the canopy to the forest floor. These heavy fogs add 130 cm or more of water to the soil each year.

Biotic Factors

Three abiotic factors nourish the evergreen giants of the temperate rain forest. The same three factors promote a rich growth of ferns, mosses, and other shade-tolerant plants on the forest floor. These factors are
- an abundance of moisture
- a high relative humidity
- a moderate (generally warm) temperature

The most characteristic of the plants of this forest are the dominant trees. There are five main species of giant conifers:
- Sitka spruce
- western hemlock
- western red cedar
- Douglas fir
- redwood

Fig. 13-12 This Douglas fir tree is over 1000 years old.

Fig. 13-13 Redwood giants like this are still common in national parks and some state parks in California.

Sitka spruce occur throughout this biome from Alaska to California. They often grow to a height of 60 m and a diameter of 1.8 m. Some even grow larger. Western hemlock, slightly smaller trees, also grow throughout this biome. Western red cedar occur mainly in British Columbia, Washington, and Oregon. These trees, like the Sitka spruce, can top 60 m and can have a diameter up to 2.4 m. Douglas fir grow throughout the biome. These trees can reach a height of 75 m or more, with a diameter of up to 2.4 m (Fig. 13-12). The real giants, however, are the redwoods. These grow mainly in a strip about 700 km long, through Oregon and California. They commonly grow over 80 m tall, with a diameter of 3 m. Occasional trees have reached 105 m (Fig. 13-13)!

Human Impact

Because of their large size and high quality, the trees of this forest are valued for lumber. Lumber from red cedar and redwood, for example, resists decay. That is, it does not rot easily when it gets wet. As a result, such lumber is used to build homes, pool decks, patios, spas, saunas, and outdoor furniture. Unfortunately, the cutting rate greatly exceeds the reforestation rate in most areas. In many places, entire hillsides have been stripped. Then the soil has washed away. Evergreen giants may never grow again in these areas.

We do need lumber for building homes. But many conservationists question cutting down 1000 year-old trees to build patios, pool decks, and saunas. Conservationists also feel that more areas of the temperate rain forest should be protected from cutting so future generations can enjoy seeing these majestic trees. What do you think about these two matters?

Section Review

1. Describe the location of the temperate rain forest biome.
2. In what major ways does this forest differ from the boreal coniferous forest?
3. **a)** Describe the climate of this biome.
   b) Explain why precipitation is so high in this biome.

Table 13-2 Trees of the Temperate Rain Forest

Species	Maximum height	Maximum diameter
Sitka spruce		
Douglas fir		
western red cedar		
western hemlock		
redwood		

4. Copy Table 13-2 into your notebook. Complete it as a summary of the sizes of the trees in this biome.
5. **a)** What are the trees of this biome used for? Why?
   b) What is the present state of this forest?
   c) What two matters are conservationists concerned about?

Comparing Two Coniferous Forest Biomes

13.3   *ACTIVITY*

The temperate rain forest and the boreal forest are both dominated by coniferous trees. And they are both governed by the same ecological principles. Yet, as you discovered, they differ in many respects (Fig. 13-14). In this activity you will investigate the reasons for their differences. By comparing them, you will better understand the ecology of the two biomes.

Fig. 13-14 The temperate rain forest (left) consists of giant conifers such as Douglas fir, Sitka spruce, red cedar, redwood. The boreal forest (right) consists of much smaller conifers such as black spruce and balsam fir.

Problem

How do the temperate rain forest and the boreal forest differ?

Materials

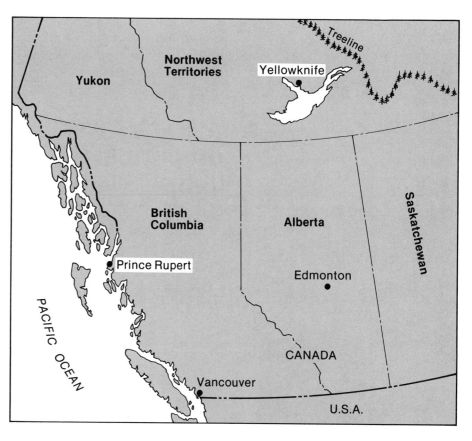

Fig. 13-15 Prince Rupert, B.C. is in the temperate rain forest. Yellowknife, N.W.T. is in the boreal forest, near the tree line.

Prince Rupert, British Columbia
Temperate rain forest

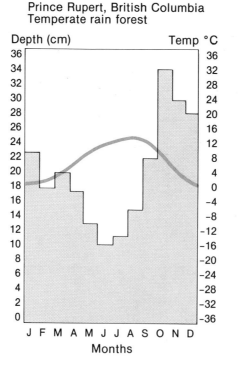

Yellowknife, NWT
Boreal coniferous forest

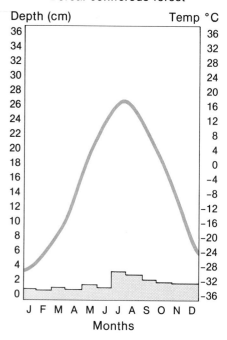

Fig. 13-16 The climatograms for Prince Rupert, B.C. (in the temperate rain forest) and Yellowknife, N.W.T. (in the boreal coniferous forest).

Procedure

a. Locate Prince Rupert, British Columbia, and Yellowknife, Northwest Territories, on the map in Figure 13-15.

b. Study the climatograms given in Figure 13-16 for Prince Rupert and Yellowknife.

c. Answer the discussion questions. Refer back to Chapter 9 and Section 13.2 of this chapter for the information you need.

Discussion

1. **a)** What biome is Prince Rupert in?
   b) Name four conifer species which likely grow near Prince Rupert.
2. **a)** What biome is Yellowknife in?
   b) Name four conifer species which likely grow near Yellowknife.
3. Compare the climate of Prince Rupert with that of Yellowknife.
4. Compare the two areas under the following headings:
   a) length of growing season
   b) annual precipitation
   c) annual snowfall
   d) month with heaviest precipitation
   e) month with lowest precipitation
   f) distribution of precipitation over the year
   g) annual temperature extremes. (How much does the temperature vary over the year?)
   h) warmest month
5. **a)** What would be the best time of year to visit Prince Rupert? Why?
   b) What would be the best time of year to visit Yellowknife? Why?
6. **a)** In which area are summer temperatures higher?
   b) What is the reason for this?
7. Calculate the average annual temperature and precipitation for each area.
8. **a)** What is the major difference between the conifers in Prince Rupert and those in Yellowknife?
   b) What are the reasons for this difference?
9. Forestry plays a major role in the economy of both areas.
   a) What aspect of forestry is most important at Prince Rupert? That is, what are the trees used for?
   b) Repeat part (a) for Yellowknife.

13.4   Two Semi-Arid Biomes

Two small biomes, both semi-arid, are found in North America. These are the chaparral and the semi-desert shrubland. Find them in Figures 7-14 and 7-16.

Chaparral

The **chaparral biome** occurs mainly in the rain shadow of the western coastal mountains. It runs in a strip from British Columbia in the north to California in the south. The chaparral has mild winters with abundant rainfall. But the long summers are dry and hot.

California has about 2 300 000 ha of hillsides covered with chaparral. The dominant vegetation is of two main types:

- xerophytic broad-leafed evergreen shrubs
- dwarf trees not over 2.5 m tall

Fig. 13-17 Sagebrush dominates the vegetation of the chaparral in the Great Basin.

Among the shrubs are chamise and mazanita. They often form very dense stands. Among the trees are oaks such as Gambel oak. They grow as shrubs or small trees. In the Great Basin to the north, the dominant shrub is sagebrush (Fig. 13-17). Most chaparral communities have little litter (unde-cayed plant matter). Also, understory plants are few.

Fire seems to have played an important role in the maintenance of the chaparral. The shrubs and trees are very flammable in the dry season. Fires have roared through the chaparral for centuries. These fires burn away old plants and return nutrients to the soil. They also keep trees from dominating the shrubs because shrubs recover faster from fires than trees do. Fires are also necessary before some seeds will germinate. They weaken the seed coats. After a fire and the rains, new sprouts become food for brush rabbits, mule deer, and other animals.

In California, people have built large homes in the chaparral. To protect their homes, they have controlled the fires. But their action allows the chaparral to grow thicker and taller. Sooner or later, a fire breaks out. And, as you might have heard, disastrous fires often sweep this area. In other places, people have planted fruit orchards on the slopes. The chapparal plants were destroyed so the fruit trees could be planted. With the ground cover gone, the soil erodes easily. Every now and then, a heavy rainfall sends entire hillsides sliding into the valleys below. Homes and orchards on the hillsides are destroyed. Homes and orchards in the valleys below can also be damaged.

Semi-desert Shrubland

The **semi-desert shrubland biome** is a narrow strip around the western and northern edges of the desert biome. In this biome, shrubs such as those of the chaparral intermingle with cacti and other desert plants. Unlike in the desert, however, the shrubs dominate this biome instead of cacti.

Section Review

1. Name North America's two semi-arid biomes.
2. **a)** Describe the location of the chaparral.

b) What two main types of vegetation grow in California's chaparral?

c) What shrub dominates the chaparral of the Great Basin?

3. Describe the role of fires in maintaining the chaparral.

4. What problem has arisen because people built homes in the chaparral?

5. What problem have fruit orchards caused in the chaparral?

6. a) Describe the location of the semi-desert shrubland biome.

b) How does this biome differ from the desert?

13.5 The Warm Temperate Evergreen Forest Biome

Fig. 13-18 Everglades National Park at the tip of Florida has examples of the broad-leafed evergreen forest that makes up this biome.

North America's smallest biome, the warm temperate evergreen forest, occurs at the tip of Florida (see Figures 7-14 and 7-16). This biome is dominated by broad-leafed evergreen trees and shrubs (Fig. 13-18). Among the trees are live oak (one of the few evergreen oak species), magnolias, hollies, and bays. Most of these species also grow along the Gulf and up the Atlantic coast.

Several tropical tree species also live here, such as the gumbo limbo and strangler-fig. A few palms also grow here. A mat of vines covers the trees in many areas. Numerous epiphytes also live on the trees. (An epiphyte is a plant which lives on another plant but does not take nutrients from it. It gets its nutrients and water from the air.) Among the epiphytes are orchids and ferns.

Of the 4 000 000 ha of southern Florida, only about 50 000 ha of true evergreen forest remain. Fires have prevented the rest from reaching this climax stage in succession. Further, land development schemes are still reducing the warm temperate evergreen forest.

Section Review

1. Describe the location of the warm temperate evergreen forest.

2. a) What tree species are found here and elsewhere in the United States?

b) What tropical tree species grow here?

3. a) What is an epiphyte?

b) Name two epiphytes of the warm temperate evergreen forest.

4. Why is there not more of this forest in Florida?

13.6 The Tropical Rain Forest Biome

North America has no tropical rain forest. However, because of its importance to the world, a brief description is included here.

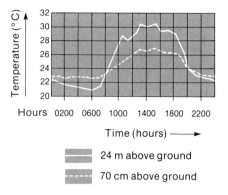

Tropical Rain Forest Temperature — The upper canopy traps most of the sun's heat by day and is exposed to heat loss by radiation at nights. Since little sunlight penetrates the understory, the daily temperature change is less. Temperature varies by nearly 10° C at 24 m but by only 4° C at 0.7 m.

24 m above ground

70 cm above ground

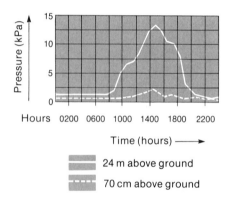

24 m above ground

70 cm above ground

Tropical Rain Forest Humidity — In the canopy, humidity nears saturation during the cooler night. The heat of day causes humidity to fall. In the shaded understory, the air is constantly near saturation with moisture. This graph measures humidity in kilopascals (barometric pressure)—as humidity increases, the reading decreases.

Fig. 13-19 Variations in tropical rain forest temperatures and humidity.

Broad-leafed evergreen tropical rain forests occur in low-altitude regions near the equator. They occur in three main places on earth (see Figure 7-14):

- in South America (the Amazon and Orinoco River basins) and up into Central America
- in Africa (the Congo, Niger, and Zambezi River basins of central-western Africa)
- in Asia (Indonesia, Malaysia, the Philippines, Burma, and parts of Bangladesh, Pakistan, and India)

All three areas receive over 200 cm of rain a year. This rain is well-distributed throughout the year. Usually, though, there are one or two dry seasons when precipitation is less than 12 cm a month. The species differ among the areas of the tropical rain forest. But their general ecology is similar. Let's take a look at it.

These moist, warm tropics provide the most favourable environment on earth for terrestrial life. The supply of radiant energy continues throughout the year because the noon sun is always within 23.5° north or south of the zenith. The daily rainfall keeps humidity high. Temperatures vary little within a 24 h period. This happens because the sky is often cloudy during the day and the high moisture content in the air reduces heat loss by radiation at night (Fig. 13-19). The tropical rain forest is dominated by broad-leafed trees. However, they are evergreen because of the constantly favourable growing conditions.

Although natural growth flourishes, tropical forest soil is infertile for agriculture. The rich humus quickly decomposes when exposed to sunlight. Also, the heavy rains wash away nutrients essential for agriculture. The natural growth of the tropical rain forest includes a great variety of plants that normally occur in five distinct strata within the mature rain forest (Fig. 13-20). This stratification increases the variety of niches available to animals (Fig. 13-21). Hence, species diversity is greater than in other land biomes. However, individual populations are often low in numbers and widely scattered. Since plant production never ceases, more animals can specialize in a particular food such as nectar or fruit. Non-flying animals must climb to reach most of their food. They tend to be small, agile, and well-adapted for moving about in the trees.

As a result of the lack of seasonal variation, many tropical species have no precise breeding time. In the humid forest, some amphibians lay their eggs on land rather than in pools of water. This step eliminates the larval stage of their life cycle. The high temperature and humidity favour insects and other invertebrates. Their constantly high metabolic rate stimulates growth. And it produces giant specimens of many species. Life cycles and hence reproduction are speeded up. More rapid evolution is possible since the greater numbers of new generations increase the chances of genetic variation. Many forest dwellers have keen colour vision and bright distinctive features. These markings help attract a mate and discourage rivals.

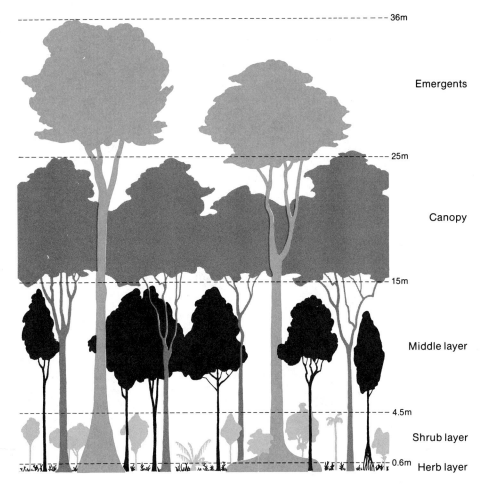

Fig. 13-20 The five main tropical rain forest strata. A: the tallest emergent trees. B: the continuous canopy. C: the middle layer of smaller trees with long narrow crowns for maximum use of poor light. D: a sparser layer of shrubs and dwarf trees. E: a ground layer of herbs.

36m

Emergents

25m

Canopy

15m

Middle layer

4.5m

Shrub layer

0.6m Herb layer

A special animal habitat is provided by the **epiphytes**. (Remember: These are plants which grow up or on other taller vegetation to reach sunlight.) Many epiphytes have dangling roots which absorb moisture from the humid air. Debris accumulates around these roots, forming humus in which many invertebrates thrive. Some ferns and orchids are epiphytes.

Currently, the earth's tropical rain forests are being destroyed at the rate of over 0.5 ha each second! (A football field is about half a hectare in size.) Much of this forest is being cut for lumber and pulp. But even more is being cleared by "slash-and-burn" methods to form agricultural land. However, as we mentioned earlier, this land only lasts for a short time as a producer of food. And, unfortunately, it seldom returns to tropical rain forest when it is taken out of agricultural use.

These forests play an important role in the earth's climate. Through transpiration (the giving off of water vapour), they moderate the high temperatures of the tropics. They also return water vapour to the air. It falls as precipitation further downwind. Yet, through careless use, these forests are being rapidly destroyed. And with the trees gone, untold numbers of plant

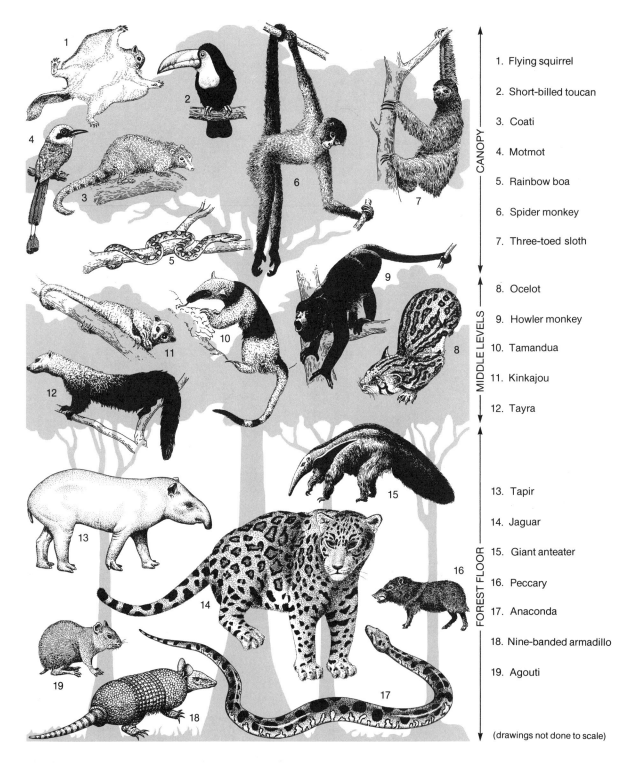

1. Flying squirrel

2. Short-billed toucan

3. Coati

4. Motmot

5. Rainbow boa

6. Spider monkey

7. Three-toed sloth

8. Ocelot

9. Howler monkey

10. Tamandua

11. Kinkajou

12. Tayra

13. Tapir

14. Jaguar

15. Giant anteater

16. Peccary

17. Anaconda

18. Nine-banded armadillo

19. Agouti

(drawings not done to scale)

CANOPY

MIDDLE LEVELS

FOREST FLOOR

Fig. 13-21 Each stratum seems to have its own characteristic animal life. Although most animals can easily move between strata, they tend to live and feed at one particular level. Why? How does this distribution affect competition?

and animal species become extinct each year. Thousands of species which humans have never even named have already vanished from the face of the earth. And dozens more join them every day. More species live in the tropics than in all the other biomes combined. Most of them still haven't been seen and named. Yet humans, through greed and carelessness, are driving many of them to extinction. Think about why we are doing this. Is there anything we can do to end this destruction?

Section Review

1. What are the three main places that have broad-leafed evergreen tropical rain forests?
2. a) Describe the climate of the tropical rain forest.
   b) Why is the temperature fairly constant during each 24 h period?
   c) Why are higher levels of rainfall needed to support large tree growth in the tropical rain forest than in the northern coniferous forest?
3. a) Why is a tropical environment the most favourable for terrestrial life?
   b) Give two reasons, other than climate, why species diversity is greatest in the tropical rain forest.
4. a) Why is tropical rain forest soil not suitable for agriculture after clearing?
   b) Humus is organic matter that is resistant to decay. Decomposition of litter in tropical forest soils is so rapid that no appreciable humus layer forms. State two reasons why decomposition is so fast.
5. a) Describe three characteristics of most non-flying animals in the tropical rain forest.
   b) Discuss three effects of the tropical climate on animal reproductive cycles.
   c) What is the function of colourful animal markings?
6. Explain how the tropical climate affects poikilothermic organisms with respect to metabolic rate, growth, life cycles, and genetic variation.
7. a) What are epiphytes?
   b) Describe their role in the tropical forest ecosystem.

Main Ideas

1. Mountain biomes have zones that resemble the earth's circumpolar biomes.
2. Alpine tundra resembles arctic tundra but differs from it in several ways (biotic and abiotic).
3. The temperate rain forest is dominated by giant conifers.
4. Climate is largely responsible for the difference between the conifers of the temperate rain forest and those of the boreal forest.

5. Two semi-arid biomes exist in North America: chaparral and semi-desert shrubland.
6. A warm temperate evergreen forest biome occurs in Florida. It is dominated by broad-leafed evergreens.
7. The tropical rain forest biome contains more species than all other biomes combined. But it is threatened by human activity.

Key Terms

alpine   krummholz
epiphyte   timberline

Chapter Review

A. True or False

Decide whether each of the following statements is true or false. If the sentence is false, rewrite it to make it true. (Do not write in this book.)
1. Alpine tundra often occurs on tall mountains just above the timberline.
2. The photoperiod in the alpine tundra is longer in the summer than that of the arctic tundra.
3. Most alpine tundra plants are perennials.
4. All alpine tundra animals move to the valleys when winter comes.
5. The temperate rain forest receives its heaviest precipitation in the winter.
6. Broad-leafed evergreen trees and shrubs grow at the tip of Florida.

B. Completion

Complete each of the following sentences with a word or phrase that will make the sentence correct. (Do not write in this book.)
1. The timberline on a mountain corresponds to the ▒▒▒▒▒ of the boreal coniferous forest.
2. The light intensity is ▒▒▒▒▒ in the alpine tundra than in the arctic tundra.
3. Two characteristic trees of the montane zone are ▒▒▒▒▒ and ▒▒▒▒▒ .
4. The conifers of the temperate rain forest reach their giant size largely because of the ▒▒▒▒▒ .
5. The ▒▒▒▒▒ biome has the greatest diversity of organisms.

C. Multiple Choice

Each of the following statements or questions is followed by four responses. Choose the correct response in each case. (Do not write in this book.)

1. The tree species in the subalpine zone of a mountain resemble most closely those of the
   a) boreal forest
   c) temperate deciduous forest
   b) temperate rain forest
   d) warm temperate evergreen forest
2. If you went for a hike at the timberline, you would most likely be among
   a) large Englemann spruce
   c) krummholz Englemann spruce
   b) large lodgepole pine
   d) stunted Douglas fir
3. An area has mild wet winters and long, hot, dry summers. It is dominated by broad-leafed evergreen shrubs and dwarf trees. This area is in the
   a) grassland biome
   b) warm temperate evergreen biome
   c) desert biome
   d) chaparral biome
4. Which one of the following is the main factor preventing the replacement of shrubs by trees in the chaparral?
   a) high temperatures
   c) fires
   b) heavy summer rains
   d) long dry summers

Using Your Knowledge

1. Alpine sorrel is a plant found in both the Arctic and alpine tundra. The Arctic variety shows adaptive differences from the alpine variety. Using your knowledge of these two regions, explain each of the following.
   a) The Arctic variety reaches a maximum rate of photosynthesis at a lower temperature than the alpine variety.
   b) The alpine variety requires a higher light intensity than the Arctic variety.
   c) The Arctic variety requires a longer photoperiod.
   d) The alpine variety produces a greater number of flowers.
   e) The Arctic variety develops more rhizomes (underground stems used for food storage).
   f) The alpine variety reproduces by seedlings; the Arctic variety relies on vegetative reproduction.
   g) Roots of the Arctic variety are short and quickly replaced; the alpine variety develops deep, long-lived roots.
2. Compare the Arctic and alpine tundra as a habitat for birds.
3. Make a list of what city dwellers could do to help conserve the giant conifers of the temperate rain forest.
4. Many foresters maintain that mature trees, such as the giant conifers of the temperate rain forest, should be harvested. They say that such trees, left to age and eventually die, are wasted resources. Evaluate this opinion.

5. Why are reptiles, amphibians, and invertebrates such as insects more numerous in the temperate rain forest than in the boreal forest?

6. The evergreens of both the boreal forest and the temperate rain forest keep their needles during the winter. But the reasons they do this are different. What are they?

7. The tropical rain forests of the world are being rapidly destroyed. It is easy to sit here in North America and criticize the countries with these forests for letting this happen. Evaluate their reasons by answering the following questions.

   a) Why do countries use "slash-and-burn" agriculture? What alternatives are available?

   b) Why are the governments of tropical countries developing their forest industries as rapidly as possible?

   c) Imagine that you live in Brazil. You are unemployed and unable to feed your family. A forest company offers to log the area you live in and give you and other local people jobs. What would you do?

   d) What role do we in North America play in the destruction of tropical rain forests?

   e) What can we do at home and abroad to help conserve these forests?

8. Why does it matter if species which have never been identified or studied are lost forever?

Investigations

1. Design and conduct an experiment to compare the ability of different woods to resist weathering. Include in your test redwood or western red cedar. Include as well wood from local conifers and deciduous trees.

2. Select one of the following conifers from the temperate rain forest: Sitka spruce, western hemlock, western red cedar, redwood, Douglas fir. Write a report of about 200 words on this conifer under the following headings: distribution, appearance (size, identifying features), uses of wood, ecological status, areas where giant specimens are preserved.

3. Spanish moss (*Tillandsia*) is an epiphyte. It is commonly found on trees such as live oak in the warm temperate evergreen forest. Research this plant under the following headings: its taxonomy (classification), its symbiotic relationship with trees, its sources of water and nutrients, its effects on the trees, its ecological roles.

4. Research a major land development project in the Amazon Basin (such as Ludwig's). Discuss the goals, difficulties faced, and outcome of the project.

Index

NOTE: The pages in **boldface**
indicate illustrations.